Alfred Wilks Drayson

Sporting Scenes Amongst the Kaffirs of South Africa

Second Edition

Alfred Wilks Drayson

Sporting Scenes Amongst the Kaffirs of South Africa
Second Edition

ISBN/EAN: 9783337123772

Printed in Europe, USA, Canada, Australia, Japan

Cover: Foto ©Andreas Hilbeck / pixelio.de

More available books at **www.hansebooks.com**

SPORTING SCENES

AMONGST

THE KAFFIRS OF SOUTH AFRICA.

BY

CAPT. ALFRED W. DRAYSON,

ROYAL ARTILLERY.

"Afar in the desert I love to ride,
With the silent Bushboy alone by my side;
Away, away, from the dwellings of men,
By the antelope's haunt and the buffalo's glen;
By valleys remote, where the ourebi plays,
The gnu, the gazelle, and the hartebeest graze;
Where the gemsbok and eland unhunted recline,
By the skirts of grey forests o'erhung with wild vine."

Second Edition.

ILLUSTRATED BY J. WOLF.

LONDON:
ROUTLEDGE, WARNE, & ROUTLEDGE,
FARRINGDON STREET;
NEW YORK: 56, WALKER STREET.
1860.

PREFACE.

NEARLY every person with whom I have conversed since my return from South Africa, has appeared to take great interest in the Kaffirs, the wild animals, and other inhabitants of that country.

I am not vain enough to suppose that my friends have merely pretended this interest for the sole object of allowing me an opportunity of talking, and have thereby deluded me into a belief of affording amusement. But I really think that the opinions which they have expressed are genuine, and that perhaps the same wish for information on the subject of the Kaffirs, or the wild beasts of the Cape, may be more widely extended than I have been able personally to prove.

Most men who have written on South Africa, have been either sporting giants, scientific men, or travellers who have gone over ground never before trodden by the white man. I am neither of these.

The first I am not, for the blood spilled by me was but a drop compared to the ocean that many have caused to flow in this land.

Unfortunately I am not scientific; but, perhaps, from this very defect, I may become the more intelligible to the general reader of the following pages, who may comprehend my simple names for simple things, rather than those of a polysyllabic character.

I know that I have sunk miserably in the opinion of *savans*, in consequence of my inability to tell whether or not the *Terstrœmiaceœ* grew luxuriantly in Africa. I only knew that the plains bore beautiful flowers, and I learnt their Kaffir names; that the bush had fine trees, some with sweet-scented blossoms, others with fruit, and I knew which fruit was good to eat.

By travellers, I may be considered presumptuous in attempting to write on South Africa, when I never crossed the Vaal river or penetrated far into the interior; but I must trust that they will pardon my temerity. I was obliged, from circumstances, to pursue the game nearer my home, which required "more patient search and vigil long," for the creatures had become more wild or savage than those animals in the interior that were seldom disturbed.

From sketches and a rough journal compiled on the spot, I have formed this book.

CONTENTS.

CHAPTER I.

Voyage to the Cape—Discomforts of a long voyage—The wolf turned lamb—Porpesses and Portuguese men-of-war—The mate's story—Catching a shark—An albatross hooked—Cape Town—Algoa Bay—Ox-waggon—South-African travelling—Obstinacy conquered—Expeditious journeying—Frontier of the colony.—*Page* 1.

CHAPTER II.

Dutch and Kaffir words—Frontier Kaffirs—Kaffir women—Kaffir soldiers—Cattle-stealing—Bush-fighting—Colonel Napier's opinion—Equipment of English soldiers—A British soldier in the bush—Kaffir manoeuvres—Corn-pits—Treatment of Kaffir thieves—The assagy and other weapons—Moral qualities of the Kaffirs—Native marksmen—Power of the chiefs—Religious opinions—Hottentot soldiers.—*Page* 18.

CHAPTER III.

Narrow escape—Sandilli goes home—Voyage to Natal—My fellow-passengers—Tempting viands—Property overboard—Natal Bay—The "tick"—Beauty of the vegetation—Dolce far niente—Cape horses—Points of a Cape horse—Shooting-ponies—Mode of journeying—The "sickness"—Training a shooting-horse—Endurance of Cape horses—A rough journey—A stormy night—Agreeable termination.—*Page* 41.

CHAPTER IV.

Warnings against the bush—Search after a leopard—Unsteady hands—Methods of hunting elephants—Speed of the elephant—Bush-travelling.—Traces of the elephants—Solitude of the bush—Tracking the herd—Charge of angry elephants—The horses reached—Search for the wounded elephant—The successful shot—An unwitting escape.—*Page* 75.

CHAPTER V.

Necessity of a gun—Strange footstep—A disappointment—Vicinity of the Umganie—Duiker buck—Matuan the Kaffir—Vocal telegraph—Reitbok—A human pointer—Singular conversation—Apathy of the residents—Kaffir messengers—Buck-shooting—The buck's tenacity of life—A buck on three legs—Dangerous country—A sporting red-coat—Strange sportsmen.—*Page* 89.

CHAPTER VI.

Eland-hunting—Beautiful country—Telescopic eyes—Loading at a gallop—The Dutch Boers—Speed of the eland—Eland-hunt—Unsuccessful result—Signals of distress—African Nimrods—A herd of elands—Better luck this time—An accident—The Slough of Despond—A "Sticks bullet"—In at the death—A bivouac—Air-pillows.—*Page* 109.

CHAPTER VII.

The Dutchman's stratagem—Wild-boar hunt—A vicious pigling—Hartebeest-chase—Hide-and-seek—The organ of "locality"—Fatal curiosity—An escapade—A false alarm—Baboons at home—A tame baboon—The baboon and the crow—Literary and scientific tastes—A leopard shot—Unpleasant journey—Conflicting opinions.—*Page* 127.

CHAPTER VIII.

The Bivouac—Hotman's story—Terrible misfortune—Both sides of the story—How to find water—Kemp's story—Death of Mabili—Single Elephants to be avoided—Hendrich and the Leopard—A struggle for life—A weary night—A poisonous companion—The rescue—Savage hermits—The "Trek-boken."—*Page* 143.

CHAPTER IX.

Bush-shooting—Silent walking—How to cock a gun—How to sit down—Delights of the bush—How to obtain honey—The honey-bird—The grey monkey—Ball better than shot—Variety of bush game—Hardening bullets—The alligator—The Pouw—Boldness of the eagle—The Osprey.—*Page* 160.

CHAPTER X.

A shooting-party in the bush—Elephant "sign"—The elephants heard—Caution in the bush—Approach to a wary elephant—The better part of valour—Traces of the wounded elephant—Sic vos non vobis—Acute ear

CONTENTS. xiii

of elephants—The elephants' signals—More of them—Tree'd—Teaching the young idea—A family picture—Chaffed by monkeys—A sharp lookout—The disadvantage of "crackers"—A Kaffir coward—Capricious temper of elephants—Elephants in the "open"—An awkward position—Sharp practice.—*Page* 174.

CHAPTER XI.

Journey to the Zulu country—Hunger the best sauce—A popular song—An unexpected guest—Panda's regiments—His pet vultures—An ingenious scarecrow—Another reit-buck—The telescope—A lesson in spooring—A trial of nerves—Intruding leopards—A Kaffir feast and concert—Baked, blinded, and poisoned—Pesbauna, a Kaffir belle—Kaffir lovetale—An abduction and a rescue—None but the brave deserve the fair.—*Page* 196.

CHAPTER XII.

A Kaffir hunt—A battue—Fire-making—A lunch *al fresco*—Troublesome invaders—Flight of locusts—Crows outwitted—Alligator shot—A lion-chase—Strength of the lion—A slight mistake—Snuff-manufacturing—A proposal of marriage—Kaffir kindliness.—*Page* 215.

CHAPTER XIII.

The Natal Kaffirs—Pseudo-Christianity—Ideas of a future state—The Kaffir prophets—Black lawyers—A wife's true value—Husband and wife—White savage *versus* black—Injustice towards the Kaffirs—Nobody wrong—Necessity of an army—Mr. Holden's opinion—Severity sometimes necessary—Real character of the Kaffir.—*Page* 229.

CHAPTER XIV.

A buffalo-hunt—A sudden meeting—A Kaffir's advice—Buffalo killed—An African race-course—The start—The run—The charge—Won at last—Unpleasant neighbours—The single spur—Light-coloured Kaffirs—Know thyself—Neglected education—Black and white—Too knowing by half—The fool's argument.—*Page* 243.

CHAPTER XV.

Kaffir killed by a snake—Medicine necklaces—Narrow escape—Puff-adders—Adventure with a black snake—Snakes distressed by their own poison—Poison-spitting snake—A day's sport—Boa-constrictor killed—Its mode of attack—Size of the slain snake—Secretary-bird.—*Page* 260.

CONTENTS.

CHAPTER XVI.

An invitation—Terrific storm—Silent eloquence—Mounted Bushmen—The Bushman as an enemy—A Dutch hunter—Gallant defence—A Cockney traveller—Boer incredulity—British disbelief—Adventure with a Bushman—African rivers—Change of sentiments.—*Page* 272.

CHAPTER XVII.

African moonlight—Poor Charley—Want of patience—Blue light in the Bush—Buck killed by a leopard—Strange followers—Porcupine-hunt—Practical joke—Foolhardy conduct—A mistake—Kaffir prophet—A dark patriarch—Conjugal authority—Strong-headed individual—Harbour sharks—Fish-spearing—Intoxicating root—A suggested experiment—Variety of fish.—*Page* 287.

CHAPTER XVIII.

Steeple-chase at D'Urban—The last day's sport—The bar at Natal—Reach Table Bay—Impertinent "pike"-keeper—Chased by a policeman—Dishonest auctioneer—St. Helena—Turtle-catching—Waterspouts—Cintra—Lisbon—Best weapons for the bush—Extra gun-stocks necessary—Recommendation to "used-up" individuals.—*Page* 307.

ADDENDA   ..   ..   *Page* 323

Sporting Scenes

AMONGST THE

KAFFIR TRIBES IN AFRICA.

CHAPTER I.

Voyage to the Cape—Discomforts of a long voyage—The wolf turned lamb—Porpesses and Portuguese men-of-war—The mate's story—Catching a shark—An albatross hooked—Cape Town—Algoa Bay—Ox-waggon—South-African travelling—Obstinacy conquered—Expeditious journeying—Frontier of the colony.

To an indifferent sailor, a long voyage is not by any means a pleasant thing; and I quite agree with the sage who said that a man on board a ship was a prisoner, with the additional risk of being drowned. One feels a continual yearning for the green fields, fresh butter and milk; and the continual noise, confusion, and other disagreeables, are more trying to temper and patience than can be imagined by a quiet stay-at-home gentleman.

We left England in the coldest weather that had been remembered for years. A month's daily skating on the Serpentine was a bad preparation for a week's calm, under a burning sun, within a degree of the line, twenty-seven days afterwards. The frames of Englishmen, however, appear to be better adapted for the changes of climate than are those of the inhabitants of any other country.

We passed the Bay of Biscay with the usual rough weather, had a distant look at Madeira, and entered the trade-winds, without having met with any other disaster than a sort of mutiny amongst the crew, who, headed by a contumacious coloured giant, refused to attend divine service on a Sunday. A detachment of half a dozen men, with the captain and the mate at their head, soon brought the gentleman in question to reason; forty-eight hours in irons, on bread and water, entirely changed his view of the matter, and he came out from the encounter a very lamb.

I frequently remained on deck in the first watches of the night, during the pleasant sailing in the trade-winds, between the Canary Islands and the west coast of Africa, a part of the world that has always been remembered by me for its beautiful climate. The light breeze caused little more than a ripple on the water, which sparkled with millions of phosphorescent lights, and the slow, easy motion of the vessel, with the occasional groaning of the blocks and bulk-heads, as a stronger puff of wind than usual caused an additional strain upon them, was like the heave and swell of some leviathan lungs, while the graceful curve of the studding-sails, spreading far out on each side, gave to the ship the appearance of some vast animal, intent on a journey of mystery and importance, and busy in thus muttering to itself a rehearsal of its mission.

I preferred resting in the stern-boat, and watching the space around, to breathing the close atmosphere of the badly-ventilated cabins, with their odours of bilgewater and mouldy biscuit, or tossing about restlessly in the narrow berth, to the disturbance and sometimes death of vagrant cockroaches, who had trespassed under the blanket, and whose number was legion.

In the surrounding water, one could trace the meteor course of some monster of the deep, whose dive left behind a long brilliant stream of fire like a rocket. Suddenly the ocean would apparently become alive with these flashes of light, as a shoal of porpesses dashed into sight with the velocity of a troop of wild horse, leaping and shying in their merry race. They cross the brilliant wake of the ship, and, with a regular wheel, like a squadron of cavalry, charge after her. The ten knots per hour that the log has given as the gallant ship's speed, make but little difference to these aquatic rovers. They open their line as they near, and now they are under the stern; in a second they have passed, in a few more are far on ahead, jumping about near the bows, and taking each valley of the rolling sea in true sporting style. Then, with another sweep, they dash down upon us, and, after inspecting the ship for a minute, disappear with the same reckless speed, leaving two or three outsiders, who, not getting a fair start, appear to ply whip and spur to regain their position with the main body. The sea is then doubly dark and mysterious.

The morning light would show the ocean covered with the beautiful little Portuguese men-of-war (*Physalus*), whose brilliant reflection of the prismatic colours would raise a feeling of ambition for their capture. An hour was passed in the endeavour to become more closely acquainted

with them, by means of a little net over the ship's side—
the result, like many others in this world, was disappointment. A man-of-war is caught, but, upon its reaching
the deck, is found to consist of a small bladder, now
destitute of those attractions that had tempted our eyes,
and a few long muscular strings, that raise a red smarting
line wherever they touch the skin. This curious creature
declines exhibiting its beauties during captivity.

I had many theoretical lessons in seamanship from the
mate during this fine weather, and many interesting
anecdotes of whaling adventures. He was very anxious
to pass safely round the Cape, and, upon my inquiring the
reason, he gave me the following account of his last trip,
which had taken place some four years before:—

"It was on a miserably cold day in February that the good
barque *Emerald*, in which I was second mate, weighed
her anchor from the mud opposite Gravesend, and commenced her voyage for the Mauritius. I had sailed with
the captain (Wharton) to the West Indies on a former
voyage, and had been asked by him to take the second
mate's place on this trip, although I was only twenty-one
years old at the time. I thought it a good berth, and
accepted it, although I disliked the man. He was a good
sailor, there was no denying, but a bit of a bully, and, I
always suspected, drank a good deal when quiet in his
cabin. He had been married just before our voyage, and
his honeymoon was rather curtailed by the hurry of our
departure. I saw his wife several times before we left
England, for she was staying at Gravesend, and had also
come on board while we were lying in the docks. She

was a very pretty young girl, and seemed to be too quiet and good for the skipper, who, I thought, did not treat her as he ought to have done. She told me that she was going to take a cottage at Gosport while her husband was away, and asked me, if I had time, to write her a few words to say how the ship got on, in case we met any of the homeward-bound, or stopped at any port. I believe, when she shook hands with me, and said, 'Good-bye, sir; a happy voyage to you,' I felt much inclined to do her any service, and pitied her lonely situation more than her husband did. She had told me that her only relation was an aged aunt. Well, we floundered across the Bay of Biscay, and ran down the trades, and in twenty-seven days from leaving England with a freezing north wind, we were baking under the line with 95° in the shade shown on our thermometer. The skipper had shoved a couple of our men in irons for very slight offences during our run, and seemed to be a greater brute than ever. He was one of those fellows who acted like an angel on shore, so pleasant and kind, but when he got afloat in blue water, he wasn't an angel exactly, at least not the right sort of angel.

"We jogged on, however, till we passed round the Cape; we gave it a wide berth, and kept well off the bank, to avoid the current that runs from the east all down that coast for seventy miles' distance. We were about off Cape L'Agulhas, when the north-west wind that we had carried with us from near South America, turned round and blew right in our teeth; we had plenty of wind in our jib then, it blew great guns, and we were under close-reefed topsails for a week. One night I was on watch, and finding that it was blowing harder than ever, and the ship was making very bad weather of it, I thought I would go down and ask the skipper's leave to lay-to. I dived down the hatchway and knocked twice at the captain's cabin-door before I received an answer; at last I heard his 'Come in.' I opened the door and was about to report the gale increased, but was stopped by the appearance of the captain. He was as white as a sheet, and his eyes were staring like a maniac's. Before I could speak a word, he said, ' Have you seen her?' I did not know what he meant, but said, ' Beg pardon, sir, the ship is making very bad weather of it.' He cursed the weather, and repeated, 'Did you see my wife as you came in?' I said, 'See your wife! No!'

" He stared at me for an instant and then dropped on his couch, and said, 'God have mercy on me.' It was the first time I had ever heard him use that sacred name, although the evil one's was pretty often in his mouth. I then asked him about the ship, when he told me to go and do what I thought best. I went up and took all the canvas off, with the exception of the mizen-trysail. I got the peak lowered down to the deck and showed but a pocket-handkerchief sort of sail; this kept her head to wind. I had a guy made fast to the boom, which kept it firm, and lashed the helm; we then rode like a duck on the water.

" I turned in as usual after being relieved, and said nothing to any one about what I had heard. In the morning the captain sent for me, told me not to speak about what he had said last night, but that he had been told that his days were numbered. He pointed to the log-book, in which he had put down, that he had seen his wife come into the cabin, and that she spoke to him, and told him something about himself. He then requested me to sign his statement in the book, and ordered me not to say a word to any of the men as long as he lived. I told him not to think anything about it, as such things were only imaginations, and were caused by the stomach being a little out of order. I did not think it at the time, although I thought it would quiet him by telling him so.

"We lay-to all that day; the captain came on deck once, but spoke to no one. In the afternoon I went down to him to ask about getting a little sail up again; I found him reading his Bible, a thing that I had never heard of his doing before. He put it down and came on deck; ordered me to get up the fore-topsail; I went forward to see about it, and the skipper walked on to the poop; the helm was still lashed, and no one was there but him. I was giving the men orders to go aloft, when I heard a crack astern, and felt a jar through the whole ship. I turned round and found the pitching had caused the heavy boom of the trysail to break the guy that fastened it, and it was swinging from side to side with every lurch of the ship. I ran aft with all the men, and with great difficulty made it fast again; it took us some time to settle, and I then went down to tell the captain. His cabin was just as I had left it before, and no one in it; I came out and asked for him on deck, but no one had seen him there. The men said that he was on the poop when the guy gave way; there was a general call throughout the ship, but the captain was not found.

"The first mate and I then went on the poop, and looked well all round. On the bulwarks near the stern there was a slight dent, and close beside it a streak of blood: there was no doubt that the boom in its first swing had knocked the skipper clean overboard, and the chances were, had smashed some of his limbs too. We never saw him more. The first mate took the command, and I told him about the captain's vision; he laughed at me, and told me I was a fool to believe in such rubbish, and recommended me not to talk about it. I quietly tore the leaf out of the log-book, and have got it now. I will show it you." Saying this he went down to his cabin and brought me up the sheet of paper; which I read, and found it as he had described. "We went on to the Mauritius, loaded, and returned to England. I had no opportunity of fulfilling my promise of writing to the captain's wife, so immediately I could leave the ship I started for Gosport to tell her about his loss.

"I found her house from the address she had given me, and walked once or twice up and down to consider all I should say to her. It was any way a difficult thing and one I did not like doing, having to relate the death of her husband; and besides, women are inclined to think there is always some neglect in others if an accident happens to those they love. At last I plucked up courage and knocked at the door. A decent-looking servant came, and upon my asking if Mrs. Wharton were at home, she replied, 'Mrs. Wharton don't live here. Mrs. Somebody or other lives here, and she ain't at home.' I asked if she could tell me where to find Mrs. Wharton, and was informed by the maid that she was a stranger and knew nothing; but the baker over the way, she thought, could tell me. I went over and asked the baker's wife, and she informed me that Mrs. Wharton had been dead nearly five months, and her aunt had moved away. I was thunderstruck at this intelligence, and immediately inquired the date of her death; she looked over a day-book in the drawer, and told me. I put it down in my memorandum-book, and when I got back to the ship I found the date the same as that noted on the leaf of the log-book as the one that the captain had seen her off the Cape. Now, I never was superstitious before this, nor am I alarmed now at the idea of seeing ghosts, but still there is a queer sort of feeling comes over me when I think of that night.

"When I got home to my friends, I told the clergyman and the doctor what had been seen. The first explained it to me as an optical delusion, but acknowledged that it was very curious; the other looked into my eyes as though he were trying to see some signs of insanity, and told me it was very likely that the captain's supper had disagreed with him that night, or that he was half-seas-over.

"Now, I haven't much learning myself, but I do despise what I have seen called science; men who study books only, can't know so much as those who see the real things; I haven't patience with men who, never having travelled much, or been across the oceans, quietly tell the world that what a hundred sane men's experienced eyes have seen and known as a sea-serpent is discovered by their scientific reasoning to be a bundle of seaweed, or a shoal of porpesses, because they saw once at Brighton one or the other, when even a land-lubber could hardly have been mistaken. My wise doctor tried to prove that what the skipper had seen with his own eyes was nothing but the result of a supper he hadn't eaten, or the fumes of some grog that wern't swallowed; because it happened not to be accounted for in his fusty old books in any other way—I would sooner be without science, if this is the result.

"Bless you, sir, I never yet saw one of your great learned sailors worth much in an extremity. Give me a fellow who acts from his practical experience. A man much given to be particular about 'how the log-book is kept,' about dotting i's and crossing t's, is generally struck of a heap, if the ship happens to be taken aback, or a squall carries away her gear. While he is going over his logarithms to know what should be done, the commonest seaman on board could set all to rights. Mind I don't run down any book-learning you may have, but I only say it ain't equal to experience, and it never will convince me that, if I see a square-rigged ship a mile off, I am only mistaken, and that a man in London knows by science that it was a fore-and-aft schooner and close to me; or if I see a school of whales, he knows they are only flying-fish, because science tells him the whale does not frequent the part where I saw them; and that my supper caused me to mistake one for the other." With these sentiments the mate ended his tale, and I now proceed with the narrative of the voyage.

While near the line, we caught a shark, which was the first animal bigger than a hare that I had ever assisted in destroying. As the method employed on this fellow was of a more sporting character than usually attends the capture of this monster, I will give in detail our proceedings.

Our voracious friend having been seen some hundred yards astern steadily following in our wake, we procured two joints of a lightning-conductor (that had lain in the hold since our leaving England, and which was intended to protect the ship from the fluid that makes so excellent a messenger but so direful an enemy), and lashed a large hook on to one end. The copper wire was stout enough to resist the teeth of the monster, and a common log-line was made fast to the wire, with a second line in case of his requiring much play. Over the stern went the hook, baited with a most tempting piece of pork; the ship was just moving through the water at the time, the whole sea looking like a vast lake of molten silver.

We watched our cannibal as the bait came near him; he did not keep us long in doubt, but with a rush put his nose against the pork, pronounced it good, turned on his side, and both pork and hook disappeared. We gave a smart tug at the line, and found him fast.

I expected a tremendous trout-like rush, or some great display of shark force; but he merely gave a wag of his tail, lowered his dorsal fin under water, and steadily dragged back on the line. We met him with a firm pull, and brought him near the ship, when he made a sudden dive directly downward, nearly carrying out both our lines.

I feared now that we should lose him, but he seemed to have gone deep enough to suit his taste, and turned slowly up again; all his movements could be seen as distinctly in this transparent water as those of a bird in the air. One or two more dives of a similar character at length tired him, and he was brought close to the vessel. One of the seamen then sent a harpoon with deadly aim right through him, which caused a furious struggle, by which the hook was snapped short off from the wire. The harpoon, however, held firm, and its rope served to guide a bowling-knot, which caught under the shark's fins, and he was dragged on to the deck. A storm of blows and a chop on his tail soon reduced his strength, which had shown itself in struggles and leaps; his demise was then peaceful. He was fully seven feet long, and seemed a string of muscles. He disappointed me by his craven surrender; a salmon would have given far more play.

Great interest was shown in inspecting the shark's interior; a button marked V R or R N might have caused endless speculation, and wonderful tales to be invented. Alas! his stomach contained nothing but a bundle of feathers! A roar from the whole crew was given at this discovery.

What could he have been about? — acting a fishy pantomime as a pillow, or turning himself into a comfortable resting-place for Mrs. Shark's head? The fact was, that there had been a great deal of poultry plucked within the last few days, and the feathers were thrown overboard. Sharky being unable to grab either the fowls or their masters, had been obliged to satisfy the cravings of his hungry maw with this unsatisfactory substitute. I cut a slice out of him; it was like a skein of wire, so tough and unfishlike.

Some preserved salmon that we had for dinner on the following day was pronounced by a youngster " very good indeed, and better than he could have fancied a shark would taste:" and he very likely believes to this day that boiled shark is very like salmon, as we were all careful not to inform him of his error.

As we neared the Cape, we were occasionally inspected by some gigantic albatrosses, whose spectral appearance, as they sailed rapidly along with outstretched and rigid wings, and passed from side to side of the horizon in sweeping circles, seemed like the ghosts of ancient mariners thus condemned monotonously to pass their time till the day of judgment.

When near the island of Tristan D'Acunha we caught one with a little hook and a line; we brought him on deck, and, after inspecting his personal appearance and ten-feet-wide wings from tip to tip, threw him overboard, when he was furiously attacked by his cousins, who, Chinaman-like, seemed to think death the only fit reward for his having dealt with the white travellers.

We entered Table Bay in the night, just in time to escape a strong south-easter that sprung up at daybreak, enveloped the Table Mountain with its dense white cloth of clouds, and sent volumes of dust from the flats pouring into the town, to the blinding of every unfortunate out-of-door individual. On disembarking in any foreign land, one is naturally amused with the curious costumes of the people; and when the country happens to be that of a coloured race, this peculiarity is still more striking. The people here were of every colour and denomination,—English, Dutch, Portuguese, Chinamen, Malays, Negroes, Kaffirs, Hottentots, Fingoes, and Mohammedans, white and black, red and yellow, with every intermediate shade.

The head-dresses showed in the greatest variety. Some heads had nothing on them, not even hair; others had a small rag. Hottentot and Malay women's heads were extensively got up with red and blue handkerchiefs; some wore English straw hats or coverings shaped like rotundas; others had plumes of ostrich-feathers, wide-awakes, &c. Most of the women and boys danced round us when we first landed, and I felt like Sindbad the sailor being welcomed by the beasts on the magician's island.

I rather liked Cape Town; there was a good library, very fair balls, pretty women, and a pleasant country near, well sprinkled with good houses, the hospitality of which might well be introduced in place of the oyster-like seclusion of many homes in England.

Three months after landing in Table Bay I again embarked for Algoa Bay, *en route* for the frontier. We had a pleasant calm voyage, keeping the coast in sight during the whole passage, and putting into two or three bays, where a delay of a few hours enabled me to haul on board a good dish of grotesque-looking fish, and some crayfish: the latter were excellent eating.

On the sixth day we landed at Port Elizabeth, Algoa Bay, whence I started without delay; sand, swindling horse-dealers, naked Fingoes, and drunken Hottentots being my principal sights at this town. I managed to obtain a mount from a friend who had voyaged from Cape Town with me, and thus reserved my selection of a quadruped until I arrived at Graham's Town. We examined the surrounding country for game, but saw only a hare, a few quail, and one buck. I was told that ostriches were within a few miles, and that elephants had been seen near the Sundays river a day or so past.

The ox-waggon of the Cape is a four-wheeled vehicle with a canvas tilt; it is completely a necessary of the South-African resident: it is his house, his ship, and in many cases his income. Until he builds a house, he lives in the waggon, keeps all he possesses there, and travels from spot to spot independent of inns or other habitations. From the general suppleness of the vehicle, owing to the very small quantity of iron which is used in its construction, it is well adapted for the purposes of crossing the steep-banked rivers and stony roads that are here so frequent.

Fourteen oxen are generally used for a team, each having his regular place, and answering to his wonderful name. A miserable Hottentot boy or Fingoe is employed to perform the part of leader: he is called "forelouper;" his duty being to hold a small rope that is fastened to the horns of the two front oxen, and to lead them in the right road.

The inspanning or coupling completed, the rope by

which the team pulls the waggon is then stretched, and the driver, whirling his gigantic whip round his victims, and with a shrill yell that a demon might utter, shouts, "Trek! Trek! Achterman! Roeberg!" (the names of two oxen) "Trek ye!"

The long whip is then brought down with a neat flip on the flank of some refractory animal who is hanging back, and out of whose hide a strip of several inches in length is thus taken.

A shout at Englishman—generally so named from being the most obstinate in the team—Zwartland, Wit Kop, &c., is followed by a steady pull all together, and the waggon moves off. When the driver has flogged a few more of the oxen to let off his superfluous anger, he mounts on the waggon-box, and exchanges his long whip for a short strip of seacow-hide, called the "achter sjambok," with which he touches up occasionally the two wheelers. Lighting his pipe, he then complacently views the performance of his stud through its balmy atmosphere. Should there be an ox so obstinate as to refuse to move on, or wish to lie down, &c., who can paint the refined pleasure this same Hottentot driver feels in thrashing the obstinacy out of the animal, or how entire is his satisfaction as he kicks the poor brute in the stomach, and raps him over the nose with the yokes-key, or twists his tail in a knot, and then tears it with his teeth. Martin's Act is a dead letter in Africa.

A few days in Graham's Town were quite enough to satisfy my curiosity; in this part of the world, the sooner one gets beyond the half-civilization the better.

I joined two friends, and started for Fort Beaufort, a day's ride distant. I was much amused at the cool manner in which our dinner was provided at the inn on the road. " What will you have, gentlemen ?" was asked: " beef, a turkey, or—" "Turkey roast I vote," said one, in answer to the landlord's question. " Piet !" cried the landlord, " knock over that turkey in the corner." "Ja bâs," answered a Hottentot servant. A log of wood flew at the turkey's head indicated, and, with unerring aim, he was knocked over, plucked, drawn, and roasted in about an hour and a half, and was very good and tender.

The frontier of the Cape colony is a very wild and rather barren district, and in many parts there is a scarcity of water and verdure. At certain seasons of the year quail come in abundance, thirty or forty brace for one pair of barrels being by no means an uncommon bag. One or two of the bustard tribe are also found here, and are called the *diccop, coran,* and *pouw*. I saw but little game besides those creatures which I have just mentioned, as we were at war with the Amakosa tribes, and it was not prudent to venture far from our forts. I employed my time in making portraits of the friendly Kaffirs who came in to see us, and also in acquiring their language, which struck me as particularly harmonious and expressive. Frequently thirty or forty men would come in of a day under some pretence or other, and I had good opportunities of watching their manners and attire, the latter, by the bye, being particularly simple.

CHAPTER II.

Dutch and Kaffir words—Frontier Kaffirs—Kaffir women—Kaffir soldiers—Cattle-stealing—Bush-fighting—Colonel Napier's opinion—Equipment of English soldiers—A British soldier in the bush—Kaffir manœuvres—Corn-pits—Treatment of Kaffir thieves—The assagy and other weapons—Moral qualities of the Kaffirs—Native marksmen—Power of the chiefs—Religious opinions—Hottentot soldiers.

THE different terms that I shall employ, viz., Kraal, Spoor, Kaffir, and Assagy, are not known to the Kaffirs themselves, except through their commerce with the white men; but as the words are in general vogue through the colony, I am forced to use them.

Kraal is a Dutch term, and means an inclosure for animals. I fancy that they call the Kaffirs' residences by this name to indicate their contempt for the people; the Kaffirs call their villages "*umsi.*"

Spoor is also Dutch: the Kaffirs speak of spoor as *umkondo.* The footmarks of a particular animal are then named as *Amasondo injlovu,* footmarks of elephants; *umkondo* being the singular,—one footmark.

"Kaffir" is also a term unknown to the men so called; they speak of themselves by the designation of the tribe. *Kosa* is a frontier Kaffir, *ama,* the plural, being prefixed, makes *Amakosa* Kaffirs; thus, *Amazulu, Amaponda,* &c. A Hottentot is called *Umluo.*

An assagy is called *umkonto;* the plural is here irregular, *izakali* being assagies. A kaross is called by Kaffirs *ingubu.*

The frontier Kaffirs are fine athletic men, and stand generally about six feet in height: they are nearly black, and have woolly hair, although the features are in many cases almost European. The *intombi's*, or young girls, are often quite pretty, with wild, free, dark eyes, that may well plead as excuses for the young Kaffirs' propensity for cattle-stealing, the decimal coinage of Kaffirland being 10 cows = 1 wife.

One very soon gets over the prejudice of colour, and after having looked for some time on the rich black of a Kaffir belle, a white lady appears bloodless, consumptive, and sickly in comparison. The hard work that an *umfazi*, or wife, has to perform very soon spoils her girlish figure and appearance, and she then becomes a haggard, wrinkled, repulsive old witch. The coolness of all these women is often surprising. A skirmish with the Kaffirs and our troops might take place on one day, and on the next the women belonging to the Kaffir men engaged would come into the camp and offer wood or milk for sale, calling to us to "*tenga*" (buy). I suspect that these women are often sent in merely as spies.

There is a great mistake prevalent in the minds of most English people, and that is, their habit of underrating the Kaffir as a foe. He is looked upon as a naked savage, armed only with a spear, and hardly worth powder and shot. But in reality the Kaffirs are a formidable race, and, from their skill in many arts in which we are deficient, are much to be dreaded. Nearly every frontier Kaffir is now provided with a gun, thanks to the English traders, and very many have horses. The

Kaffirs, being also particularly active and always in excellent training, make splendid light infantry. I believe it was Napoleon who remarked that legs won as many battles as arms: should this be true, the Kaffirs certainly have a great advantage over us, as they can go three miles at least to our two.

Although indifferent marksmen, they are not inferior to the average of our private soldiers, and they are fast improving. Their training from childhood consists in a course of assagy-throwing and a cunning way of approaching and surprising an enemy. As they are in such cases destitute of clothes, they move through the thorny bush with great ease, and are in such light marching order that their impediments are nothing in comparison with those of our soldiers, heavily burdened and tightly strapped. A Kaffir is also seasoned by hardship from childhood, and keeps fat and sleek on the roots and berries which he picks up, occasionally eked out with scraps of meat; while Englishmen rapidly lose their form and flesh by living on the tough old ox that is killed and immediately served out to them as rations.

The individual courage of the frontier Kaffirs is undeniable, and they have given many proofs of it. One case I may mention, which will show the great risk which they will run for their favourite stake, cattle. It was related to me by an eye-witness.

During the time that there was encamped on the Debe flats a force consisting of upwards of two hundred men, the cattle were inclosed nightly in a kraal, formed of bushes and trees cut down, and inclosing a space of some forty yards in diameter. Sentries were placed round this inclosure, in spite of whom, for two nights, the bushes had been removed and two or three oxen taken away. There had been a slight disturbance amongst the cattle each night, but upon inspection everything seemed right. To prevent a third robbery, a number of Hottentots were placed round the kraal and ordered to lie down under the bushes, and to keep quiet. They remained nearly half the night without seeing anything, when one wily fellow noticed a small black object on the ground at a short distance from him, which he thought he had not observed before. Keeping his eyes fixed upon it, he saw a movement when a sentry walked away from it, and a stillness as he approached. The Hottentot remained perfectly quiet until the black object was a few yards from him, when he called out in Kaffir that he was going to shoot. The black object jumped on its feet, whirling an assagy, but only in time to receive a heavy charge of buckshot in the breast, followed up by a bullet, which terminated the career of a Kaffir well known for his daring and cattle-stealing propensities.

That the frontier Kaffir is, in nearly every case, a rogue, a thief, and a liar, no one will, I believe, deny; there is a great deal, however, to be said in excuse for him. He is a savage, uneducated, and misled by the bad example of his forefathers, and he is gradually encroached upon by the white men, who, after a war, most unceremoniously appropriate a certain number of square miles of territory, and tell the original owner that he must either move on, or that he is only a squatter on sufferance.

The Kaffir has had one or two severe lessons, showing him that he is no match for the white man in fair open fights, and so, gathering experience from these lessons, he now rarely runs an open risk, but confines himself to attacks where he has every advantage of numbers and position. His great stronghold is the bush, and without doubt he is there a most dangerous animal. Active, unencumbered with clothing, and his colour well suited for concealment, he glides about like a snake; the knowledge he has gained in surprising the quick-sighted and sharp-eared animals of his country, he now applies to the destruction of his enemies. Hiding himself amongst the roots and underwood, he waits patiently his opportunity, his gun in readiness and his assagies handy. It is not at all remarkable that the raw soldier, whose early training has been the plough or a shop, or some other occupation as little likely to fit him for bush-craft, falls a victim to the hidden foe. The scarlet coat of the British soldier makes him a capital target, while his belts and other trappings retard his movements most effectually.

Lieutenant-Colonel E. Napier, in his work entitled "Excursions in Southern Africa," has described the effect of the trappings of the English soldier in so able a manner, that I am afraid to attempt any further description, but must e'en pirate this author's words, and beg his pardon for the theft:—

"The 'Rode Bashees' of the party, as the Kaffirs denominate our gallant red-jackets, to distinguish them from the 'Amabula' (Boers) and the 'Umlaou,' or Hottentots, of the force, had previously, as much as possible, divested themselves of those old-fashioned 'pipeclay' trammels, only calculated, when on service, to impede the movements and check the brilliant valour of the British troops. Tight tape-laced coatees (scarlet in leprosy) were cast aside, and shell-jackets, well patched with leather, generally speaking, had become the order of the day. Blue dungaree trowsers were substituted for white prolongations. The heavy knapsack had been left at head-quarters, and was replaced by a small canvas bag loosely slung across the right shoulder. Few stiff, leather dog-collars,—most appropriately called 'stocks,'—now answered the roll; and the crown of that very essence of discomfort and uselessness yclept the 'chako' being kicked out, had made way for the rather more sensible head-dress of the 'forage-cap;' whilst, horrible to relate! many a sunburnt, weather-beaten English phiz,—long a stranger to razor or soap-suds, and spite of 'whisker' regulations,—wildly peeped through a bushy jungle of untrimmed beard and luxuriant moustache, which, though rather, it must be admitted, brigand-like appendages, were undoubtedly found more comfortable by the respective wearers than an equal proportion of sores or blisters, with which the 'pale faces were sure to be covered if deprived in this fiery clime of that protection so kindly afforded by Nature.'

"The above is, generally speaking, a correct representation of the British soldier when on actual service; and only shows how completely unfitted are his every-day dress and appointments (though perhaps well enough adapted to the household troops) for the roughing of a campaign; particularly such campaigns as he is most likely to be engaged in, against uncivilized barbarians, under a burning sun, and amidst the abrading effects of dense and thorny jungles.

"No; if the pipeclay martinets, the gold and tape-lacing tailors of the army, cannot bring themselves to study utility and comfort a little more, in the every-day dress of the *working* part of the army, let them, at least, when our brave fellows are called upon for such roughing as that required in the last Kaffir campaign,—let them, I say, safely deposit all these gingerbread trappings in store; rig out our soldiers in a fashion that will afford *some* protection against climate; not impede the free use of their limbs; and give them a chance of marching under a broiling sun, without a *coup de soleil;* or of coming out of a thorny jungle, with some small remnants of clothing on their backs.

"What, with his ordinary dress and accoutrements, was often the result, to the British soldier, of a Kaffir skirmish in the bush? Seeing his Hottentot *compagnons d'armes* dash into the dense thorny covert, and not wishing to be outdone by these little 'black fellows,' he sets its abrading properties at defiance, and boldly rushes in on their wake. His progress is, however, soon arrested; an opposing branch knocks off the tall conical machine curiously balanced, like a milkmaid's pail, on the top of his head. He stoops down to recover his lost treasure; in so doing his 'pouch-box' goes over his head, his 'cross-belts' become entangled. Hearing a brisk firing all around, and wishing to have a part in the fun, he

UNFITNESS OF THE DRESS.

makes an effort to get on to the front, but finds himself most unaccountably held in the obstinate grasp of an unexpected native foe. The thick-spreading and verdant bush, under which the 'chako' has rolled, is the *wacht-een-beetje,*' and, to his cost, he feels in his woollen garments the tenacious hold of its hooked claws; for the more he struggles to get free, the more he becomes entangled in the thorny web. He now hears 'retire' echoing through the adjoining rocks; and his friends, the 'Totties,' as they briskly run past, warn him, in their retreat, that the enemy—who knows right well our bugle-calls—is at their heels. Exhausted by his protracted struggle, whilst maddened at the thought of falling into the power of his cruel foe, the poor fellow makes a desperate effort at escape. In so doing, the ill-omened 'chako' is left to its fate; the *wacht-een-beetje* retains in triumph part of his dress. As he 'breaks covert,' the Kaffirs, with insulting yells, blaze away at him from the Bush; and, scudding across the plain, towards his party, with the ill-adjusted pouch banging against his hinder parts, the poor devil,—in addition to the balls whistling around him,—is also exposed, as he approaches, to the jeers and laughter of his more fortunate comrades!

"Far be it to attempt here to detract from the efficiency and merits of our gallant troops, whose services—spite of every obstacle raised in their way—have been so conspicuous in every part of the globe; I merely wish to point out how very much that efficiency might be increased, by a little attention to the dictates of reason and common sense."

Lieutenant-Colonel Napier evidently does not consider a man who carries weight ought to be matched against one unhampered by such a retarding influence, and he appears also to believe a man would be able both to fight and to march better, if he were not half-choked, or half-crushed, by his accoutrements. In olden times, the armour of a knight, whilst it so fettered him as to almost prevent him from injuring his enemy, still protected his own person. The trappings of the British soldier of the present day merely perform the former half of this service.

The Kaffir is accustomed to act on his own responsibility, is full of self-confidence, and is a kind of independent machine in himself; the common English soldier is trained *not* to think for himself, but to do what he is ordered,—no more, no less. When, therefore, he finds himself separated from his companions, which frequently happens in bush-fighting, surrounded by a dense thicket, a brier under his arm, a mimosa-thorn sticking in his leg, and half a dozen wait-a-bits holding his raiment fast, there is but little blame due to him if he is assagied by his unseen dark-hided foe, who has been long watching for this opportunity.

When provisions or stores are sent from one part to another, the ox-waggon of the country is made use of. A convoy of twenty waggons, and sometimes more, are sent together, an escort of fifty or one hundred men accompanying it. These waggons, each with its team of oxen, cover a great distance, and the road being frequently lined with bush, impenetrable except to a Kaffir, several opportunities of course occur for advantageous ambuscades, where overwhelming numbers can be at once concentrated on any particular spot. To be completely guarded against these Kaffir surprises is next to impossible, the whole thing being done in a few minutes; and, perhaps, during that short time, two or three spans of oxen are whisked off, which one might as well attempt to follow as to chase clouds.

If Kaffirs are attacked in the bush, and they find that they are likely to get the worst of the fight, they do not hesitate a moment about retreating. There is no false delicacy with them, and they are away as fast as their legs can carry them to a more secure and distant locality, only to return again on the first convenient opportunity.

Attacking and destroying their villages inflicts no great loss upon them, for their houses are rebuilt in a few days. The only time when they are likely to suffer is near their harvest season, for their crops then would be destroyed. If they once gather the corn, they soon have it well concealed in holes made for this purpose, which are circular and deep.

I was nearly terminating my career in a corn-pit at Natal, and was therefore well acquainted with its construction. As I was riding round amongst some old deserted kraals looking for bush-pigs, my horse suddenly stumbled; he partly recovered, and then came down on his head; I thought he had the staggers, and tried to jump off. I felt him sinking behind me, and as he was struggling, I had great difficulty in getting clear. I had just got my foot out of the stirrup and was throwing my leg over him, when he fell down several feet, with me on the top of him. The whole of this took place in a few seconds. The dirt, dust, and an avalanche of broken sticks, came tumbling down, and blinded me for a moment. Upon looking about me, I found that we had sunk into an old corn-pit, about twelve feet in depth and seven in diameter. The sides were as hard as stone, for a fire is always kept burning for a day or so in the interior when the pit is first made.

Fortunately, during the fall I was uppermost, otherwise our mingled bones might have been the only intimation that my friends would have had of this misfortune, as the hole was in a very out-of-the way locality.

My pony struggled at first, but, being a very cool hand, soon became quiet. His hind legs were bent under him like those of a dog when he squats down, his head resting against the side of the pit. I could not reach the top to get out, so I set to work with my knife and cut some holes in the side of the pit, and worked my way out as a New Zealander gets up a tree. I then ran to the hut of a squatter about a mile distant, and obtained the aid of half a dozen Kaffirs with spades and picks. We set to work and dug a sort of ramp, which allowed my horse to walk out. He was very much cramped and rather stiff; but after walking about a little, seemed to be all right, and no ill effects followed from the fall, with the exception of a quantity of hair rubbed away, and the fracture of the saddle-tree. Some Kaffirs had covered this pit over with sticks and turf in hopes of earthing some game. It was fortunate there was no sharp stake driven at the bottom of this pit, as is frequently the case; one, if not both of us, might then have been impaled.

It is a difficult thing to surprise Kaffirs, for their spies are always on the alert, and the movements of the main body are made with great rapidity. If a large force invades their country, the Kaffirs will retreat with their cattle to the most inaccessible places; if attacked there, the men fight as long as is prudent, and then beat a retreat, leaving some of their cattle and driving away others. Thus they harass the attacking parties of their enemies during their return, lining every drift (crossing of river) and every bit of cover, firing away like fury, and ready for a rush should an opportunity occur.

After this the Kaffirs break into small bands and invade the colony, burning, murdering, and cattle-lifting. They are sometimes gainers by this system of reprisals, at least until a large force is raised, or extra troops arrive from England. The Kaffirs then eat a little humble-pie, pay a fine in cattle, which they most probably steal again soon, and peace is once more restored. No great punishment is inflicted on these rascals, they being difficult to catch. And when they are caught, and such a lesson could be given them as would act as a caution for years, the English authorities have great fear that any severe punishment which they might inflict would bring the whole of the good but mistaken peace-loving folks of Exeter Hall in full cry on their heels. Moreover, although these philanthropists have a splendid field in England upon which to exercise their feelings, such as prisoners in Newgate who have committed crimes small by comparison with those of the Kaffirs, still the far-off land of Africa must be chosen by them, and the savage, whose great delight, from habit and taste, is to murder and steal, must needs be protected, when he ought to be hung or shot without mercy. If some of these misled and misinformed people were aware how much harm they really did to the savage, and the vast number of lives that have been sacrificed by a want of firmness and of *apparent* cruelty on the part of those intrusted with Kaffir government, they would cease to do wrong out of piety, and would leave the entire management of these matters in the hands of merciful men, who may be on the spot, and whose experience would lead them to discover that a few lives taken without hesitation at the commencement of disputes would eventually prevent the loss of many hundreds.

The policy of showing mercy to the frontier Kaffir murderer is similar to that of allowing a mad dog to run at liberty and bite people rather than to commit the cruelty of knocking it on the head. At the present time, the prompt and decided conduct of the able governor of the Cape appears to have checked a most threatening demonstration of the frontier Kaffirs. The Dutchmen, who are far up in the interior, keep their black neighbours in better order. When there is any just cause for going to war, such a severe punishment is inflicted by them on the Kaffirs, that a score of years will not wipe out the moral effect of the dread that these Dutchmen have inspired. I am convinced that by this apparent severity lives are eventually saved.

Almost all the disasters that we have met with in Africa have been caused by underrating the enemy, or fancying security where there was danger. Perpetual caution and watchfulness are the only safeguards.

THE ASSAGY.

Many people under English dominion have a desire for war, on account of the advantages which they thereby derive, their waggons and oxen being frequently let for months at a time to the commissariat, &c., and standing idle, but well paid for. The more troops there are in the colony, the more money is brought to the inhabitants.

The unfortunate individuals who are settled on the outskirts of the colony, or in situations liable to be attacked, are the great sufferers during war time. In each successive war the Kaffir tribes are found to be better armed and more formidable. Young Kaffirland likes excitement, and having little to lose and everything to gain, trusts to his luck for a *coup*.

The assagy is a formidable weapon in the hands of a Kaffir: it is a light spear about five or six feet long; an iron blade, of nearly two feet in length, is fixed in the wood while the iron is red hot, and the socket is then incased with the fresh sinews of some animal, which hold all firmly together as they contract. When preparing to throw the assagy, the Kaffir holds it about an inch on the wood end of the balance, the back of the hand down, the first finger and thumb grasping, and all the other fingers resting on the wood. He continues jerking the assagy about, to give it the quivering motion that renders it difficult to avoid; while he occasionally pretends to throw it, to put the man aimed at off his guard. All this time he continues jumping about, rushing from side to side, but getting gradually nearer.

Having generally five assagies, he launches them, one after the other, with great rapidity and certain aim, and with sufficient force to drive the iron through a man when thrown from fifty to eighty yards' distance, while some experts can throw them a hundred yards. An assagy may be dodged when it comes singly, and is seen, but a Kaffir prefers throwing it when your back is turned, and generally sends a shower of them. Fortunately the Kaffir nations consider that to poison spears is despicable. When an assagy is quivering in the hand of a Kaffir, it appears to be alive: the quivering motion given to it just before casting continues to affect it during its aërial course.

The *knob-kerries* (sticks with large heavy knobs on the end) are also very favourite weapons, and are thrown with great precision. It is a frequent practice for a dozen or more Kaffirs to go out after quail, and to knock over great numbers of birds with their sticks.

The Kaffir men assume a vast amount of dignity, and look down upon the Hottentots, Fingoes, &c., as a very inferior race to themselves. Gratitude they scarcely seem to know, and charity is looked upon as a weakness.

I saw a Kaffir come into the commissioner's residence one day to sell some horses; he made out a most miserable story of his distress, stating that his cattle had been taken by our soldiers, although he was a most peaceably disposed man: he was in consequence very hungry, having really little or nothing to eat.

Trading at this time was forbidden between the Kaffirs and the colonists, and this man wanted to go into the colony to turn his horses into cash. The commissioner, thinking the Kaffir's account was untrue, refused him this permission, although the applicant talked most eloquently for two hours in support of his case, frequently complaining of his hunger. He was told, at length, by the commissioner, to eat his horses if he were starving. The Kaffir, giving with his tongue a loud click (always expressive of disgust and indignation), sat silent for nearly a minute, he then stood up to his full height, and wrapping his blanket round him, told the commissioner, with a grand air, that he was not a Hottentot: he here referred to the practice these men have of eating the *quagga*, or zebra.

Finding all the talking of no avail, the Kaffir at length squeezed out a few tears; they appeared so genuine that an officer who was present gave him a shilling to get some meat. The Kaffir quietly pocketed it, and, looking round to one of his followers, said, in a low tone, "What does this fool of an Englishman expect to get from me?"

The horses which the Kaffirs use are small, underbred, but hardy animals. A Kaffir soon ruins them, as he surely gives the horse a sore back, and always rides at full gallop. He considers a horse to be of no use unless it is ridden fast, as he can go along on foot at six miles an hour.

These Kaffirs think that it is vulgar to appear in a hurry to talk about any subject, however important it may be to them. A party coming in to see the interpreter on business, rush up at full gallop, their blankets flying out behind them, and their whips busily at work. They pull up close to the talking-house, jump off and fasten their horses to a bush, or turn them out to graze, they themselves quietly sitting down to smoke. In about an hour the chief man gets up, stretches himself, as though much fatigued and lazy, and quietly walks to the house of the interpreter, giving him the usual salutation, and talking at first on indifferent subjects. When the Kaffir considers that there is a good opening, he broaches the matter for which he came, but with an assumed air of indifference and carelessness. When it has been fully discussed, he quietly walks out and sits talking the whole matter over with his councillors; all the black party then mount, and dash off with the same reckless speed.

The Kaffirs are most daring riders. They will ride at full speed down the steepest and most dangerous hills. It is true that they frequently get most fearful *"purls,"* but their neck-joints appear to be more firmly constructed than ours.

Some of the friendly Kaffirs who came in to see us were very good shots. Kona, one of the chiefs, fired at a quart bottle stuck up at a hundred yards, sending all his bullets within a few inches, and at last knocked the neck off. He sat down on the ground, and aimed by resting his left hand on the ramrod, which he stuck in the ground for a support; this sort of shooting would be quite good enough to annoy troops in a thick bushy country.

I think that the next Kaffir war, which is now nearly due, will be a very severe one, unless some individual out there thinks of *" burning the bush "* that these black fellows hide in; a method that was suggested by some wise head in England, who condemned the stupidity of the Capites for not having done it before. Surely there has been enough intellect in South Africa to have thought of this long ago, had it been possible. Unfortunately, the greater part of the trees are evergreen, and therefore rather unfit for a blaze. Let the wise proposer try his success on his boxwood hedges, or his rhododendrons, and then imagine patches of forty square miles of similarly constituted vegetation; he will at once see that burning is not so very simple a process.

It is scarcely to be wondered at that in civilized countries, man should bow to his fellow-man, and quietly submit to be his slave, as very many are compelled thus to cringe for their daily bread. But it does appear extraordinary that amongst savages this same submission and obedience should be practised, as the chief is frequently undistinguishable from his commonest man, and the latter is independent of the former as regards food, clothing, or any other of the world's goods. Yet no clansman in Scotland yields half the homage to the head of his clan that the African savage does to his chief. This feeling of obedience would render almost useless any attempt to employ the Kaffirs as our soldiers, a plan that appears now to have some supporters in England. We might give our orders to these black troops, but if a chief winked his eye, or held up his finger, not a man would obey us until he had received his chief's permission.

The Kaffir's ornaments are simple, but characteristic; such as strings of beads interspersed with the teeth of wolves, lions, or hyænas, while necklaces made of the claws only are generally worn by chiefs of distinction.

The white beads and teeth contrast strongly with the dark skins of these people, and produce a very good effect. Round their wrists they wear rings of brass, which are welded firmly on, and extend sometimes nearly to the elbows; higher up the arm rings of ivory are worn, which are punched out from the tusks of elephants. Both the teeth necklaces and the ivory rings are much valued, and cannot readily be purchased. I possess a specimen of both ornaments; the former I with great difficulty obtained for eight shillings, a sum nearly equal in value to a cow.

There appears to be great doubt, even amongst the best-informed, as to a Kaffir's religion; that the Kaffirs have a belief in the future state, there is, however, no doubt; but in what way they really look on this state it is difficult to determine. They believe in apparitions and the return of the spirits of their departed friends after death. *Shulanga* is the term which they use to express this idea, and a Kaffir attributes most of his successes and escapes to the thoughtful watchfulness of a friendly spirit. They are believers in witchcraft to an unlimited extent; but what they understand by the term is very difficult to say. I once obtained the character of a wizard by mixing a seidlitz-powder, and drinking it off during effervescence, for the spectators took for granted that the water was boiling. The rain-makers have enormous control over the tribes at times; but acquaintance with the white man lessens the faith in these wizards.

The Hottentots are certainly the ugliest race on earth, and the first view of them causes a feeling of almost horror. Men they are, without doubt, but many look more like baboons; their high cheek-bones, small eyes, thick lips, yellow mummy sort of skin, with a few little crumbs of hair like peppercorns stuck over their heads and chins, give them a most ridiculous appearance. Their short stature, rarely over five feet, and frequently less, with the rough costume of untanned leather breeches, &c., would make but a sorry spectacle were they to be paraded in Regent-street on their rough-looking Cape horses beside a troop of Life-guards. But still greater would be the ridicule were a troop of the latter to be transported to Africa, and then told to follow these active little Hottentot soldiers through the bush, and to attack the band of Kaffirs hidden in the dark kloof above: each is good in his calling.

The Cape corps is almost entirely composed of Hottentots, and they are right well fitted for the work of fighting the Kaffirs. Courageous and cunning, endowed with a sort of instinct that seems superior to reason, they can hear, see, and almost smell danger in all shapes, and are ever on the watch for suspicious signs. No footmark of Kaffir, wolf, lion, or elephant is passed unnoticed; no bird is seen to flit away from a distant bush without apparent cause, but a careful watch is at once set up; not a dog lifts up his ears, but the Totty—as the Hottentot is familiarly called—is also suspicious.

The wild life led in Africa causes even one lately removed from civilization to feel his instincts become rapidly keener.

A man who has been born and nurtured in the wilderness, therefore, must be far superior to the freshly transplanted European, who finds that he has to commence the A, B, C, under these very men whose appearance would at first produce only a feeling of contempt for their prowess.

A deadly hatred exists between the Kaffir and the Hottentot, and both are equally expert in the bush, where an Englishman is so rarely at home.

In fair fighting the British soldier has proved that no country produces men fit to cope with him; but let him be cautious of ambuscades and bush-fighting.

A naval officer, who was in a fort on the west coast of Africa, happened to be attacked by the natives, but as his fort was a stronghold that the barbarians could make nothing of, they were easily repulsed. Elated with his successful defence, he sallied out, and gave them a good drubbing on some open ground near. But not contented with this triumph, he must needs follow them up into the bush, where he was defeated with great slaughter. His jaw-bones are now said to be beating the big drum of Ashantee.

Our victories over the barbarians of Africa have not been so very great, but that we might condescend to take a useful lesson from these men, savages as they are.

Any man who has seen the Kaffirs or Hottentots approach dangerous game,—their perseverance, courage, activity, and hardihood, combined with caution and cunning, may easily understand that they could employ these gifts in a manner that would make them anything but despicable enemies.

There is a recklessness about the Hottentot which the Kaffir does not possess, the former being a thorough spendthrift. Give him ammunition for his defence, and he will blaze away at tree or bush, air or ground, until it is all expended, and with no other object or reason than for amusement, or thinking that a Kaffir *might* be near.

I had the following story from a Kaffir, one of the actors, who remarked to me the great quantity of ammunition that had been wasted in a skirmish.

Three Kaffirs were hidden behind some rocks on a hill, watching the advance of a party of the Hottentots who were sent out to take cattle. As this party entered a ravine below the Kaffir spies, one of the latter crept down in the bush, and, taking care to get a safe place, fired a shot. A volley from the Hottentots was the response, and they continued firing into the bush, from which no return came, until the whole of their ammunition was expended. The Kaffir remarked to me that, had his party been larger, he could then have attacked the lavish invaders at a great advantage.

I always admired the neat little double-barrelled carbine of the Cape corps; it is light, effective, and, being double-barrelled, is far more destructive where snap-shooting is all the chance one gets. I never thoroughly understood why the whole army should not have double-barrelled guns.

It is a difficult matter at first to tell the Fingo from the Kaffir, but after a little practice one soon sees many distinctions. The Fingo, for instance, always bores holes in his ears, and frequently carries things in them, which is not the case with the Kaffir.

The frontier bush is principally composed of the mimosa and wait-a-bit thorn; the fish-hook-like shape of the latter, and the long spears of the former, make a journey through the bush very destructive to clothes: one ought to have a suit of armour to get on comfortably.

CHAPTER III.

Narrow escape—Sandilli goes home—Voyage to Natal—My fellow-passengers—Tempting viands—Property overboard—Natal Bay—The "tick"—Beauty of the vegetation—Dolce far niente—Cape horses—Points of a Cape horse—Shooting-ponies—Mode of journeying—The "sickness"—Training a shooting-horse—Endurance of Cape horses—A rough journey—A stormy night—Agreeable termination.

AFTER about eight months of frontier life, which was little better than so much banishment, I had directions to leave the colony and embark at Algoa Bay for conveyance to Natal. I had to wait in the wretched town of Port Elizabeth for a period of three weeks, during which time I was nearly drowned in the bay, owing to swimming out too far, and forgetting the strength of the current which set along the shore. While waiting there, I visited the pretty little village of Uitenage, with its neat houses, gardens, and tree-lined streets.

On the road to Graham's Town, I met a large party of Kaffirs, galloping along as usual, leaving a cloud of dust behind. They pulled up as I met them, when I recognized the great Gaika chief Sandilli, Anta the giant, a splendid fellow nearly seven feet high, and all the aristocracy of Kaffirland. They had been for some time prisoners in Graham's Town for their rebellious conduct in not stopping the cattle-stealing of their men, but had now been let out, and allowed to go home, on condition of promising to be good boys in future, and kissing the governor's great toe. They appeared to be in high spirits, and, in answer to my "*Uya pina?*" (Where are you going?) shouted with exultation, "*Goduka*" (Going home).

The little ship that carried me and my goods from Port Elizabeth was badly supplied in every way. The captain was a happy bridegroom, and because he had been living for a fortnight on love, seemed to think that others should have equally as refined an appetite. I thought that even our start was bad, for there was something wrong in getting the anchor up.

The other passengers were two in number,—the one a jolly fat Dutchman, who used to sit in his little chest-of-drawers-like bed-place, and tootle unknown airs on a flute; and the other a carpenter well to do at Natal, who never changed his clothes, and talked through his nose.

As the cabin was only eight feet square, there was no place for the latter individual to sleep upon but the floor. He shook down a blanket for his bed, and regularly at about ten o'clock became horizontal, and, looking at me with only one eye open, remarked that he "turned in all standing like a trooper's 'orse." This he repeated with precisely the same expression of face every night, till at last it made me quite nervous, and I used to remain very late on deck for the sole object of escaping this infliction. When he did not use his nose for talking, he still prevented it from lying silent by snoring through it with a sound like a locomotive engine blowing off steam.

The distance from Algoa Bay to Natal was but 600 miles, and yet we were twenty-three days on that tempestuous coast, most of the time half under water. A hurricane blew during the greater part of the voyage, and in ten days after leaving Algoa Bay we were off Cape L'Agulhas, or 300 miles further from our destination than when we started.

I should not have been so much annoyed, had there been anything to eat or drink; but the beer was all finished in three days: wine there was none, with the exception of a composition of Cape stuff, that had been shaken up into the appearance of a pot of blacking, and was very like vinegar in taste. A dish of pork swimming in its own fat was our usual meal, with the exception of some mutton, which I declined, in consequence of having seen the sheep die a death all but natural. This fate was only prevented by the wonderful activity of a sailor, who acted as butcher, and who, on seeing from aloft the state of affairs, came down one of the back stays by the run, and stuck his knife into the—I am afraid to say which —sheep, or mutton. He declared, however, that it was sheep, while the fat Dutchman "verdamt" it was mutton. A jury of the captain and mate was called, who took evidence, and decided that the sheep had been fairly killed.

Another delicacy with which we were favoured was some water in which a cabbage was daily boiled; this composition the captain dignified with the name of soup; it came day after day, and was worse each time—while around the taffrail ten more cabbages hung.

I was sitting one day beside the Dutchman, improving my knowledge of his language, when I noticed that he had been for some time looking with a melancholy sort of face at this row of esculents. Our eyes met, and he asked me, with an expressive voice, " if I liked cabbage-soup?" I met him more than half-way, and said, " No; and if you are only a man, we won't have any more." We understood one another immediately, and met on that evening by appointment, when the halter of each vegetable was quickly cut, and they all dropped with a cheerful splash into the sea. Suspicions there might be, and were, respecting the guilty party, but no certainty.

We were all alarmed one day by the mate reporting that there was a deal of water forward amongst the coals; so all hands set to work to get the coals out, and then to look for a leak; which proceeding was not accomplished without considerable risk, as the sea was tremendous, and the little brigantine, being only about 140 tons, made very bad weather of it. Fortunately there was no leak, the water having come from above instead of below, owing to the heavy pitching.

We envied the fine-looking Indiamen, who frequently rolled past us with their stun'-sails set and every sail drawing, while we were pitching and tossing, and making scarcely any progress. "More wind in your jib," was frequently applied by our sailors to the vessels that met us, and at length was responded to by the south-east gale changing to a north-west, which enabled us eventually to reach the wished-for Bluff of Natal, where we were boarded by the port-boat. With only one bump on the bar, we passed to the smooth water inside, and, sailing along the narrow channel, obtained a sight of the glorious bay of Port Natal.

It is difficult for any pen to give an adequate idea of the beautiful view, and almost impossible for one as unskilled as mine, to convey to the imagination of the reader even a slight impression of the glorious reality that was presented by the bay and surrounding country of Natal. It broke suddenly upon the wearied eye after three weeks' perpetual contemplation of leaden-coloured water had tired the vision and caused a thirst for the green and earthy.

On our left, as we entered, rose the bluff, densely wooded to the water's edge, the branches of the trees, with their rich foliage, almost brushing the vessel's yards. Two hundred and fifty feet of this nearly perpendicular vegetable-clad wall formed our foreground, while the middle distance was represented by the calm and brilliant waters of the bay, with two or three thickly-wooded islands. Numbers of wild fowls floated about, and among these the delicate colours of the flamingo and the grotesque forms of the pelican were conspicuous, the white plumage of some cranes standing out like stars in the blue waters. In the distance were seen the densely wooded hills of the Berea and the white chimneys of a few of the plastered houses of D'Urban village; while little wreaths of light smoke coming through the trees gave indication that the culinary processes of a habitation were being carried on.

The waters of the bay extend nearly six miles inland, and at the extreme end, the refraction from heat, &c., caused some of the mangrove-trees that lined the banks to be magnified or inverted, while others appeared to be suspended in the air, and to have no connection with the earth below. We dropped our anchor in this smoothest of harbours, where no wind could move the ship. As we were within a few yards of the shore, we soon received visits from several residents, who came to the vessel for the latest news.

I was so ill when I landed, on account of the confinement on board and our bad provisions, that I was obliged to remain in bed for several days at the miserable "hotel" of the village: I was kindly attended by the resident surgeon of the troops, under whose skilful hands I soon recovered.

Having regained health and strength, I began to look out for a horse, but had great difficulty in getting all that I required; at length an animal was offered me at a reasonable price, and he became my property. He merely served for riding about in the deep sandy roads near, or for saving me from the persecution of a little animal called a "tick," whose armies were quartered upon every blade of grass and leaf of tree. On the first opportunity these little creatures transferred their adhesive qualities, with great delight, to the most retired situations of a newly-arrived victim; there they would bury themselves under the skin, and before their invasion could be discovered, produced an irritation and a sore that enlarged with great rapidity and became a serious evil.

A thorough inspection and frequent bathing were the two best antidotes; the leaf of the Kaffir gooseberry I also found very effective; it should be bruised, laid over the part bitten, and held on by wrappers of linen.

BEAUTY OF THE VEGETATION.

Each ride that I took brought more beauties before me; the sterile appearance of the frontier was here exchanged for the most luxuriant and fragrant vegetation. Forests appeared, hung with creepers and scented blossoms; undulating grassy slopes, with detached and park-like clumps of trees. Here and there the calm silvery water of the bay was seen in the distance through openings in the forest, or under the flat horizontal foliage of the umbrella-acacia, whose graceful shape, combined with the palm, the gigantic euphorbias, and the brilliant Kaffir-boom, formed the characteristics of this bush. Let the admirers of architectural art talk of their edifices and public buildings, they are not equal to a single tree. Bricks and mortar, stones, plaster, chimneys, &c., are heaps of rubbish when compared to a natural forest, every leaf and flower of which is a witness and an evidence of that mighty Power who creates with as much ease the endless worlds about us as the minutest details of vegetable and animal life, the perfect working and machinery of which are more than wonderful.

The annoyance to which an individual must submit during a voyage over nine thousand miles of ocean is well repaid by a scene of this kind, that scarcely needs its accompaniments of many animated specimens of nature, in the shape of birds, bucks, and monkeys, to enliven it. Still, however, there are some human natures so dead to the purely beautiful, and so entirely fettered to the things less pure, that all the beauty I have so feebly described is passed over unadmired and almost unnoticed; and the same round and routine is carried on in the leisure hours of such men as though they were in Portsmouth, Plymouth, or some other well-peopled town.

"How do you pass your time?" I asked of an intellectual looking gentleman with whom I dined soon after landing.

"Oh, I backy a good deal, and bathe sometimes, but it is too hot to do much," was his answer.

"Do you sketch?"

"Well, I'm no hand at that."

"Is there no game about? I have heard that bucks were numerous and elephants very near."

"Well, if you bother about them, I dare say you may see lots; but it's too much trouble for me, and I am no shot."

Poor miserable man! he took no interest in anything; he had no pleasure in viewing the most wonderful and beautiful works of nature, and had no gratification in placing on paper even a poor representation of the scenes before his eyes, for the future amusement of friends less favoured by locality. No! there was trouble or bother in it; there was neither, he thought, in smoking tobacco, and drinking brandy-and-water: the first habit, however, has ruined his health, the latter his prospects and character.

I know many men who through their devotion to field-sports have avoided many of those evils which others, through nothing but a life of idleness, have incurred.

I was soon fortunate enough to purchase a very useful second pony, which was an accomplished animal in every way: he would stop immediately when I dropped the reins, or crossed the gun over the saddle, or rested my hand on his neck, or even if a buck sprung up in front of him. He would stand fire like a rock, and would not shake his head or start on any account, nor did he care for elephants or anything else. He was a most useful auxiliary, and from his back I shot elands, hartebeest, reitbok, ourebis, steinbok, duikers, &c. He would allow small bucks to be put up behind the saddle, and would carry them quietly.

I passed a month in making myself acquainted with the country around D'Urban, its rivers, paths, and kloofs, and also in studying the Zulu language, which I found to differ slightly from the frontier Kaffir. I always carried a dictionary with me, and, upon meeting any natives, sat down, and, pulling out my book, asked word for word what I wanted. I rarely failed in making myself understood, and then the Kaffir would repeat my words, giving the correct pronunciation and grammar. If, for instance, I was thirsty and wanted some milk, I would look in my dictionary for "I want." *Funa*, I would find, expressed to want; *amasi* or *ubisi*, milk (the first being sour milk, a very refreshing drink, and the latter sweet milk); *uku posa*, to drink. "Funa ubisi uku posa," I would say. The Kaffir would give a kind of intelligent grunt, such as *er-er*, and say, "Wena funa posa ubisi." I then repeated the sentence after him, putting *di*, I, for *wena*, you, and bore in mind that "Di funa posa amasi (*or* ubisi)," was I want to drink some sour (or sweet) milk. By this means I was soon able to ask for everything I wanted, and in six months could talk the language with tolerable freedom.

I found it of inconceivable use in my solitary trips, as I was then independent of Dutch farmers, English squatters, &c.; a Kaffir kraal always supplying the few things I wanted; and I was by its aid enabled to see and hear more than by any other means.

I recommend every person who may be in a strange country at once to set to work and acquire its language; it turns out generally a most useful amusement.

By these Kaffirs I was taught the art of spooring; my lessons were learned over the print of some buck's foot on the bent-down blade of a bit of grass. Spooring requires as much study and practice as any other science, and a professor is often required to decide some knotty point, such as the number of days since a buffalo passed, or at what hour certain elephants rolled in the mud. It first appeared to me very much a matter of guess, but I afterwards saw the reasons throughout for the Kaffirs' conclusions.

A few rough outlines, showing the spoors of some of the different South-African animals may be useful to an inexperienced hunter.

A is the footprint of a Bull Elephant (circular).
B   ,,   Cow Elephant (elliptical).
C   ,,   Rhinoceros.
D   ,,   Hippopotamus.
E   ,,   Buffalo. The animal can also be known by its dung being different from that of the antelope.
F   ,,   Eland.
G the footprint of antelopes of different species, such as the Hartebeest, Reitbok, Duiker, and Bush-buck; practice will alone enable the sportsman to distinguish between each.
H is the footprint of a Wild Pig or Vleck Vark.
I   ,,   Ostrich.
K   ,,   Hyæna.
L   ,,   Leopard; the Lion's is similar but much larger.

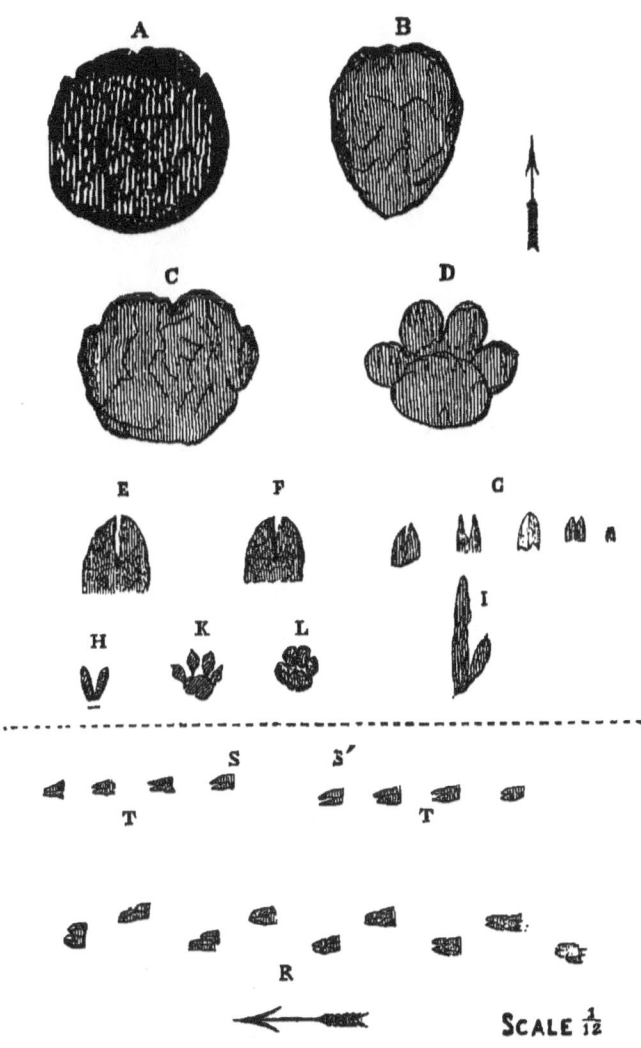

The pace at which an animal has travelled may be judged by the impressions of its footmarks, or the position in which these impressions lie.

T would indicate that an animal had galloped or cantered, the distance between S and S' being great or small, in proportion as the animal had moved fast or slowly.

R would indicate that the animal had walked or trotted; if it had moved at a trot, the toes of the hoof would be seen to have indented themselves in the ground more deeply than had the heel, and most probably some grass, gravel, or soil, would be found lying on the ground, they having been kicked up by the animal in its rapid passage. Practice alone enables a man to judge of the length of time that has elapsed since the animal passed. A good plan is to scrape up the ground with the foot and compare this "spoor" with the animal's footprints.

When judging of elephants, it may be concluded, that if they browsed, they must have moved slowly; if they are found to have passed through the forest in Indian file, they travelled at a quick walk; and if they disregarded old paths and smashed the branches or trees in their course, that they moved very rapidly. Other signs the hunter will soon learn by experience, that best of all instructors.

The Kaffirs in this district are most quiet, harmless, honest people, living in small villages, each of about twenty kraals. These they build in a ring, the place for the cattle being in the centre. The houses of these people are composed of wicker-work and thatch. One or two stout poles are driven into the centre of a circle of about fifteen feet in diameter; round the circumference of the circle, long pliable sticks are stuck into the ground, and then bent over and made fast to the top of the pole or poles driven into the centre, which are left about eight feet out of the ground. This framework gives the skeleton outline of a beehive-looking hut, which the builders cross with other pieces, and finally thatch with long grass.

The furniture consists generally of two or three assagies, some club-sticks, a pipe made from an ox's horn, some skins, a few dried gourds to retain the milk, a wooden pillow, some beads, and small gourd snuff-boxes. These habitations are certainly snug, warm when a fire is lighted, and cool without one. They are entered by a small opening about three feet high, which is closed by a wicker-work door. The whole clump of huts is surrounded by high palings.

Although they numbered near seventy thousand souls, if not more, these Kaffirs lived together, and with the white intruders, in the greatest harmony. Scarcely a case of theft or crime was known amongst them during my residence of two years and upwards. Many of them have run away from the tyranny of the Zulu king across the Tugela river; and finding safety in the protection afforded by the presence of the white men, they live a pastoral and harmless life.

I have trusted myself alone amongst them, many miles from any other white man, and never met with anything disrespectful or annoying in their treatment. If much accustomed to deal with white men, they are given sometimes to ask for presents; but the less they know of the whites, the less I always found the Kaffirs so disposed. As auxiliaries in the bush they were unequalled, and I rarely moved without taking at least two with me. Enduring, cheerful, sensible, and unassuming, they were thoroughly skilled in tracking game; they could be sent home with a buck, and the horse thus be kept unincumbered, or the hunter himself free for more sport.

I was always gathering some lesson from them either as to the animals which we pursued, their habits or their trail, the things good to eat in the forests or those to be avoided. The Kaffirs' ambition was limited, a cow or a blanket being sometimes the extent of their desires.

In a country of this description one has the pleasure of great freedom. It is certainly pleasant for once in a life to feel like a wild man,—to throw off all the restraints imposed by the rules of society, and to wander, unwatched, uncriticised, amongst the wonders and beauties of nature. Dress, that all-important subject in civilized countries, and about which the minds of hundreds are wholly engrossed, is here a dead letter, or nearly so. Could a man dye his hide a dark brown, he might walk about with a few strips of wild-beast skins hung around him, and not attract particular attention. Novelty has certainly a wonderful charm, and perhaps it may be for this reason that a man fresh from civilization feels so much pleasure in sharing the pastimes and excitements of the savage. A wet tent is by no means an agreeable residence, and frequently during the heavy rains that visited Natal, I shouldered my gun, and paid an afternoon call to some Kaffirs who lived a

mile or so from my camping-ground. We had plenty of conversation, and could afford mutual instruction about many subjects on which we were each respectively ignorant. I believe that, if we inquire without partiality, we shall find no man so ignorant but that there is some one subject upon which he can instruct us. I rarely found a Kaffir who could not afford me a vast amount of information on many subjects; and all the cunning and art of an English lawyer would scarcely improve the Kaffir's style of reasoning. I believe that common sense is more admired by the savage than the civilized man; it certainly is by the savages with whom I have conversed. While in civilization the most sensible and sound arguments or advice are " pooh-poohed" or neglected, because they happen to come from one who is unknown in the world for wealth, position, or fashion, amongst savages these same arguments or advices are received at their proper valuation, irrespective of the soil from whence they spring. The words of a chief or *induna**
are generally worth hearing, and consequently receive their proper respect; but if the logic used by either happens to be unsound, any common man whose capacity is equal to the competition may enter the lists, and come out victorious; a Kaffir is not too bigoted to acknowledge that he may have been wrong. The man who thus gained a victory by his more sensible argument would neither be much elevated nor proud in consequence, but would merely consider himself as a man who had pointed out a by-path that had been overlooked by the tra-

* Councillor.

veller. The Kaffirs easily appreciate reasoning by analogy; I frequently tried its powers upon them, and with invariable success. On one occasion an old Kaffir laughed at me, because of a mistake that I made in speaking his language. I used the word *inyama* to express *black*, when I should have used *mnyama*; the former word signifying *flesh* or *meat*. After he had laughed immoderately, I asked him how long he had known Englishmen; he said, many tens of moons. I then said, "How much English do you speak?" "None." "Why not?" "Because I cannot hear the Englishman's words." I then told him that I had known Kaffirs scarcely twenty moons, that I could speak my own language as well as he spoke his, and, in addition, I could speak his sufficiently well to converse. Therefore he ought to laugh at himself for knowing nothing of my language, not at me for knowing so little of his; besides which, as his hair was grey, he ought to possess more wisdom. He was much struck by the argument, and repeated it to several other Kaffir men, all of whom appeared equally to appreciate it. I doubt whether a civilized man would have been as much affected by this reasoning as were the Kaffirs; for how often do we find that foreigners are ridiculed by the ignorant Englishman because they cannot speak English correctly, the quiz forgetting at the same time that he cannot utter two words correctly in any other language than his own, and that he very frequently fails even in that.

But it is the vulgar error to laugh at people as ignorant because we may discover that they know less on some one subject than we do. Some of our most scientific men would be sad "pigeons" and regular dunces, were they to show in the ring at Epsom, and few of our celebrated statesmen would be equal to the savage in the crafts necessary in an African forest. The savages rarely make the blunder of choosing the wrong man; they are very excellent judges of character, and consequently would not choose a man to fire a long shot or fight a battle because he was a good hand at stringing beads together, or talking at their council-fires. They select the man on account of his fitness for the post. Here savages have a great advantage over civilized men. Amongst the latter, individuals are frequently chosen in the most fantastic way;—mere theorists are used for practical purposes; and men placed in positions where quick decision and energy of character are all-important, and where trifles should not be allowed to interfere, because perhaps these men have excelled in the minute details of some office, or are famous for increasing a correspondence already too large. We might as reasonably select a man to ride our racers simply because he had studied and understood the anatomy of the horse. While the learned theorist was arguing about or reasoning on which muscle or nerve ought to be excited, the practical jock would be busy at the "pull and hustle," and would win as he pleased. The Kaffirs, from whom my experience was gained, however low they ranked in savage society, had none of the offensive or presumptuous manners that are met with so frequently amongst the vulgar in civilization. They never pretended to more than they possessed in any way, or by a system of deceit, lying, or false appearance, endeavoured to persuade others that they were really more than simple savages.

Let us now contrast these men with a civilized house. On one occasion I paid a visit to the house of a settler, who was clothed in white linen jacket, straw hat, fustian trowsers, and coarse shirt, and was busy at work in his garden. His wife met me, and, being acquainted, we at once entered into conversation. I wished to hear about the soil, the thriving of poultry, &c.; but at first this would-be great lady could utter nothing but apologies for being so " dreadfully dressed." She then gave a long history of the number of her great friends in England, and described the astonishment of these aristocrats were they to hear of *her* being in such a wilderness. Then, pointing to her husband, she said, "Ah, dear me! to see —— now, you would scarcely imagine what a stylish man he was formerly. In England, he used to wear his hair long, and when he had greased it, and put on a clean shirt on a Sunday, there was not a more gentlemanly-looking man in London." With some difficulty I immediately invented a story, at which I pretended to laugh immoderately, and thus concealed my want of appreciation of the former elegance of her dear, fallen spouse.

The extremes on very many occasions appear to meet. The perfectly uncultivated man is certainly nearer perfection than he who has picked up a little knowledge, and is puffed up in consequence. We see this in so many subjects. In music, for instance, it is sweeter to hear a person (who may be ignorant of the science) play by ear an air, than listen to the struggles and unmusical contortions produced by some beginner trying to play by notes, on scientific principles. When one advances, and makes the acquired knowledge subservient to the natural, the admired effect is then produced.

A ring, composed of grease, wax, and wood, is worn on the head of the Kaffir men. I believe it to be a sign of a man having arrived at the dignity of marriage; it is called *esikoko*, the two *k*'s signifying two clicks of the tongue.

This clicking is a peculiarity of several South-African languages. The Bushmen, Hottentots, and Kaffirs have each several clicks. The Natal Kaffirs use but three, and these not frequently, as there are few words but can be understood without the click. In the Bushmen's language, very many are used, and I have heard that a Bushman is not considered to speak his language elegantly until age has deprived him of all his teeth. These curious little men use a great deal of action during their conversation; and it is said, that if a Bushman wishes to talk during a dark night, he is obliged to light a fire, to enable the listeners to see his action, and thereby fully to comprehend his meaning. A deadly hatred exists between the Kaffirs and the Bushmen, and war to the knife is the result of any chance encounter, always supposing that neither party can retreat, as they have a mutual dread of each other.

I soon made inquiries with reference to the game in the Natal district, and was informed that the following were the principal animals that were plentiful; viz.,— snipe, quail, partridges of three species, pheasant, two species of Guinea-fowl,—one that was generally found in the plains, the other in the forests: the latter was a very fine bird, excellent eating, and very handsome; he had a fine top-knot on his head, but was otherwise similar, only superior in size, to that of the plains. Two species of bustards were common; viz., the coran and the pouw, both excellent eating, the latter frequently reaching to a great size and weight. Ostriches were sometimes met on the plains near the Draakensburg Mountains. Many birds, brilliantly adorned, frequented the forests, amongst which the golden cuckoo and the lowry were conspicuous. Eagles and hawks of all sizes sailed around in search of prey, while the little sugar-birds, with their long fluttering tails and their dazzling plumage, gave an appearance of life to every bush.

Three species of bush-buck were plentiful in the forests along the coast. The finest is the black bush-buck (*Tragelaphus sylvaticus*). The male is three feet high, and about five feet long; he is very elegant, and stouter than the generality of antelopes; his horns about a foot long, nearly straight, and wrinkled near the base; the general colour is dark chestnut, black above, and marked with a streak of white along the spine, with several white spots about the body: the female is similar, but lighter-coloured, and without horns. The ears, large and round, are well adapted for the bush, and the hunter must be an adept who approaches these antelopes without causing them alarm; few shots are obtained at them, owing to their watchfulness. The red bush-buck (*Oreotragus griseus*) is a very common antelope in the wooded tracts up the south-eastern coast. The male is about two feet high, and about three in length; small horns, three inches long, smooth, round, and vertical; large ears; colour deep reddish-brown : the female similar, but hornless. The foot of this buck, between the division of the hoof underneath, has a small hole that reaches to the fetlock-joint; a straw can be pushed up in it to that extent. I cannot conceive its object. The blue buck (*Cephalophorus cæruleus*) is a beautiful creature; the male is scarcely more than a foot in height, and about two feet three inches long; ears like a rat's, but much larger; small and conical horns, two inches in length, closely annulated; colour dark blue, or mouse-colour: female hornless and smaller, otherwise similar. These three bush-bucks were solitary, and very wary. The latter antelope was very difficult to distinguish in the gloom of the bush, his colour suiting well for concealment. The duiker (*Cephalopus mergens*) : most frequently found amongst bushes, or long grass; about two feet high, three feet eight inches long; horns four inches in length; colour dun: female with smaller horns, otherwise similar. The steinbuck (*Oreotragus tragulus*): about twenty-one inches high, and three feet in length; horns four inches long, wrinkled at the base, slender and pointed; colour brownish-red, with belly white: female hornless, otherwise similar. Generally found in bushy ground along the hills. The ourebi (*Oreotragus scoparius*) : two feet high at shoulder, and four in length; horns annulated, and about five inches long; colour pale tawny, with white belly: female similar, but hornless and smaller.

Generally found in the plains in pairs. The reit-buck (*Eleotragus reduncus*) : three feet high, nearly five feet in length; horns one foot long, and annulated near the base; ears six inches long; colour ashy grey, white beneath: female smaller, but hornless, otherwise similar. Resides variously in reeds, grass, and near bushes. Generally found in pairs. He frequently lies down in a small patch of grass, and, from his colour, is overlooked by the sportsmen.

The leopard (*Felis leopardus*) : male two feet six inches high at the shoulder, and seven feet in extreme length; armed with long teeth and retractile claws; colour tawny and reddish-brown; the chin, breast, belly, and inside of extremities white, irregularly marked with spots of black, which vary in size and colour at different ages and states of condition; tail nearly four feet long: female similar, but smaller. Found in thick coverts, either bush or reeds. Destructive to poultry, cattle, and game; generally seizes its victim by the back of the neck.

The spotted hyæna (*Crocuta maculata*) : height about two feet six inches, sloping towards the rump; length about five feet ten inches; colour brown, with blotches of circular black spots; white under; head short and broad; feet like a dog's; common in bush and plain: female similar. Destructive to sheep, calves, and foals; seizing them by the flank, and holding on until the piece gives way or the animal falls. This animal possesses a wonderful strength of jaw, grinding the bones of the largest animals to powder: it is very cowardly. The *Crocuta brunnea* was also common, but did not very greatly differ in habits or appearance from the spotted hyæna.

The wild hog (*Sus Scrofa*) : height two feet six inches; extreme length about five feet; canine teeth very strong, those in the upper jaw projecting horizontally, those in the lower upwards; colour dirty brown; bristles long; tail a foot long. Inhabits the forests (gregarious).

The African wild boar (*Phacochærus æthiopicus*) :. height two feet six inches; extreme length six feet; colour reddish brown; covered with bristles; canine teeth, very large, curved upwards, forming a semicircle; head very large, a large fleshy wen behind each eye, and an excrescence on each side of the muzzle; tail tufted with bristles, two feet long, straight. Gregarious; found in the plains; retreats into holes in the ground when pursued; dangerous when wounded.

The reh-buck (*Eleotragus villosus*) : male two and a half feet high, about five feet in length, slender, and neck long; horns about nine inches long, straight, pointed, and slender; colour greyish-buff, white beneath: female similar, but hornless and smaller. Found in troops of from six to twenty, generally on the rocky hills.

The hartebeest (*Acronotus Caama*) : male five feet high, and nine in extreme length; head long, horns forming nearly a right angle, rising above the head about eight inches, and then turning backwards; colour bright sienna, with a red shade, black stripes down the back of the neck, on the fore-leg, and on the hind-leg: female smaller, with more slender horns, otherwise similar. Found in large herds in the plains.

The eland (*Boselaphus oreas*) : male six feet high at the shoulder, and about twelve feet in length; horns two feet long, with a ridge ascending in a spiral direction about half-way up, the spiral making two turns when the male is an adult; appearance like a bull, a broad dewlap hanging to the knees; tail two feet six inches long; general colour dun, or ashy-grey, with a blue tinge when heated: female smaller and slighter, with more slender horns, and without the ridge; no dewlap. Found in large herds in the plains.

The buffalo (*Bubalus Caffer*) : male about five feet six inches high, twelve feet in length, very heavily made, neck short, breast dewlapped, head ponderous, eyes nearly overshadowed by hair and the heavy dark-coloured horns, which are nearly in contact at the base, spread out horizontally, and curve round and inwards; hide bluish black, without hair: female similar, but smaller in every way. Found on the plains and forests in herds, and often a solitary bull in the forests; very dangerous.

The hippopotamus (*Hippopotamus amphibius*): four feet six inches high at the shoulder, ten feet long; body ponderous, legs very short, head thick, eye small, and placed in a prominence; ears small and round; the upper incisors and canine teeth large,—the latter may be called tusks; skin very thick and tough; colour pinkish-brown: female smaller. Amphibious; found in the rivers and lakes; several still remain in Sea-cow Lake, about six miles from Natal, and in several of the rivers up the coast. The ivory is valuable, as it is curved in the shape of the nautical sextant, and being very hard, is especially adapted for the fine lines used upon Vernier scales; the skin is cut up into whips, called by the colonists *sjamboks*; the flesh is good eating, tasting when salted something like pork.

The elephant (*Loxodonta africana*): male twelve feet high, droops towards the tail; extreme length eighteen feet; colour blackish-brown; tail short, tufted with coarse hair at the end; ears very large, and front of head round; tusks large, from three to seven feet in length, weighing nearly a hundred pounds: female smaller, with tusks, except solitary specimens. Gregarious; found in large troops in the forests; wary, fierce, and vindictive.

Besides the animals that I have described, there were baboons, monkeys, rock-rabbits (the *hyrax*), a species of hare, porcupines, the ratel, many small vermin, such as the ichneumon, &c., in great numbers. All these animals were to be found in the Natal district in numbers, whilst across the Drookensburg Mountains were camelopards, rhinoceros, zebras, koodoo, wildebeest, gnoos, sassybys, water-buck, roan-antelope, blesbok, springbok, pallahs, ostriches, and many other magnificent animals, in countless herds.

A curious creature inhabits the African forest,—many specimens were found by me in the Berea, near Natal; it is called the Manis. It looks like a large and scaly lizard, being covered with hard scales, or plates, like thick short leaves; when lying on the ground motionless, it resembles a vegetable. Its body is long; tail twice the length of body; total length, about four feet; it is toothless.

The Cape horses have been universally praised by travellers; they are particularly hardy, game, and docile. The climate in many parts of the colony is well suited for breeding; and although inland but little attention is paid to this important matter, still it is a rare occurrence to find an animal, however ugly or misshapen, without its redeeming quality. At Cape Town and the immediate neighbourhood, the horses generally are like those of England, with a slight trace of the Arab in their head and hind-quarters; the breed, in fact, is a compound of the English thoroughbred and the Arab. Several well-known English horses have found their way to the Cape, having been purchased for exportation when they were stale or broken down; Fancy Boy, Battledore, Rococo, Gorhambury, Evenus, and many more, having acted as fountains for supplying a stream of pure blood through the equine veins of Africa. Nearly a hundred horses of tolerable English fame have been landed at the Cape within the last twenty years.

In many parts of the colony races are held, and the stakes are sufficient to repay the winners for their expenses in training and breeding. In Cape Town horses of good appearance fetch from twenty-five to sixty guineas, and very much larger prices are frequently given. The stallion is all-in-all with Cape breeders, the mare being considered as quite a secondary item. The consequence is, that from the frequent disproportion between the dam and sire, awkward-looking animals are common, more especially inland, where the science of breeding is less understood: a horse is frequently seen with fore-quarters equal to fifteen hands, and hind-quarters only large enough for a pony. In Africa many animals have a tendency to largeness about the fore-quarters; the elephant, wildebeest, and hartebeest appearing unnaturally heavy in front, and as though they required but a push from behind to send them on their noses. Whether the climate has anything to do with this peculiar form I know not, but the horses are seldom too large in their hind-quarters, although the Hottentots and the Cape sheep are in this particular absolutely ponderous.

The Hantam and Swellendam districts are celebrated for their breed of horses, and these supply great part of the colony. The qualities most esteemed amongst the Cape breeders are,—small head, small ears, large nostril, small muzzle, broad chest, large bone in the leg, short in the cannon and pastern, toes rather turned in than out; well ribbed home (many Dutchmen would not buy a horse that allowed more than four fingers to be placed between the last rib and the hip-bone); broad behind, with the tail set on very high (this last is a *spécialité*); cow-hocks are detested. Several small peculiarities are esteemed at the Cape that are not even observed in England; for instance, a Dutchman once told me that he knew a pony of mine must be enduring, from the small size of the corns on the inside of the hindlegs; he assured me that, when this was the case, a horse rarely tired, while, when the reverse, he generally shut up with only half a journey. I must own that I found this man's theory correct, as far as my experience carried me.

The Cape shooting-ponies are most extraordinary animals. In a country of this description, where every small journey, or even call, is made on horseback, the pony is more convenient than the horse; he is more easily mounted, is cheaper both to keep and buy, and is generally more manageable and teachable. Beauty forms no necessary item with a shooting-pony; he is often ugly, misshapen, big-headed, and small in girth; but upon examining him closely, the large bone of the leg, game head, and large nostril, with several other recommendations, cancel the imperfection of want of beauty. His action also is peculiar; he rarely walks, his mode of progression being a sort of tripple, at which he travels about six or seven miles an hour: trotting is not admired by the Boers. When the pony gallops, he shows good action, and his activity in scrambling down the hills that are covered with loose stones, rocks, and holes, is something marvellous; he is seldom shod, his hoofs being as hard and tough as iron. I usually shod the fore hoofs, as the roads were sometimes hard in or near the towns; but inland, where the country was nearly all grass, even this was unnecessary. The hardiness of these ponies was extraordinary; they frequently had but little to eat, and less to drink, were ridden long journeys, and then, while covered with sweat, turned out on a plain to pick up a very scanty meal. Their principal forage was fresh air and a roll in the sand; and upon these they thrived very well, while grooming was considered quite an unnecessary labour, and a proceeding that did more harm than good.

When a Boer takes a long journey, he rides one pony and leads two others, changing his saddle from back to back, as each animal has done its share. Riding for two hours, and off-saddling for half an hour, is the usual arrangement; six miles an hour being the general pace. When a traveller halts in Africa, which he does in a well-chosen spot, near water and shade if possible, he takes off the saddle and bridle, and knee-halters his horse; this last affair is nothing more than fastening the animal's head to its leg just above the knee; the leg is lifted up, and the halter passed round, and formed into a clove hitch: thus held, the animal is unable to move away quickly, and can be caught when required: the halter does not slip, or gall the leg. As soon as the pony finds himself at this partial liberty, he searches for a dry, sandy place, scrapes the ground a little, and then enjoys his roll; he gets up covered with dust and dirt, takes a drink, and loses no time, but at once picks up as much grass as the place affords. When the traveller is again ready, the animal is up-saddled, and the journey continued. Few of the colonial settlers have stables; the pony, on completing the journey, is turned out to graze until evening, when it is driven into an inclosure fenced with palings or brushwood, and thus left uncovered and uncombed. In the morning, it is turned out for the day. The better-kept horses have oats, barley, and Indian corn; oats being expensive in many parts of South Africa, barley is obliged to supply its place, and the horses consequently suffer in condition; the Indian corn is fattening, but is very inferior to oats; it is also dangerous by blowing out horses; and if they are allowed to drink much after eating it, they sometimes die from the swelling of the corn inside them, or the gas there generated.

About the coast of Natal, horses did not thrive well; the climate was rather relaxing, and "the sickness," as it is called, sometimes attacked them. The enormous number of ticks that transferred their adhesive properties from the grass to the hides of the horses, and then sucked the blood, was a species of outlay that few of the hard-worked quadrupeds could afford. If a horse were turned out to graze in the morning, he would before evening be covered with hundreds of ticks, each of which, by burying itself under the horse's skin and sucking the blood, becomes distended and increased from the size and appearance of a common bug to that of a broad-bean. A Kaffir would be nearly an hour in clearing a horse from these animals, and after all overlook scores, whose distended hides would appear in the morning. The sickness that I refer to was very fatal: a horse would one day appear well, but perhaps a little heavy in hand; the next day he would be down on his side, and dead before the evening. I attended the *post-mortem* of one or two animals that died in this way, but could discover nothing decidedly unhealthy: this, however, was most probably owing to my want of experience in the veterinary art. The Boers are frequently unmerciful to their horses, and I seldom rode a horse that had been very long in the possession of a Boer, but I found its mouth like iron and its temper none of the sweetest. The Dutchmen frequently train their shooting-horses to stand fire by galloping them for two or three miles and then firing twenty or thirty shots from their backs. If these horses are at all frisky under the discharge, the merciless riders, plying whip and spur, take another gallop, and repeat the performance until they conquer the restlessness of their steeds. This is certainly not a proceeding likely to improve the temper of any animal, particularly if well bred or having any fire in its composition; but rough-and-ready is the great thing in Africa.

When well trained, the Cape shooting-pony is worth his weight in gold; he is treated more like a dog than a horse, knows when he is spoken to, and obeys orders, fears nothing, and seems to delight in sport. I possessed a pony that was so easily managed and steady, that I frequently shot snipe, partridges, and always buck, from off his back. He was my daily companion for two years, and rarely played me a trick. He had a queer temper; but, knowing this, I made due allowance, and we always managed things well. If I spurred him, or pulled the rein, when he approached a hill, he would stop and refuse to advance; but a word or two in Dutch, in place of the assault, would make matters progress satisfactorily. I heard that his career after I left was unfortunate; he passed through one or two hands who could not have understood him, and was finally killed by a lion in the interior. I can easily imagine that such would have been his fate, should he be in the vicinity of a hungry lion, as he never showed fear of elephants or any other animal,

ENDURANCE OF HORSES. 71

and was not alarmed by the smell of a fresh lion's skin past which I rode one day.

The Boers are generally very heavy men, and the small shooting-ponies that they ride appear fearfully overweighted: a pony of twelve or thirteen hands is ridden long journeys, and hunted, by a Boer of some fourteen or sixteen stone weight. The game little animal does its work well in spite of the weight it carries; and one of the surprising facts to an ·Englishman fresh in the African hunting-field is the pace at which the Boers thus mounted go across country. Neither whip nor spur is spared during a chase, and, not contented with the day's hard work, these Boers sometimes on returning home take a half-mile gallop as a test of the enduring qualities of their ponies. During my experience in Africa, I was but once unfortunate enough to have a horse that I was riding knock up with me: the animal was a new purchase, and had led a life of idleness during some previous weeks. The results of its failing me were a thorough ducking and a very unpleasant journey of near five miles. It may give an idea of the manners of the civilized man of South Africa, if I detail the circumstance. I left Pietermaritzburg about three o'clock in the afternoon, and purposed resting for the night at Stony Hill, the distance being twenty-five miles. About eight miles had been accomplished, when I was attracted by a grand fight between two bulls. I watched the struggle for a considerable time, and admired the courage of each combatant : sometimes they would charge each other, and, falling on their knees, roar and bellow with mingled rage and pain. Victory for a long time was doubtful, until the strength of one appeared to be failing, and then, turning tail, he galloped off, followed by his conqueror. Finding that the sun had moved a considerable distance while I was engaged in watching the bull-fight, I pushed on faster than the usual African travelling-pace, and found, before twelve miles were ridden, that my horse appeared much distressed. The day was intensely hot, and I thought an "off-saddle" for half an hour might refresh the animal; but upon again starting I found it difficult to spur even a trot out of him. I dismounted and tried to lead him, but found he was one of those brutes that will not follow. He stuck his head out as I drew the reins tight, but would not stir an inch. Remounting, I managed to hustle him along at a smart walk; but even this I did not accomplish without considerable manual and spur labour. I had nearly five miles before me, and the sun was within half an hour of setting. Had the night been fine, a ride would have been pleasant during the moonlight; but the dark heavy clouds that were gathering round, and a drop of rain that fell occasionally, gave earnest of a coming storm. No house or resting-place was there on the road, except that for which I was making my way, and Botha's, which latter was five miles farther. I reached Stony Hill soon after dark, and was preparing to dismount at the door of the inn, near which I noticed two waggons; when the man who kept the establishment came out, and said, "Who's that?" I told him that I wanted a dinner, a bed, and stabling. I heard him make a remark in Dutch to some person within the building, and distinguished "verdamt Englishmensch" as two of the words. He then turned round to me, and said, "I can't give you a dinner or a bed." I told him that I was not particular about what I ate, but, as my horse was knocked up, I could not go farther. He said, "Well, you shan't stop here; and if you didn't mind sleeping in the pigsty, I wouldn't even let you have a bed there." I was very angry with him, and high words ensued; and I am afraid that deeds would have followed the words, had not a Hottentot near me whispered that I had better not strike the man, as he would not hesitate to use the knife when he was half-drunk. I therefore turned my tired horse again into the road, and, with a vigorous dig of the spur, retreated from the conflict. I had now five miles of a very rough road before me : it passed over stony hills, and wound round the side of others. The night was dark as Erebus, and the road, or rather beaten track, could only be distinguished during the flashes of lightning, which now came with blinding brilliancy. My horse slipped down on his side, and nearly broke my ancle, as we were passing round a hill on the side of which the road sloped; the rain, that now fell with rapidity, having made the track greasy and slippery. Dismounting, I drove the horse before me, but had great difficulty in getting him to keep the beaten track; sometimes he would turn to the right or left, and the long grass brushing against my legs would alone make me acquainted with the fact of having left the road. I then waited for a fresh flash of lightning to enable me to regain the pathway. Strange and indistinct forms would be seen as the surrounding country was electrically illuminated; the wild animals always choosing rainy or stormy weather to wander forth from their rocks, holes, and coverts. Nearly two hours were passed in the midst of the most vivid lightning and deafening thunder, while the rain poured upon me in torrents. At the end of that time I reached Botha's Hotel: I had to knock up the landlord from his bed; but this civil and obliging man lighted a fire for me, and brought the better half of a chicken-pie; in the enjoyment of which luxuries I soon forgot the previous disagreeables; and throwing off my wet garments, and fastening a blanket round my neck, and wrapping myself in its folds Kaffir fashion, I feasted like a Zulu chief.

CHAPTER IV.

Warnings against the bush—Search after a leopard—Unsteady hands—Methods of hunting elephants—Speed of the elephant—Bush-travelling—Traces of the elephants—Solitude of the bush—Tracking the herd—Charge of angry elephants—The horses reached—Search for the wounded elephant—The successful shot—An unwitting escape.

I HAD received so many accounts from different sources as to the great dangers that were certainly to be met in the dense bush of the Berea, and also the part that extended across the Umganie for several miles up the coast, that I had hesitated attempting so rash a course as entering it until I had gathered experience from trying cautiously at first what dangers I was likely to encounter. "Elephants would catch me; tigers (*i. e.* leopards) becroup (*i. e.* stalk) me; snakes bite me," &c.: these and other horrors would be sure to entail my return on a shutter. I frequently rode round and looked for a short distance into different parts of the bush, gathering confidence each time.

One morning early, a Hottentot man came to tell me that his master had sent him to ask if I would like to join a party going out after a leopard that had destroyed several chickens, and had also breakfasted on a half-grown pig on the said morning. I was glad of this chance, as I hoped to see some sport, and immediately shouldering my gun, and fastening a large clasp-knife in my belt, joined my guide, who led me to a house on the outskirts of the village of D'Urban, where I found a party of ten or twelve as rough-looking customers as one could desire to see: I am sure a leopard would not have had courage even to look at them. If beards or dirt made African sportsmen, I thought I must be in a very hot-bed of them. I soon saw that the party were more of the style of *sporting-men* than *sportsmen*; they were liberally imbibing brandy and water, which they wanted to force upon me to steady my nerves; an auxiliary I begged to decline, first, on account of the hour (10 A.M.), and, secondly, because the shaking hands of many present made me doubt its steadying qualities. We started in two divisions, one taking the trail into the bush where the pig had been made pork, while the other entered where the leopard generally came out.

The cover was so very dense and thick that we were obliged to crawl on all fours, great care being necessary to prevent the triggers or cocks of the gun from getting set and caught: we were all particularly requested to be silent; but the hairy men *would* talk. After creeping 150 yards, we came to some of the bones of the pig, evidently just left by the leopard: we watched carefully every gloomy part of the surrounding bush to discover the leopard, but could see nothing. Suddenly a bird flitted away close to us, and one of the bearded gentlemen, who had appeared the greatest swaggerer, called for us to look out, as the leopard was coming. I immediately heard the click-click of double-barrelled guns coming to full cock, and saw a gentleman a few yards to my right pointing his gun straight at me; I shouted to him to mind what he was about, when he coolly told me he was only getting ready in case the leopard sprung; his shaking hands, however, were certainly not pleasant masters of a trigger, the slightest pressure on which would have sent an ounce of lead through me.

I withdrew as soon as possible, as I was convinced there was no chance of seeing sport with these cock-tail gentry, who, it is almost needless to add, saw nothing of the wild animal, and returned soon to their nerve-steadying specific. The leopard had been seen retreating by two Kaffirs, who happened to be passing on the opposite side, immediately we entered the bush: we could not have been within 300 yards of the monster, therefore, at any time.

With most South-African sportsmen the elephant is one of the last of the wild animals which he is fortunate enough to see: it was my first. The view was not a long one, still it is well impressed on my memory.

I received a note one morning before breakfast from a true sportsman, informing me that he knew of a large herd of elephants in the Berea, and, if I would join him, he hoped that we might get a shot at them. This proposition, from our ignorance of all the artifices necessary in the bush, was rather rash, as elephant-shooting is always dangerous sport, and when attempted by novices on foot in a dense bush against a very savage herd, it becomes still more so.

Elephants are generally hunted in Africa on horseback. The Dutchmen, who frequently obtain their living by this sport only, are amongst the most accomplished hands; they make periodical trips into the uninhabited districts, or where elephants are numerous, and the country open or park-like. When a herd of elephants is discovered, these Boers make a plan of attack, either to drive the herd of game to a better and more open country, or to prevent them from retreating to the dense bushes near. As soon as everything suits, they mark out the leader of the troop, generally the biggest bull-elephant. They then ride up as near as they dare, and give him a volley; if he falls, they can manage the remainder more easily, as, missing their chief, some confusion takes place. Should he, however, be only wounded, turn savage, and charge, as is most frequently the case, they close together, and gallop away for a hundred yards or so, when, at a given signal, they separate, and ride round in different directions. This diversion generally puzzles the elephant, and, before he has made up his mind what to do, another broadside is poured into him. Two or three volleys are generally sufficient to quiet the big bull. I have been assured by many old elephant-hunters that they have frequently seen a herd of elephants stand with their heads together, after the leader has been killed, as though in despair, and they would not make a rush: these may be pleasant, but are undoubtedly rare, chances for the pot-hunter. Gordon Cumming's plan of lying in wait for the elephants at their drinking-place was a bold and successful plan. I cannot but think him a very lucky man never to have had a wounded bull charge him then; had one done so, I fear we should not have had his amusing lectures, or his own account of his wonderful sport.

Many methods of elephant-hunting may never have

come to light, owing to the enterprising sportsman having been crushed to death by his infuriated game before he had an opportunity of making public his experience.

An elephant can run very fast, and moves with surprising ease and silence.

I remember hearing tales as a boy of the elephant's beginning to turn early in the morning, and managing to finish his gymnastic performance by mid-day; the wily huuter, therefore, by keeping behind, him was always safe.

My own experience is very different from this: I have seen them turn round and crash away through the forest with nearly the rapidity of a large buck; and a man's speed stands but a poor chance in comparison with theirs. In the thick underwood or reeds a man is continually impeded, while an elephant walks through everything with the greatest ease; a horse, however, in open ground gets away from an elephant, especially when going up hill, the weight of the latter being much against it on rising ground.

The elephant stands very high in the class of wise animals, and, I believe, is as fully susceptible of a moral lesson as is a schoolboy. When a large herd is but seldom disturbed by man, but on each visit five or six elephants are killed, and two or three more die of their wounds, the remainder then have a very great dread of the smell of a biped, and the report of his gun; but when elephants are disturbed very frequently, and only one shot obtained at them, which wounds and annoys, but may not kill, they become very savage, and, upon smelling their teasing enemy, are at once furious and vindictive. The herds that came into the Natal bush were of this latter disposition; they were frequently disturbed, and sometimes fired at, but without any great result, as the density of the cover rendered it almost impossible to get more than one shot; and a single bullet rarely carries immediate death.

The bush for many miles up the Natal coast was impenetrable, except by the paths that the elephants had made; and in which they had stalked to and from water, and from place to place, in Indian file. It was difficult for a man, when moving along these paths, to see many yards on either side, the underwood, briers, and parasitical plants, being matted together like a hedge. In many parts one has to force himself through places where he cannot see a yard around him. Here he must trust to hearing, and almost to scent, or he will not long be left to enjoy the excitement of the sport, which, when once indulged in, produces a bush-fever that leaves as lasting an impression as the similar disease caught on the prairies of the Far West. Patience, caution, keen senses, and experience, are the requisites for this work; and unless a hunter possesses the whole of these qualities, he will give but a sorry account of the fun to be had in the bush; the general cry being "that no game is to be seen there."

I soon joined my friend, who, although a thorough good sportsman, and a slayer of nearly all the large game of Africa, was still not quite up to the precautions necessary in thick bush-work, I at the time being grossly ignorant of everything connected with it.

We cantered over the Natal flat, and entered a small,

narrow bush-path, that led to the top of the Berea. On the way, my friend told me how he had become acquainted with the position of the herd we purposed encountering.

His Kaffirs had discovered the traces on the road to Pietermaritzberg, which they had crossed during the night. He himself had examined the road leading to the flagstaff at the top of the Berea, and found that they had not passed this; so he knew that they must be between the two roads mentioned. He therefore concluded that we should find them about half-way between the two, and near a large umbrella-looking tree, which plainly showed itself from all parts of the surrounding country.

Unfortunately, as both our guns were of small calibre, being fourteen-bore only, I was recommended to put in two tops of powder, instead of the usual charge of one, and also to use my friend's bullets, as they had been prepared with one-eighth of tin, to harden the balls, and prevent them from flattening against a bone.

The Berea in this part was about two miles broad, and was very thick, with plenty of underwood in most parts.

On reaching the top of the woody hill, we found an open space of some twenty yards in diameter, where we dismounted, and left our horses, taking care to fasten them to a tree by the head-stalls, which are generally allowed to remain on the head, either for the purpose of fastening up a horse, or for knee-haltering him. M—— (my friend) showed me the fresh indications of the elephants. The grass was trodden down in every direction, and in some places it was torn up, as though a heavy piece of timber had been dragged along over it. One or two places, which were destitute of grass and rather clayey, retained large circular and oval-shaped impressions, which M—— explained to me as belonging,— the circular to the bull, and the oval to the cow elephants; the height of the respective elephant being about six times the diameter of these impressions. We measured one foot-print, which gave us an answer of twelve feet, a height quite sufficient to satisfy the fastidious in this sort of sport.

A strange mysterious feeling came over me in being thus brought for the first time on the fresh traces of evidently a numerous herd of these gigantic animals. I began to ask if it were not great impertinence for two such pigmies as we now seemed, to attempt an attack upon at least forty of these giants, who, by a swing of their trunks, or a stamp of their foot on us, could have terminated our earthly career with as much ease as we could that of an impertinent fly? There is also an utter feeling of loneliness, and self-dependence, in treading the mazes of these vast forests. One mile of bush always appeared to remove me farther from man and his haunts than twenty miles of open country. One is inspired with a kind of awe by the gloom and silence that pervade these regions, the only sounds being the warning note of some hermit-bird, or the crack of a distant branch. The limited view around also tends to keep every other sense on the alert, and the total absence of every sign of man, or man's work, appears to draw one nearer to the spirit-world, and to impress us with a greater sense of the Divine presence.

Our advance was rather quick, as we did not pay sufficient attention to the signs and noises as we approached the elephants. Scarcely thirty yards had been gone over when I looked round to the spot where our horses stood; the thickness of the intervening bush, however, prevented me from seeing them. Several large branches had been broken off the trees, the ends eaten, and then cast across the path in different directions. Either in play or rage, the elephants had entirely destroyed two or three trees of a considerable size, that stood near their path, peeling the bark off in many instances for several feet up the stems.

We steadily continued our advance, following in the footsteps of the elephants; the freshly-trodden course of the gigantic animals being clearly indicated.

I was much surprised at the silence that reigned in the bush. I expected that a herd of wild elephants would indicate their presence by noises audible at a great distance. M—— told me, however, that during the day they usually remained quiet, especially when they knew that they were in a suspicious neighbourhood, or where they had lately smelt traces of man. This cautious proceeding I have since discovered to be invariable.

We trudged on steadily for about a mile, creeping under the branches that crossed our path, and removing others which had apparently been dropped by the elephants. We were at length stopped by observing the branches of a distant tree violently shaken. We watched them for a considerable time, and listened, but only heard a queer sort of rumbling noise for which we could not then account. This, as I afterwards knew, was caused by elephants; but seeing a couple of monkeys jumping about in a distant tree, we thought that it was caused by these little animals, and therefore proceeded.

About one hundred yards farther the bush became very dense, long creepers growing all over the shrubs, matting and tying the underwood together, so as to render it quite impenetrable, except where the elephants had forced a path. We moved through these passages quickly, and of course caused some noise. I was about two yards behind M——, and scarcely expected anything could be near, when suddenly the bushes on our right and close to us were violently shaken, and a deep sort of growl was uttered, that sounded much like a lion's roar. M—— jumped forward, and raised his gun to fire; I was going to follow him, but on looking a little to our left, I saw a huge elephant, about ten yards distant, striding towards us, with his trunk coiled up and ears erect. At the same instant M—— fired to his right, and springing past me, shouted, "Run for your life!" I did not stop for another look, as I then heard, almost over me, the terrific shrill trumpet of the animal which I had seen charging, in addition to the growl of the wounded elephant and the answering shrieks of several others who were round us.

Our burst for the first hundred yards must have been fine, but we had nothing to spare, as I looked round soon after starting and saw the big elephant coming after us as if he really meant mischief, and but a short distance behind us.

I lost my hat, but we rushed on, diving under some

branches, hopping over others, dodging this way and that, until I was completely blown, and called for a halt, as, having both barrels loaded, I was anxious for a shot. M——, however, would not hear of stopping, but still recommended that we should clear out of the bush with the greatest quickness, as the herd had shown themselves so savage. I bowed to his superior judgment, knowing that he combined true courage and daring with a sufficient caution to prevent recklessness for the mere sake of display. We at length came to our horses, and I must own I felt more comfortable when my leg was over my stout game little pony, than I did when on foot within a yard or so of the elephant's trunk.

We stopped to listen, and heard the shrieks and trumpets of this wild troop, and the crashing of the bush, which showed that they had not yet entirely given up the hope of trampling to death their insignificant but annoying enemy. I had, as I before stated, dropped my hat during the first hundred yards' rush, and I did not care at the time to stop to pick it up.

M—— soon told me that he thought we should find his elephant dead if we returned, as he had killed rhinoceroses, and thought the growl we had heard was indicative of a death-wound. As he had aimed behind the shoulder, he considered such a result probable.

Upon riding clear from the bush, we found on the Natal flat a Hottentot, who was quietly sitting down mending his only pair of trowsers; he looked at us very knowingly and said, *"Olephants barnie qui bas"* (Elephants very angry, sir). Upon asking him how he knew this, he told us, that although he could only just hear the report of the gun, he could still plainly hear the elephant's trumpet, and he knew from the tone how savage they must be: this man was at least a mile distant from the scene of our encounter. On that evening it was decided that early on the morrow we should retrace our steps, and follow up the wounded elephant until we found him, in case he happened not to be dead on the spot; and also that we were to divide the ivory, as, although I had not actually fired, I had still aided and abetted in the affair. While we were thus quietly counting our chickens, this tough old African giant was most probably walking away through the forest, with no more idea of dying than we had; little cared he for a fourteen-to-the-pound bullet!

This was my first introduction to the South-African elephant, and I may say to South-African game.

On the following morning, the dew had scarcely been dried by the sun before we entered the bush on our traces of yesterday. We brought with us an English settler, an experienced elephant-hunter, two Kaffirs, and a Hottentot. We were uncertain about bringing a hatchet for the purpose of cutting out the teeth, in case the elephant was dead (the tusks, I should here remark, are commonly called the teeth, while what in England are called the teeth are really the grinders). We saved ourselves a vast amount of ridicule by leaving the hatchet at home.

We had no difficulty in at once recognizing the spot on which our yesterday's scene was acted. Had we been in doubt, the discovery of my hat would have settled the question; it had been knocked out of the path, and its broad brim was smashed considerably. No doubt the big elephant, in his charge, had accidentally trodden on it, and kicked it on one side.

We went to the spot on which M——'s elephant had stood. I certainly was disappointed to find that he had not even fallen on receiving the shot. None but an experienced eye could tell that anything extraordinary had even taken place here; but both Kaffirs and Hottentot at once saw, by the traces, all that had happened. These sharp-sighted savages pointed to the spot from whence M—— had fired, and then to where the elephant had stood. They said he had turned round and rushed headlong towards the smoke of M——'s gun. He there stopped, and then slowly retreated, keeping himself away from the remainder of the herd.

We followed his traces, and soon found blood, both on the leaves and branches, as also on the ground, but not in such large quantities as I should have supposed. We followed this spoor for some distance; but the blood soon ceasing, and the wounded elephant's traces being crossed by other feet, we saw no more of him.

We discovered, however, that, during our advance on the previous day, we had passed three elephants within fifty yards without being aware of their vicinity. The noise which we had heard and the rumbling sounds were caused by them. They thought it prudent to remain nearly still; and their plan was successful, as they were undiscovered by us.

We also saw that three or four elephants, that were feeding close to the spot from whence we had fired, had chased us for at least two hundred yards. Fortunately, one of the sharp turns which we had taken threw them out in the chase, and very probably saved us from being acquainted with the weight of their feet.

I must say that this little adventure somewhat cooled my ardour for a second meeting with these angry brutes. Interviews, however, frequently did again happen, as will be seen by the future pages.

CHAPTER V.

Necessity of a gun—Strange footstep—A disappointment—Vicinity of the Umganie—Duiker buck—Matuan the Kaffir—Vocal telegraph—Reitbok—A human pointer—Singular conversation—Apathy of the residents—Kaffir messengers—Buck-shooting—The buck's tenacity of life—A buck on three legs—Dangerous country—A sporting red-coat—Strange sportsmen.

AFTER this attack on and by the elephants, I devoted my time to the pursuit of the reit-buck (*Eleotragus reduncus*), the ourebi (*Oreotragus scoparius*), the duiker (*Cephalophorus mergens*), &c., all of them found within a few miles of Natal. As these days' sport are, with little exception, repetitions of each other, and therefore possess interest only to the person concerned, I will select one or two incidents, that stand well out in my memory, as amongst the most interesting.

It is always advisable, in a country of this description, where the game wanders and its locality is uncertain, never to be out without a gun. You may wander for many miles and not see a single head of game in a country that ought to be teeming with it; but you may stroll out one hundred yards from your house and meet a noble buck who has come to take a peep at you. He, of course, will not accept your invitation to wait until you go in for your gun.

Scarcely an individual whom I ever met, and who had been long resident in Natal, did not remark some time or other to me, "Oh! if I had had my gun the other day, I would have shot so and so." In time, also, the gun becomes no more troublesome to carry than a walking-stick.

I can mention many instances with regard to myself, where, not thinking it at all probable that I should see anything worth shooting, I left my gun at home. I have then had some teasing buck jump up in front of me, and stand looking for half a minute, as if quizzing me, at perhaps forty yards' distance, and then quietly canter off. "Oh! if I had my gun," I moodily exclaimed. At last, I was rarely seen without it. "Going out shooting?" was often asked me from this circumstance. "No; only for a walk, or a bathe," I would answer. "Why have you your weapon, then?" was generally considered a cutting remark. Many a small pair of pointed horns, and many skins, would have answered the "why." I generally came across something without looking for it.

The greatest annoyance that I met with from not having a gun was when riding one day, with an officer of the commissariat, on the beach between the Umganie and Natal Bay. I remarked some curious footprints on the sand, and dismounted to see what they were. I could not identify them, although I was well acquainted with most South-African trails. My friend called my attention to their impressions all along the sand, and far on ahead. As we looked in advance, we saw a large black object moving nearly half a mile before us. We started off immediately in chase, and soon neared it. I then saw that it was covered with long fur, had short legs in front, and a kind of finny organ behind. It appeared about ten feet long. Immediately it heard us galloping, it made for the water.

We were going so fast that we could not pull up, and went past between the animal and the sea; so that before we could return it had gained the water, and, taking a look at us, dived and disappeared. Had I had my gun with me, I could have stalked to a spot within thirty yards of it, by means of the sand-hills near the beach, and a couple of bullets would no doubt have made us better acquainted. I described this animal to several people, but none had seen a creature like it. The Kaffirs had seen the spoor before, but had no name by which to designate it.*

The country across the Umganie river was thickly wooded, but inland it was either open, or of that park-like description so common in many parts of Africa. About eight miles across this river an English settler lived, who had frequently asked me to put up at his house in case I went for a day's shooting in his neighbourhood. I usually preferred availing myself of some Kaffir's kraal; as the wild uncivilized native I found more agreeable company than the general class of English or Dutch emigrants: the naked savage was frequently the more gentlemanly fellow of the two. In the present instance, however, my host was an exception; he was an unassuming, hard-working man, and I accepted his proffered offer of a shake-down, with thanks.

I sent on one of my Kaffirs with my shooting-pony the previous day, and at daybreak, on a lovely morning in October, started from my tent for a day's sport in this district. I had scarcely ridden half a mile from our

---

* I have since seen descriptions and paintings of a sea-lion that frequents some islands to the north-west of the Cape, and am inclined to think that this creature was a traveller of that species.

encampment on the Natal flat, when I noticed a small animal jumping over some bushes that bordered the road about 150 yards in front. Upon reaching the road, it stopped, and looked at me, and I then saw that it was a duiker. I had placed a bullet in each barrel, and immediately took a shot at the buck. I saw that the animal stumbled as I fired, but it cantered on to a thick patch of bush on my right. I wanted to salute it with the second barrel on its coming out, but, after waiting half a minute or so without seeing it, I dismounted, and crept up to the bush. On peeping in, I saw the duiker, lying on his side. I made ready for a shot, and gave a loud whistle, but it did not move. Upon crawling into the bush, I found that the buck was quite dead, the bullet having gone through its ribs. I was not certain I had hit it at first, although, when I fired, I fancied I heard the "thud" of the bullet. I applied the knife, and carried the buck to the thick bush close by, where, selecting a forked tree in a shady dell, the venison was hung up. From information that I sent my Kaffirs, they called for it before sunset that evening. They were too late: the intense heat, although the venison hung in the shade, had placed the meat beyond even an epicure's idea of what game should be.

I pursued my journey, and arrived soon after 8 A.M. at my host's. I took some coffee and bread, the latter made from Indian corn, and soon after, mounting my shooting-pony, I started for a kraal that had been pointed out to me as the residence of an old Kaffir who was well acquainted with the hiding-places of the bucks that frequented this locality. I soon saw him, and found he was a man of about forty. It is, however, very difficult to judge of a Kaffir's age; but he was rather grey, nearly six feet in height, very muscular, and without an ounce of superfluous fat. He was ready for sport at once, and recommended me to leave my pony to graze near his kraal, as the place where some reitboks were usually found, was so hilly and broken that he did not think a horse would be of much use. On our road to the ground which he had chosen as the most likely for game, he asked all sorts of questions about me, and volunteered much information about himself. He had committed that common sin amongst savages, of having too many cattle, which had raised the envy of his chief, who consequently accused him of witchcraft, and would have soon murdered him, had not the accused party made a bolt, and placed himself some sixty miles within the British boundary, but a beggar by comparison with his former condition. He seemed, however, contented, and had now a few cattle and goats.

This part of the country was plentifully watered, and the numerous ravines and marshy spots allowed the long reeds to escape the firés that perform the part of mowers once or twice a year. In the heat of the day the antelopes choose these cool retreats for shelter. The old Kaffir, who rejoiced in the name of Matuan, led me to the top of a slightly-wooded hill, and, pointing to an opposite ridge, nearly a mile distant, he said, "*Nànqueer.*"* I looked in the direction indicated, and there

---

* The Kaffir words that I have used throughout this work I believe are incorrect in their orthography. For the uninitiated, however, I thought it better to spell them as they sounded, as by adopting this plan, a more complete idea can be obtained of the sound of the Kaffir language.

saw a few goats feeding, and could plainly see a little Kaffir boy sitting beside them: the transparency of the air in these latitudes almost does away with the effect of distance. "*May-na-bo!*" then sang Matuan, resting very long on the *may*, in a singing sort of way; and, without any apparent exertion, a kind of shout from the boy came thrilling through the air, like the voice of a distant bird. "*Ou vel arpe umseke?*" sung Matuan. "*Empeshear kona,*" thrilled the boy. Matuan, giving a grunt of approval, moved on. This I must translate to make intelligible:— the *maynabo* was to call the attention of the boy, a kind of "Holloa!" *Ou vel arpe umseke?* meaning, Where are the reitboks gone? *Empeshear*, indicating that they were over on the other side.

I have been frequently astonished at hearing the ease with which two Kaffirs will carry on a conversation when separated by distances that would be considered by us as entirely to interrupt verbal communication. This conversation is accomplished by the tone and modulations of the voice, as also the distinct divisions in the Kaffirs' language.

We walked on for nearly two miles under a burning sun. The heat was intense, and my gun-barrels became so hot that it was with difficulty I could hold the gun. The annoyance from numerous flies and insects, whose bite was severe, added to the natural irritation that one sometimes feels on a hot day. Matuan soon showed me a long ravine, full of rushes and reeds, that looked a most likely place for a buck. We sat down beside a little rippling stream, while we refreshed ourselves with a draught of its pure water, and invigorated our spirits with a pinch of powerful snuff, without which no Kaffir is entirely happy. While we allowed time for these stimulants to produce their full effect, Matuan detailed to me his plan of operations. He said that he would go on the left of the ravine, and, keeping a little in advance of me, would shout and beat the reeds. This proceeding would probably cause the bucks, if there, to come out on the right-hand side, and run towards his kraal: he therefore recommended me to keep on the right side, and look out for my shot.

We started in the manner that he proposed, and had scarcely gone half-way up the ravine, when a doe reitbok sprang out of the cover, and cantered across in front of me at about eighty yards' distance. I fired at her shoulder, and heard the bullet strike; she staggered and nearly fell, recovered again, reeled a few yards, and came to the ground to rise no more. Matuan shouted to me to look out for the ram; we waited a few seconds, when, not seeing him, I explained to the Kaffir that I should like to load. I had just placed the bullet on the powder, when the ram burst out of the reeds, and bounding away a few yards, stopped and looked full at me. I did not wait to cap the barrel that I had loaded, but aimed with my second. Just as I brought the gun to my shoulder, he gave a sharp clear sort of whistle to call his partner, and dashed off. I let fly at him as he went, and saw a hind leg dangling useless and broken. Matuan rushed through the reeds, and was after him like a hound. I followed as quickly as I could, but, being encumbered with gun, bullets, &c., was, after a few minutes, "nowhere." I got occasional glimpses of Matuan, who kept to the ridges of the hills, and had evidently the game continually in sight. I made several short cuts, and was only about two hundred yards behind the Kaffir, when he suddenly dropped as though he were shot, and thus slipping down the hill, commenced beckoning me furiously. When I reached him, he told me that the reitbok had just lain down in some long grass over the hill, "so far," he said, pointing to a tree near.

I waited till I recovered my breath again, and having now both barrels loaded, I took off my hat, and, telling Matuan to keep quiet, crept up in the direction that he had indicated. Upon reaching the top of the hill, I slowly rose, and saw the wounded antelope standing on his three legs, looking straight at me. I aimed at the chest and fired; the buck reared straight up and fell over backwards. I knew there was not an ounce of life left in him, so I walked back to Matuan for my hat. The perspiration was pouring out of every pore of his swarthy hide and trickling over his face, as much from excitement as heat; and when he saw me thus quietly returning to him, a look of despair came over his face, and he said, "*Yena mukile*" (He has gone away). I merely said, "*Hamba si hamba*" (Let's be going), and walked to where the buck lay, completely concealed by the length of the grass around him. Matuan soon saw the reitbok, and jumping in the air with delight, shouted "*Wena shiele!*" (You have killed him!) He then sat down beside the reitbok for full a minute, gazing with delight on the anticipated steaks and chops that he hoped would soon pass from outside the ribs of this animal to the inside of his own. He pushed his fingers into the two bullet-holes, and then waved his arm in indication of the dead doe behind us; then held up his three fingers, pointing two at the wounds in the buck before us, and waving one in the direction of the other animal shot, as much as to say "Three shots, all hit." Then, as though he had satisfactorily decided an important question, he placed his hand horizontally across his mouth, looked steadily at me for half a minute, and said, "*e-ar-nesa, wena inkosi*" (In truth, you are a chief). Poor Matuan! he had not enjoyed such a feast of meat for many months as I gave him on that and the following night.

We were obliged to get aid from a neighbouring Kaffir's kraal to convey the meat home, each buck being more than we could comfortably carry. I gave part of the venison to Matuan, and retained the remainder for the benefit of my host.

A curious incident here happened, which struck me at the time as very ridiculous.

A French emigrant was stopping at this house with my host, and being unable to speak a word of English, he had great difficulty in making his wants known. It happened that on leaving England I was a tolerable French scholar, and could manage to converse; but a year of disuse, and also the study of the Hottentot-Dutch and Zulu-Kaffir languages, had driven all my French away, and upon being thus suddenly called upon, I could scarce think of a word. This Frenchman had

H

fortunately studied the Zulu language, by books during his voyage out, and by practice since his residence in Africa: we therefore carried on an interesting conversation in this language. It seemed curious that two white men, whose native countries so nearly joined, should be thus compelled to communicate in a tongue so little known in the native land of either; the Kaffirs themselves thought we were doing it merely for their amusement, and sat grinning first at us and then at one another.

On the following day I shot a reitbok, a duiker, and three corans.

Several days of good sport were yielded me in this neighbourhood. I found, however, that the bush close to Natal was teeming with buck, and a buffalo was sometimes seen there. Several unsuccessful journeys after the former taught me that more skill was required in shooting them than I at that time possessed. By patience, perseverance, and the instruction obtained from the Kaffirs, I at length acquired the art of moving with silence and watchfulness through the mazes of the forest, and was then rewarded by first-rate sport, and found this amusement one of the most fascinating in this country.

I have known many men who were good shots and able sportsmen, fail completely in the bush, from a deficiency in the qualities of patience and caution; several of whom have gone day after day, and returned, not only empty-handed, but without having seen a single head of game. Yet two or three Kaffirs or Hottentots that I could name would make certain of bagging a fine fat buck each day they devoted to the purpose, and over the very same ground that had been drawn a blank by the other sportsmen. It may be concluded, therefore, that some skill and experience is requisite in the bush-hunter of Africa. So plentiful was the game in the Natal district during my residence there in 1847, 1848, and 1849, that even around Pietermaritzburg, within a mile of the houses, I have shot bucks;—while partridges, pheasants, quail, and snipe were also common. But the use of the bullet against the larger animals is so fascinating a mode of sport, that it prevents the South-African sportsman from attending much to the feathered game, which are merely popped at for the purpose of putting them beside bread sauce and Cayenne pepper. Two or three strings of reh-boks were to be met with round the Pietermaritzburg hills, while reitbok and ourebis seemed to come in daily from the surrounding country for the sole purpose of supplying the gaps caused by the death of others of their species. There was a tolerable monopoly in the shooting line here that was curious. While the English traders, &c., still translated the national motto of "*Honi soit qui mal y pense*," as " Slave away for money as long as you live," the Dutchman merely saved his powder for a trip into the interior, and the gentlemen who had nothing to do for their living seemed to do nothing for their pleasure. The consequence was, that not half a dozen men were ever seen to go out shooting at all regularly. This may appear strange, when we consider the quantity and quality of the game; but, perhaps, the luxury of the climate relaxes the energies of those who may be long resident, and their greatest happiness, consequently, is repose; they thus wisely avoid many troubles and annoyances that more mercurial or enterprising temperaments may meet. Upon proceeding to Pietermaritzburg, I found that I had a pleasant little manor, extending for about fifteen miles in every direction, plentifully supplied with reitbok, ourebis, duikers, rhe-bok, bustard, pheasant, partridge, guinea-fowl, and sometimes a wild boar and a stray hyæna or leopard. I adopted an original plan for my day's sport. Sending for one of my Kaffirs, I would give him a pound of beef and some snuff, and tell him to go on to the top of a hill which I would point out to him, and request that he kept me in sight all day. This hill would be some seven or eight miles distant. I would then send for another Kaffir and give him similar directions, pointing to a second hill, perhaps four miles from the first.

These Kaffirs, who worked for *five shillings a month, and nearly found themselves*, were capital fellows, and obeyed orders without a murmur. Sometimes, at Natal, I would call a Kaffir, and say, "So-and-So, tabata s'incwade, musi inglovu" (this would be broken Kaffir for "Take this letter to Pietermaritzburg, wait for an answer, and come back")—*only fifty-three miles!* In about ten minutes this Kaffir would be seen going off with a little skin-bag filled with corn, the letter carefully inserted in a split stick, whilst he occasionally worked his arms about in all the pleasant imaginary castle-building of knocking over enemies or wild beasts. In three days he would come back, with the single remark, "*Fikile*" (arrived), and deliver the answer to the note.

After starting the Kaffirs to their look-out stations, I could comfortably take my breakfast, do any business that was required, and then mount my horse and canter out to the ground that might have been selected for that particular day's sport. Then riding through the long grass, and beating up the ravines, the antelope would soon be bounding away in all directions. Now came the sport. The grass being nearly five feet long, it was necessary to fire from the saddle, and it was very pretty to see the shooting-pony, with an instinct almost equal to reason, following the dog in every turn, and doing so without a touch of the reins, standing also like a rock when a buck sprang up. Away the antelope would rush, making (if an ourebi) perpendicular leaps of at least two yards in the air, and then scouring over the plain. But a quick messenger would soon be after him, and the sound of the bullet striking would be frequently the only indication of a successful aim. The buck might drop dead if struck in the neck, the shoulder, or the kidneys; if in other parts, he frequently galloped off with a doubled-up and cramped action. The hitherto quiet dog would then come out in a new character, and give chase to the buck, while the pony would have to do his best to live with the two. A mile or so would decide the thing. Upon the buck being vanquished, no trouble was then taken in cleaning him; the pony is off-saddled,—immediately takes a roll, and commences grazing, while dog and man look out for the nearest stream of water to obtain a drink and to cool themselves from the effects of the burning sun.

In about half an hour one of my Kaffirs would be seen

jogging over a hill, and making his way straight down to the dead antelope. He cleans it, and, if it is too heavy for him to carry alone, seeks for aid in the nearest kraal, distant sometimes three or four miles; by signalling, he saves himself great part of the journey. The half of the buck would be an ample reward for the service of an additional man; and the venison is thus sent home, while the pony is saddled, and the sport again proceeded with.

During the first fortnight that I was engaged at this sport I shot only three bucks, although out eight times, and having several fair shots each day. I thought that I was bewitched, and had suddenly an attack of the crooked eye; but, upon mentioning in confidence to a friend, Major K—— (as perfect a gentleman and gallant a sportsman as ever trod on African soil), what had happened, he told me that very probably I had wounded many more of these animals, but that they had dropped when out of sight. He proposed going out with me one day, an offer that I was delighted to accept;—and I may here mention that many of my earliest and best instructions were received from him. When riding a few hundred yards from Major K——, I fired at a fine ram reitbok, that got up about fifty yards in advance. I thought I saw a little lurch in his action as the bullet went by; but, not observing any other sign, I remained for an instant quite still. Major K—— then called out, "After him," with which direction I complied, and followed in the buck's wake for fully half a mile. He seemed to be going quite comfortably, and I began to think there was no use in thus pursuing, when he stopped and looked at me. I jumped off my horse, and was quickly on the ground; but the buck was down first. I ran up to him, and found that my bullet had entered the back without touching the bone or principal muscles, had passed through his body, and come out in the breast; he was bleeding at the mouth, and lay quite dead. Major K——, on coming up, told me that this apparent toughness as regarded life was, during his experience, by no means an uncommon thing. The secret of the crooked eye was now explained, and I afterwards made a practice of watching for a considerable time bucks that I had fired at, unless I was perfectly certain that I had missed them. So tough were some of these reitbok, that a gentleman once told me that he thought, after the first bullet, all others seemed to do them good. It was not quite as bad as this, although the following instance that happened to myself may give an idea of their tenacity of life.

I sighted a buck, and saw him lie down in some long grass. Leaving my pony at some distance, I stalked up to the buck; he rose, and afforded me a fair shot at twenty yards. I gave him a dose of buck-shot near the shoulder, which knocked him over. He jumped up again instantly, and went away on three legs. Not having my dog with me, I ran back to my pony, and mounting him, galloped to the hill over which the buck had disappeared. I looked all round, but could discover no signs whatever of the reitbok. I held up my hand, in order to find which way the little wind that there was happened to be blowing, and, riding with my head to the wind, went nearly a mile without seeing a sign of the buck. I was about making a fresh cast, when I noticed a few reeds on ahead; I went towards them, and, upon getting within one hundred yards, saw my wounded buck jump up and gallop off. With his three legs he could beat my pony's four. So I pulled up, and tried a long shot at him. He got it in the stern, stumbled, recovered, and held on. I loaded, and kept him in sight, thinking he would certainly drop. But no such luck; he staggered along, and was getting away from me, when I saw that he was going down a steep hill at a pace as though he had his legs sound. At the bottom of this hill there was a large watercourse, about twenty feet wide and ten deep. He could not stop himself when he saw this in front, owing to having but one front leg sound, but tried to leap it. This he failed in doing by a long way, and dropped with a crash to the bottom of the ravine. My pony had been much interested in the chase, and was nearly following suit by rushing into this watercourse. As I was going at speed down the hill, and had my gun in my right hand, I could with difficulty pull him up with my left. I jumped off, and ran to the edge of the ravine, where I saw the reitbok trying vainly to leap up the steep bank. I gave him a third shot, which dropped him dead. It was astonishing to see with what wounds he had held on; the dose of buck-shot had made his shoulder look as though it suffered from a severe attack of smallpox; and the second bullet had gone half through him,—a raking shot. Some Kaffirs who were passing soon after conveyed him home for me; and he proved to be, by scale, one of the heaviest bucks that had been shot near Pietermaritzburg for some time. Upon telling this to a facetious friend who came to look at the trophy, he said that it was no wonder, considering the quantity of lead that was in him.

I had several very pretty courses after wounded buck around the country near this village, or town as the Natalians would like it called. On one occasion, by keeping the hills, I saw my dog follow and pull down very neatly a wounded reh-bok. This dog would occasionally point, but, having a good dash of the foxhound in him, he made a useful servant-of-all-work.

If I shot a large reitbok, and could not obtain assistance from Kaffirs to convey him home, or found him too heavy to lift on to my pony, I used to take the two haunches, and pass the girths through a slit cut between the back sinews of each leg and the bone, and thus mount them astride behind the saddle, leaving the remainder of the venison either to be sent for afterwards, or as an offering to the jackals, &c.

I was walking one day about the kloofs near this town, when I heard a noise like running water; I listened attentively, and was convinced I heard its ripple, although the ground was apparently unbroken. Approaching carefully through the grass, I came suddenly to the mouth of a naturally-formed pit about forty feet deep, with a stream running through it at the bottom; the aperture was only about eight feet wide, and quite concealed by long grass; but below, it opened out considerably. This was a nice sort of place to fall into when galloping after a buck, or making a short cut at night. There is no one here to stick up a post with "dangerous" on it, or to hang a lantern near a hole of this description at night. In twelve hours, were any accident to happen, one's very bones would be picked and ground to powder by the hyænas, vultures, jackals, &c. There are many of these holes in Africa, although some are not quite so bad as the one I have described; they are still quite dangerous enough, and serve in a gallop to keep up the excitement, as well as an " in and out" or a " stiff rail," in an English fox-hunt.

I witnessed a most amusing scene on the hills, about eight miles from Pietermaritzburg.

As I was sitting down one day to allow my horse his rest and feed, I noticed a red-coated gentleman riding along in the valley below, and soon saw that he was a non-commissioned officer of the regiment quartered at the time at Natal; he had a gun, and was evidently out taking his pleasure, on leave for a day's sport. He drew all the kloofs and grass that I had tested half an hour before, unconsciously passing over my plainly written horse's footmarks, with a laudable perseverance that deserved success. Presently an eagle or large hawk flew past, and settled some distance on ahead; red-coat followed, and, when near the spot, tried to keep his horse steady; it did not seem to quite understand the matter, and decidedly refused to stand still. A little of the bullying usually practised by unskilled riders then commenced; he spurred the animal, and then chucked it in the mouth with the sharp curb; strange to say, this proceeding failed in making the stupid *equus* more quiet. At last the man dismounted, and, carefully drawing the reins over its head, and taking the saddle off, he looked at his steed in a kind of suspicious way, but left it standing, and proceeded to stalk the eagle. He got up pretty close, when the bird flew away; he took aim, and—bang, bang!—produced not even the effect of ruffling a feather. Loading his gun, this unsuccessful marksman now returned to the horse, which, giving a shake of its head, turned round and walked quietly away. I heard shouts of "Wo! wo!" sent after the horse, with a heavy charge of strong language to propel them; still the animal did not seem to understand; the soldier's walk became a run, and so the horse galloped, and won the race easily, kicking up its heels in the excess of its joy. This was more than the warrior's temper could stand; he had missed the bird, but he thought he could manage the horse. Hot and enraged, he pulled up, and let fly both barrels at his charger. He seemed to have made a better shot this time, as the horse gave a jump, and started at speed towards home, while the soldier had the satisfaction of carrying his saddle for about eight miles under a burning sun, on a day when the thermometer would have shown 95° in the shade. I would have given anything to have heard how this Nimrod described his day's sport to his comrades on his return home. Another somewhat similar case occurred about this time, with the exception that the gentleman *killed* his horse, instead of merely driving him home; and the strangest fact was, that this representative of his stud was nearly the only animal that he did kill with a gun during his residence in Africa.

After an emigrant ship arrived, strange sportsmen

sometimes were seen about the Natal bush, armed with an old gun, and clothed in cast-off garments that smacked more of Whitechapel than of African build; they would prowl about the roads in lots of two or three, shooting from their one gun by turns, at the small birds that had hitherto been left in peace. I once saw a couple of men watching in intense excitement for a shot at some poor monkeys, and utterly unconscious that half a dozen wild elephants were smashing the bush in rage, from a wound given to one of the herd by my bullet, not a couple of hundred yards from them.

ELAND HUNTING.

CHAPTER VI.

Eland-hunting—Beautiful country—Telescopic eyes—Loading at a gallop—The Dutch Boers—Speed of the eland—Eland-hunt—Unsuccessful result—Signals of distress—African Nimrods—A herd of elands—Better luck this time—An accident—The Slough of Despond—A "Stick's bullet"—In at the death—A bivouac—Air-pillows.

AT the cold season of the year the Dutchmen are in the habit of making excursions into the uninhabited plains in search of the large herds of elands and hartebeest that are there found. These excursions are made for the purpose of obtaining a supply of meat, which is dried and salted: the Boers thereby save their cattle from the knife.

The plains under the Draakensberg Mountains, and near the sources of the Mooi river, were very frequent hunting-grounds of the Boers who lived near the Bushman's river. Some of these farmers I had met on former occasions, and in consequence received an invitation to join their party, which consisted of Kemp, Pretorius, and five others: we had three waggons amongst us, and nearly two dozen horses: many Kaffirs and Hottentots also accompanied us. The country in which we purposed to hunt was covered with a most beautiful undulating turf.

Late in the autumn of the year the grass, which grows to a great length, is set on fire either by the Boers or by the Bushmen; tribes of the latter living near, in the Draakensberg Mountains. The ashes of the consumed grass make a good manure, and, after a shower of rain, the young tender grass springs up, and causes the whole plain to look glassy and brilliant, much like a vast green velvet carpet. The antelopes scent the fragrance from afar, and come many miles to graze; they then fall easy victims to the unerring aim of the Bushman's arrow or the Dutchman's rifle.

The air in this neighbourhood was particularly balmy and pure, cooled by its transit over the high peaks of the Draakensberg, that already bore traces of snow in many parts; little cascades could be seen glistening like silver wire in the different kloofs or ravines that were formed by the spurs of the mountains. These ravines were well wooded; many fine trees grew in them, the underwood being thick and matted, as is usually the case in Africa, affording a secure retreat to some angry old bull-buffalo, an exile from his family. It is well to have one's weapons and nerves in order, if this old hermit is to be bearded in his den.

Here also bush-buck, and very many of the feathered tribe are found, the latter having brilliancy of plumage in place of the gift of song. A most useful thing to have in this country is a field-telescope, as it enables one to obtain a good view of all the distant details, and thereby frequently saves one a journey after imaginary animals.

The Boers, however, made out everything wonderfully well with the naked eye; they had rules that experience had taught them; and these rules almost supplied the place of the " far-seer," as they call the telescope.

"What is there?" one of the Boers would exclaim, pointing to an object about four miles distant, and on a slight elevation. Before I had obtained the correct focus of my glass, the object would by them be decided as a hartebeest, without two opinions about it. If I looked through my glass, I always found that their decision was correct. Upon asking how they could know an animal at such a distance, they answered by giving me a great deal of valuable information, amongst which I remembered the following as the most useful:—Elands always look light fawn-coloured when they turn, whereas hartebeest look red, buffaloes black; these three animals being the most commonly met with in these plains. The wild boar (the "vleck vark" of the Dutch) is told by its dark colour, and because it is not so large about the head and shoulders as a buffalo; besides, four or five are generally found together. When the sportsman becomes acquainted with the habits of the animals, the positions which they occupy, as also their way of moving, will generally show to what class the game belongs.

All the antelopes on the flats start off, when alarmed, with their heads to the wind; they like to know what is in front of them, and, having good noses, they can discover danger better by this course.

When a herd of animals are seen on a large flat, the hunter should not ride at them immediately; he should first obtain a weatherly position, which will insure him a good start when the animals begin to move. Before alarming a herd, an after-rider should be sent away to the distance, and directed to approach the game so as to drive them towards the hunter. When a herd start off, the hunter can gradually approach them, taking care, however, that he does not ride in front, as they will then turn in a different direction. When he is within shot, he can jump off his horse, fire, and remount, loading as he rides, and taking care not to follow in the rear of the retreating herd, but to move off to the right or left, and then gallop forward: by this means the distance lost is sooner regained, as the animals do not then go on so rapidly. It is better to keep a herd on the right hand; the hunter, after dismounting, is then behind his horse, and the game consequently are not so much alarmed.

The best plan for loading at a gallop is to place the butt of the gun between the left knee and the saddle; the ramrod side being nearest the body, the left hand (in which also the reins must be held) should hold the gun at about six inches from the muzzle; the right hand is thus free, and therefore can be used for loading.

The pockets of the waistcoat that are used for ammunition should be all on the right-hand side, and lined with leather. A couple of bullets are recommended by some sportsmen to be carried in the mouth, as they can then be readily used, and do not require wadding, if fired immediately they drop upon the powder. This plan I never tried, as I did not like the risk of having a couple of such pills suddenly jerked down my throat, after a flight, spread-eagle fashion, half a dozen yards over one's horse's head. There are so many blind-holes, and other reasons for horses suddenly coming down, and turning completely over with their riders, that the Dutch ride with very long stirrup-leathers, and put just the end of their toes in the stirrups, so as to be ready for such a contingency.

We had proceeded nearly three hours without a rest,

and, as it was not usual to travel beyond that time, a halt was called; the horses were off-saddled, knee-haltered, and allowed to take their much-enjoyed roll, and to pick up a mouthful of grass; the oxen were unyoked, and turned out to graze; some dried wood was collected from a neighbouring kloof, some fires lighted, coffee ready, and pipes in full glory in a very few minutes. Most of these Dutchmen were well-to-do farmers, fat, jolly fellows, with apparently no care, enjoying everything they possessed, and wanting nothing more; they were good riders, excellent shots, and very handy men in the field. In education and refinement they were certainly limited; they were more *au fait* at spooring an elephant and skinning an eland than in solving an equation or making a polite speech; but for good-hearted, dirty, free-and-easy fellows, their equals were rarely to be met with. If a man desires to see the wild parts of a country and its sports, he cannot always have the refinements or the luxuries of civilized life at hand.

Upon continuing our journey, the Dutchmen each made one of their thinnest specimens of humanity, in the shape of a young Hottentot, mount a spare horse, and follow with a rifle. These skinny fellows were useful during a long run to provide a remount, or to turn any herd of game that was not taking a convenient direction. We were now in the game country, and had therefore to keep a good look-out all round.

The elands are well known in England, several fine specimens being in the Regent's Park Zoological Gardens. No idea of their activity can be formed from their appearance in that confined space. Give them a good run, and they would nearly leap over the palings that there surround them. Their usual pace when alarmed, is a long trot, at which they can go sixteen or seventeen miles in an hour. It is easy to ride up to them on a level and unbroken plain; but when a steep hilly country with large loose bits of rock, or heavy ground, happens to be the hunting line, it is a far different matter; they rush down the steep hills like an avalanche, making prodigious leaps to clear the large stones in their course. On rising ground the horseman has the advantage over them, but not enough to enable him to regain what he loses during the descent.

We were all riding along a little ridge which gradually sloped into the plains to our right, and dipped precipitously into a valley on our left; when a cry of "Look, look! eland's bull!" brought us all to a stand. In the plain to our right a large animal was seen pounding away, kicking up the dust in clouds as he went. If he continued his present course, I saw that he would pass over the ridge on which we then were, and at about half a mile in front of us. Taking a look at my gun, therefore, to see that all was right, I let drop the spurs into my pony and galloped forward. One of the Dutchmen then called to me to stop, and, fearing I might be infringing some rule, I pulled up, but soon found that the Boers had been obliged to wait until their after-riders could bring up their guns; and it was to obtain *a fair start* that they had detained me.

In consequence of this delay we were all fully two hundred yards distant when the eland crossed the ridge and dashed down the steep slope on our left. He showed such a splendid pair of horns as he passed, that the Boers compared them to a koodoo's. We were all obliged to dismount and lead our horses down the hill, although the antelope had rushed down like a cricket-ball.

A party of nine Boers were now mounted, and started off in chase. There was a great deal of lee-way to be pulled up, and the country was also very much against us; the hill-sides were covered with large loose stones, and the valleys in many places were so soft and boggy that the horses sank knee-deep in the mud. As I was descending one of the slopes, I thought I could see the eland inclining a little to the right: instead, therefore, of going with the remaining Boers down the hill, I kept along the ridge, thereby saving several hills, and a long course, if the game held on to his new line of country. The long grass and loose stones were unfavourable for galloping, so I nursed my horse for a turn of speed over the flat that I could see in advance.

I had lost sight of the eland for some time and began to fear that I had been thrown out of the run altogether; but by still pursuing my line, I knew I should meet some of the party. After cantering about three miles farther, I had the pleasure of viewing the game "rising" an opposite hill not a quarter of a mile from me.

The long stream of white foam blowing from his mouth, and the blue appearance that his coat had assumed, both indicated distress. My nag was unfortunately in fat condition, and had by this time begun "to ask for his mamma:" giving him a squeeze, I managed to hustle him along until I had reduced my distance from the eland to about eighty yards, when, jumping off, I fired. The previous gallop and excitement caused my hand to shake, and I heard the harmless whistle of the bullet as it sped on its course. The eland made a leap and changed his direction, giving me a broadside shot; I dropped on my knee, and sent the second bullet into his shoulder; he stumbled as the shot struck him, but still held gallantly on. Again mounting, and loading as I cantered, I kept in his wake, hoping to see him soon fall, as he was bleeding freely; but he seemed to be rather invigorated by the loss of blood.

One of the Boers, who had changed to his second horse, now passed me, and firing, placed a second bullet in the eland's shoulder. The eland still trotted rapidly away, and both my horse and the Boer's being completely blown, we could go no farther. We could see the wounded animal pass over a hill in our front, and apparently go directly down on the other side; we managed to lead our horses to the top where he had passed, and took a minute survey of the surrounding plains, but could discover no signs of our lost antelope, as the country was so much broken by clumps of trees and undulations.

The other Dutchmen soon joined us, and blessed the eland in choice language for escaping and being such a hard runner. We all spread out along the ridges, to get if possible a view, as also to search for spoor; but the hard state of the ground prevented our doing anything by the latter means.

Evening closing in, we were forced to give up, and

thus one of the finest specimens of horns that I ever saw on an eland's head was lost. The animal must have miserably perished in some ravine, and found an ignoble tomb in the maws of hyænas and wolves, instead of assisting at the festivities of our *al fresco* repast, or adding strength to the sinews of some worthy Dutch Boer, his "vrow" or "kinders."

We did not reach the outspanned waggons until long after dark, and were directed to them by the firing kept up at intervals by the Hottentots at the waggons.

There is an established custom in Africa, that when any one is absent from the nightly gathering, a man is sent on to the nearest rise, when, putting the muzzle of his gun close to the ground, he fires the two barrels in quick succession: this is repeated at short intervals, and on a still night the report is heard many miles off. Should any one be lost, or in distress, at any time, the same signal from him serves to indicate it. I asked all the Dutchmen into my tent, and we had our beef and bread brought in hot-and-hot, with a steaming basin of tea from the bivouac-fire. I had with me a plentiful supply of brandy and gin, which I distributed to my guests with a free hand. They talked a great deal, the run we had had being the principal topic; they were generous enough to say that they thought I should have killed the eland at once, had I been allowed to go off after him.

I was much amused to discover by their conversation in what poor estimation they held English sportsmen generally. Many of my gallant friends (oracles in their sporting world) would be struck dumb with horror if they knew with what contempt their performances would be looked upon, were they to show them amongst an African field. Perhaps I may clear up this apparent mystery if I relate what are considered the essentials necessary to even mediocrity in this land of sport.

It is absolutely necessary not only to be a good shot, but to be so after a sharp four-mile gallop, and from either shoulder; to load as well while at full speed as when on foot; to be able to ride boldly across country, and allow your horse to go down-hill at speed over the large stones and *with a loose rein;* to pull up, dismount, fire, and get up again with a rapidity a monkey might envy; and when an animal has been wounded and is out of sight, to lean over your horse's shoulder, and follow the spoor at a canter on the hard ground with the accuracy of a hound; and last and not least, to take care to fly clear of your horse when he turns over in a jackal's or porcupine's hole, instead of letting him come on you and smash a few ribs. These and many other qualifications, I have no doubt, most of my readers possess; but there may be some who do not, and who in consequence would not stand A 1 in the far south.

Many offers were made to me to go on elephant-shooting trips into the interior with these men, who purposed a journey during the next dry season: the Boers' anecdotes gave a great impulse to my already long-cherished wishes, but circumstances unavoidably prevented this trip.

When the Boers left my tent, I rolled myself up in my blanket, and listened to the distant shrieks of the jackal and laugh of the hyæna, while many other strange noises in the distance excited my curiosity.

I slept and dreamed not.

The cold air, just before daybreak, penetrating my blanket, awakened me, and I heard the Dutchmen and Hottentots conversing near, and was soon up and enjoying a cup of steaming hot coffee, with some beef and biscuit.

The morning sun was just showing its rays above the horizon, and the fogs were rising up the mountains, when we were once more in the saddle.

When we had ridden for nearly an hour, we suddenly saw, in a valley beneath us, an enormous herd of elands: they were scattered about grazing like cattle. The Boers' plans were immediately taken, and it was arranged that some of the party should ride at a distance, keeping out of sight, and show themselves on the opposite side, so as to drive the herd towards the waggons.

Some of the party managed this business, while I and two of the Boers waited under the hill until the elands should come past us.

After waiting some time, we could see the look-out eland get the alarm; he twisted round, swung his tail about, and trotted down to the main body, who soon left off feeding, collected together, and started off in their long trot, advancing in our direction. I admired the Boers' arrangements,—everything was so ably planned. Suddenly the leading bulls of the herd seemed to smell danger in our neighbourhood, and swerved to the right; I was afraid they were getting away from us, but Kemp, who was by be, restrained my impatience, and told me to wait. Soon after the elands had turned, a man on horseback was seen to canter over the hill that they appeared steering for; he pulled up, took off his hat and waved it, and fired a shot; he was too far off to have done much damage by the shot, but the ruse was immediately successful,—the whole herd wheeled suddenly into their old line, and came thundering along towards us. I looked at my caps to see if all was right, and rammed the bullets down tight; such a herd of game were coming on, at least two hundred of them, bulls and cows, with quite young calves.

The leaders were soon in line with us. I picked out a large fat blue-looking bull, which I saw fall dead at the shot. Most of the others, as they heard the whistle of the bullet, made prodigious leaps in the air, the effect of which was extraordinary, as, from their great size and apparent unwieldiness, these bounds seemed almost impossible. With the second barrel I pinked another bull, but he did not fall. These shots caused the elands to gallop on very fast; we mounted our horses and started after the herd, a second eland having been dropped by one of the Dutchmen, while a third was soon seen to leave the main body and stay behind, evidently in difficulties. I could not load very well while going at full speed, so reduced my pace a little to accomplish it. I had scarcely completed the operation, when my horse came down on his head with a crash, and rolled over, flinging me far from him. I came down on my hands and shoulder, and fortunately was not hurt. Upon getting up, I found, to my disgust, that I had broken the stock of my gun: the trigger-guard alone held it together. I also saw that a large jackal's or ant-bear's hole, that was concealed by the long grass, was the cause of my horse's mistake. There was no remedy but to ride to the waggons for my second gun: they were not very far distant, and nearly on the line that the elands had just taken.

I started off without loss of time, and arrived a few minutes after the herd had passed. They had been viewed from the waggons, and I was told that many were badly wounded, and that five of the Dutchmen were well up, and were, as the Kaffirs in delight said, *barnie bulalu* (much shooting) the elands: the Kaffirs were anticipating a regular cram that night. I stayed only sufficiently long to procure my sound gun, and started in pursuit of the Boers. I was much annoyed at being thus cut out of so fine a chance, and to make up my distance, I let my game little nag go his best over the springy turf that, like rolling waves, lay around. I suddenly noticed some animals nearly a mile distant that looked extremely like elands, and therefore I turned in their direction, which was nearly opposite to that which I had first pursued.

As I approached them, I made out a couple of bulls and four cow elands, with five or six half-grown calves. They went away as soon as they noticed me, and crossed a little muddy hollow, that seemed soft enough to hold them fast; they got over, however, but sunk to their bellies in the attempt, and came out on the other side with black mud-stockings. I knew that their instinct had shown them the best place for a crossing, and that if

I tried at any other, I might get pounded completely; I therefore went down to the spot, and tried my horse at it. He would not stir a step into the bog, but smelt at it in a suspicious manner: spurs and whip had no effect on him, he would not face it.

An English officer who happened to have joined our party, and who weighed upwards of sixteen stone, was now approaching at a canter: he had lost the main body of elands, and was coming after my lot.

I saw that the quiet plan was no good with my nervous brute, so, turning him round, I gave him a little canter, and brought him down again to the muddy crossing with a rush. When he found what I purposed, he tried to refuse; but I let drop both spurs into his flank with a vigorous dig, and at the same time plied the *sjambok* behind with such good effect, that he floundered into the bog, sinking to the girths. He struggled desperately, and could scarcely move. There were little round hard tufts of grass in places, that afforded him a slight footing; I therefore dismounted, and, by shouting and lifting with the bridle, managed to get him across the score of yards, the breadth of this horrid place. This struggle took a good deal out of him, and he was none of the freshest when I remounted and followed the elands, which I saw steadily trotting along a mile in advance. My horse seemed to gather strength at every stride, and by keeping him well together I hoped soon to be able to make a push and overhaul them. Two or three graceful ourebis jumped up, and flew across the plain in front of me; their beautiful movements, and frequent springs of several feet in the air, looking most interesting by the contrast which the white and fawn robes of these antelopes produced with the satiny green of the plain.

I at length closed with the elands, and turned a bull from the herd. I rode behind, and obliged him to keep at a gallop, as this pace was more distressing to him than the trot. Seeing another muddy place a short distance in front, I pulled up, and as the bull was floundering through it, I gave him the contents of both barrels in the stern. He did not fall, although I could see that he was very badly wounded. I managed to get over this difficulty with greater ease than the first, as the mud was not so deep, and commenced loading as I rode. Upon taking out my bullets, I discovered that they were for my broken-stocked gun, the bore of which was nearly two sizes larger than the one I now had with me; and this difference I had forgotten in my hurry of changing. I thought that if I rode steadily after the eland, his wounds would soon cause him to fall. I tried this plan, but at the end of two miles saw but little prospect of a successful termination. I then put the bullet in my mouth, and kept biting it to reduce its size; at last I managed just to put it into the barrel; but when there, I could not persuade it to move farther.

I could see no probability of my heavy sixteen-stone friend coming, so I dismounted, and with the aid of a flint on the ramrod hammered the bullet down about half-way, —farther, however, it seemed determined not to go. I tried without success until the skin came off the inside of my fingers.

The eland had trotted down to some water, that flowed

from a rocky ravine near, and formed a sort of court or semicircle, the back of which was high, and like a stone wall. He stood in the water, and as I approached could not retreat, as he was in a sort of *cul de sac*, and did not like coming past me. I left my horse, and came within forty yards of the antelope, to prevent his getting away, and had another try at my obstinate bullet. I could not get a move out of it, and therefore felt inclined to go in at the bull with my long clasp-knife; but a threatening kind of pawing, and a shake of the head, when I came near, made me think it more prudent "to keep off."

I now remembered a Dutchman's plan for a "sticks bullet" as they call it; viz., dropping a little water in the barrel. I went to the stream and let a few drops trickle down on the bullet. I soon found the good result, for the ball began to move, and at each blow from the ramrod went lower and lower, until the clear ring and springing of the ramrod at length showed it to be home. I then laid my impatient prisoner low with a shot behind the shoulder; he was a fine young bull about fifteen hands in height. I off-saddled and sat down near him, as I was not inclined to follow the remainder of the herd, both horse and self having done our work. After about half an hour, my heavy friend showed on the hill-top, and came galloping down and shouting to know where the elands had gone, with as much eagerness as though he had been but half a mile instead of half an hour behind. I accounted for one out of the lot, which he helped me to skin and decapitate (a proceeding that we did not accomplish before sunset), and we conveyed the head with difficulty to our outspanning-place for the night. We were welcomed by the Dutchmen, in whose estimation I found myself considerably advanced. They could not, however, imagine for what reason I had brought the head and horns, and I found great difficulty in making them comprehend that they were considered as ornaments in England and were also rarities. They inquired if we had no elands in that land, and seemed to think it a very poor place where no large game was to be found.

I tried to explain to them the glories of a good run with hounds across a grass country sprinkled with pretty stiff fences, but they could not realize its beauties. And when I told them that foxes were preserved merely for the sake of being hunted, they actually roared with laughter, and assured me that they could not live or breathe in a country so destitute of game, or be happy or feel free unless they knew that at least one hundred miles of open country were around them, about which they might ride, shoot, or live, just as they liked.

I explained to them the manner in which England was cut up by roads, and that no one was allowed to go out of these roads and ride over the country just as he might like; and that if he did by chance do so, he would probably be prosecuted for a trespass. In order to prevent any such contingency, I told them boards were always stuck up near any pretty wood or nice places, marked in large letters, "Trespassers beware," or, "Any person found on these grounds will be prosecuted." This relation made them almost furious, and they allowed their spleen to effervesce in several anathemas against the "Verdamt Englishmensch."

I have generally found that the want of a pillow is the greatest discomfort in sleeping on the ground; all persons who run the risk of passing a night out of their beds, should provide themselves with an air-cushion, for it can be filled when required, and be packed very neatly in the pocket when not wanted.

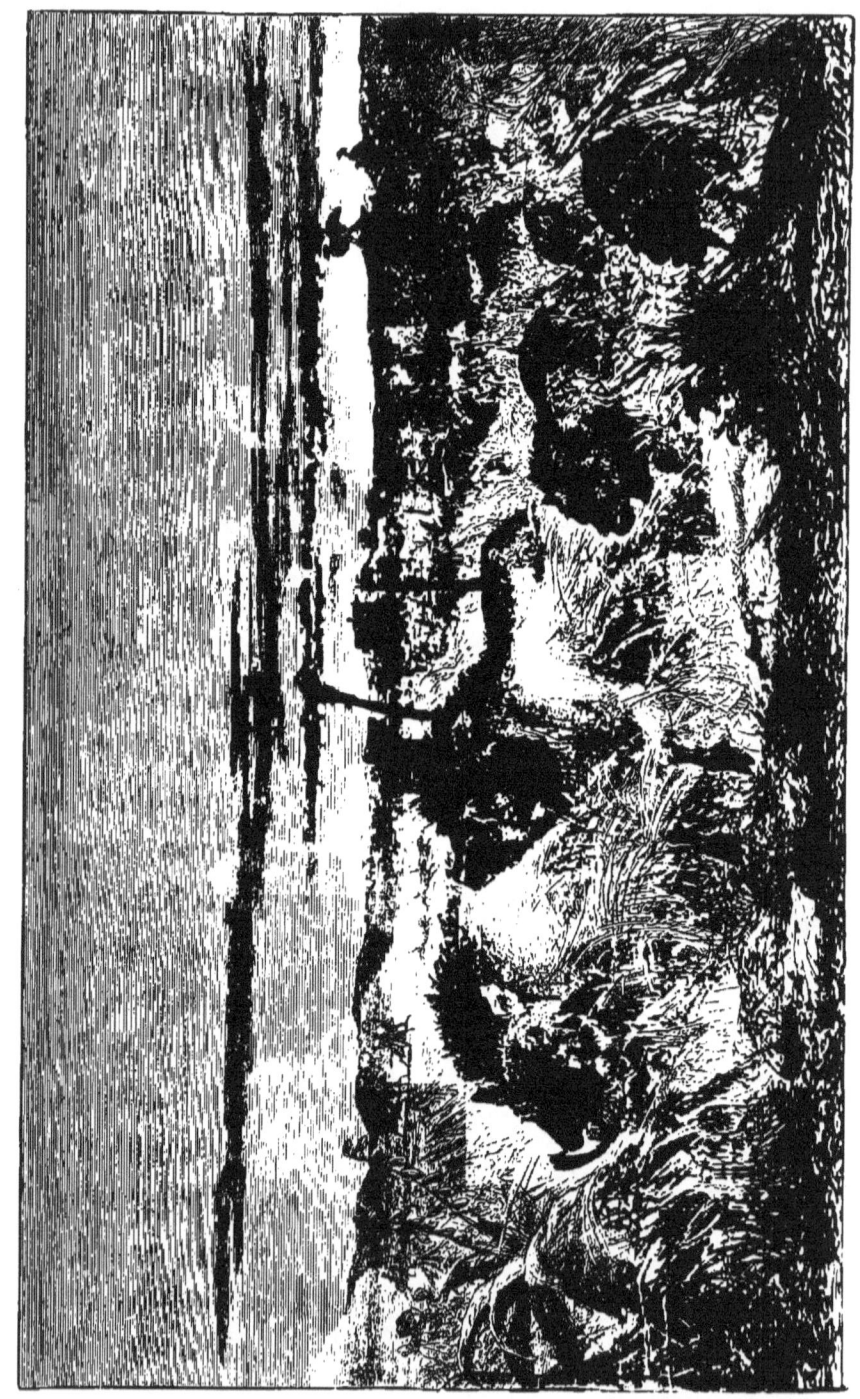

WILD BOAR HUNTING.

P. 127.

CHAPTER VII.

The Dutchman's stratagem—Wild-boar hunt—A vicious pigling—Hartebeest-chase—Hide and seek—The organ of "locality"—Fatal curiosity—An escapade—A false alarm—Baboons at home—A tame baboon—The baboon and the crow—Literary and scientific tastes—A leopard shot—Unpleasant journey—Conflicting opinions.

ON the third day we came across a troop of hartebeest, which commenced galloping round us, taking care to keep at a long distance from us. We tried one or two rides at them, but failed in getting near enough for a shot. They continued circling round us in a most tantalizing way for a long time, while we were taking shots at from five to six hundred yards' distance. Suddenly they started right away from us, and, by the straight line which they kept, did not seem disposed to return. One of the Dutchmen now told me to look out for a shot, and at the same time he fired both barrels at a high elevation, so that he sent the bullets over the heads of the troop of hartebeest, which, striking the ground far on ahead of them, sent up a cloud of dust. The result was at once seen; the troop, as they heard the whistle of the lead, and saw the dust in front, darted here and there, and then, wheeling round, came directly back to us. We fired a volley at them; but, as they were at least three hundred yards from us, and were going at full speed, one only remained on the ground; another, however, was seen in difficulties, and surrendered his stakes after a hard run of some six miles.

Towards evening, we had a brilliant affair with an old wild boar (the *vleck vark*), his wife, and children.

We were told by the people at the waggons that the brutes had passed some time before we returned to lunch, and, having a good supply of eland-beef, the Boers thought that some bacon would be very palatable. We therefore took all the curs that were with the waggons, and went out in search of the party. We got the spoor immediately, and, partly by that and partly by the aid of the dogs, we drew up to some rocky hills, that presented anything but a favourable ground for galloping. The boar was seen a long way on ahead, leading his sow and sucklings at a trot, which was increased to a rapid gallop as our approach became known to him. The pace at which the whole party went along the rocky ground was more than we could manage to beat, until a long, flat, grassy plain again became the scene of contest. As we neared, we sent the curs in advance, who, without difficulty, overhauled the chase. The movements of the boar family were most absurd; with tails sticking straight up, they galloped along, putting their snouts up in the air occasionally to have a look over their backs at their pursuers; this gave to their whole action a most absurd appearance. These creatures are obliged to do thus, because their eyes are placed so far forward, and their necks are so stiff, that they cannot see to the right or left by turning the head. On the outside of the eye a large lump of flesh protrudes, which also limits the lateral vision considerably.

As the dogs came up to the pigs, they laid hold of one of those invitingly-carried tails, and soon reduced it to a stump. The wild boar himself was armed with a formidable pair of semicircular tusks in the upper jaw, while the lower jaw was furnished with those sharp, straight, short tusks that soon rip up a dog, as they did most effectually on the present occasion a large cur which ventured to pin the pig himself. When we were close to the herd, the boar slackened his speed, and had a wicked expression about the eye that indicated a wish for mischief. Little time was given to him for consideration, as a well-directed bullet laid him low. A young pig which I succeeded in catching was a regular little varmint; he squeaked and struggled furiously, and tried to bite every hand that was placed near him. He was not much bigger than a sucking-pig. So, after tying his legs together, I slipped him into a haversack, and delivered him in safety to one of my Kaffirs, who placed him in a waggon. On the following day, he bit a Hottentot's finger, and was in consequence killed by the man. I did not know how or where the animal was for two days, as the murder was concealed from me. I regretted the loss of this savage little creature, as I had intended to send him to England.

We passed eight days in the Mooi river veldt. The weather was fine, except on the last day, when the rain poured in torrents. I sought shelter under the waggon-tilt, but was forced to lie on a mattress stuffed with eland's meat. One must not grumble in this country at having to submit to even greater disagreeables.

The air was delightfully pure and bracing on these plains, and I quite regretted that I had not a shooting-box near them, so as to be able to pass months at a time in their vicinity.

The Boers came into my tent each night, and by their conversation and anecdotes gave me a great fund of useful information on the biped and quadruped life of Africa, and on the craft that was necessary in carrying on a successful campaign against either.

Whilst on a visit to an English settler, who resided about forty miles from Pietermaritzberg, I had some good sport with hartebeest.

Having made inquiries from the few Kaffirs who lived in this neighbourhood, I found that a troop of hartebeest were usually found feeding on some table-land about twenty miles from the house at which I was staying. I therefore started alone one beautiful bright morning at daybreak to have a quiet gallop after these animals. Unfortunately, my telescope had been forgotten, and I could not scan the country with such accuracy as to distinguish the antelope from the stone on the flat distant hills. After riding an hour or two, I reached the country that had been indicated to me as the hartebeest kop; I off-saddled for half an hour to have my horse as fresh as possible, in case of a run, and then continued my ride. On rising a little stony ridge, I suddenly came on a troop of nearly forty hartebeest: they were grazing, but immediately took the alarm. As usual, they did not at once make straight away, but took two or three circling gallops round me; they kept at such a safe distance that I did not try a shot for some time; at length, seeing that they were going away, I rode at a point for which they were making. I had to keep my horse at full gallop to hold my position with them, although they seemed to be merely

cantering. There was a little opening between two hills, and for this the hartebeest appeared to be steering; making a grand push, I passed a little ahead of them, and, jumping off, got a double shot at the string as they dashed past. I saw that the result was a hind-leg of a fine bull-hartebeest broken. He went gallantly away on three legs, but I certainly did not doubt but that I should be more than a match for him with the horse's four. I lost a little ground by dismounting, and before I had loaded again, the herd had passed out of sight over some rising ground.

Upon again viewing the hartebeest, I was alarmed at the start they had obtained; they were mere specks in the distance. Feeling great confidence in the gameness of my well-conditioned, hardy little nag, I let him go over the green springy turf, and soon found that the distance between us and the hartebeest was diminishing. Seeing my horse's ears suddenly elevated, I looked round on each side, and saw my three-legged hartebeest galloping away behind, and nearly close to me; he had been lying down amongst some stones, and had allowed me to pass without moving. I turned after him, my horse seeming as anxious in the chase as a hound. When an animal is badly wounded, he usually separates himself from the remainder of the herd, as though they no longer had any sympathy with him, and he then seeks in solitude to brood over his sufferings, unwatched by the eyes of his fellows. I intended to save my ammunition until I got a fair chance of a dead shot, but after a stern-chase of more than four miles, I found that the loss of one leg did not much affect the speed of my friend; edging off a little, I made a push forward, and pulled up for a broadside-shot at little more than one hundred yards distant. As I did so, the hartebeest also stopped and looked at me, and I dropped him with the first shot behind the shoulder. The next proceeding was to get as much of the flesh cut up and put on my horse as he could manage to carry. I was anxious for the head and skin; but from want of skill as a butcher, I mauled the skin so terribly that I found it would be useless. Taking away the head and choice parts of the flesh, I looked round for my bearings, and slowly returned homewards.

To the inexperienced in this sort of travelling the road would not have been easy. The hills bear a wonderful resemblance to one another, and during the excitement of a gallop of this description, there is little time to take observations as to the course one is pursuing; a sort of instinct seems to supply the place of reason; it would be difficult to tell any one why or how we know that such a direction is the right one—we *feel* that it is so, but can give no reason why. I am confident that this is the feeling that animals have when they find their way for miles to their homes by roads on which they have never before travelled. There is a well-authenticated instance of a dog having been taken from the south of England to Scotland by sea, and returning alone by land.

On another day I went out hartebeest-hunting, and soon found a troop of these creatures quietly feeding on a level plain that extended some miles around. They were some distance from me, and my horse, not having had any good forage for four days, had lost his condition, and was not fit for a gallop after these fleet animals. There was not a stone or ant-hill near enough to get a shot from, and the grass being very short, stalking was out of the question. I left my horse, and slid along to within six hundred yards of the herd without attracting their attention, and lay down in a small patch of long grass to watch proceedings. A knowing old bull-hartebeest, however, was on the look-out, and kept moving from side to side with a careful and suspicious air. I saw that I could get no nearer, and yet did not like to try my shot from such a distance. I had often heard of the curiosity of the antelopes, and that they might be decoyed by this weakness of character. So lying down well out of sight, I took a red silk pocket-handkerchief, and, tying it to my gun, waved it slowly above the grass. The hartebeest saw it immediately, and all left off feeding; they moved about very suspiciously, keeping a good look-out at the strange object. I kept waving the flag most industriously, and soon saw that they were coming up towards it; but when about two hundred yards distant, they again stopped, and eyed my signal. Hoping that they would come nearer, I did not fire, and saw them walk knowingly round to leeward to try and get my wind. This would have ruined all, so, lowering the flag, I fired at the ancient bull and dropped him. It was the cleanest dead shot I ever saw. A Dutchman, in describing a similar event, said that "the foot that was in the air never came to the ground while there was life." I gave the contents of the second barrel to another bull; but he went away gallantly after receiving the ball in his ribs. I took enormous pains to skin and preserve the head from injury, and then went down for my nag, who had remained feeding quietly. He was a good shooting-horse, and generally behaved well; but when he saw me coming, he gave an impudent sort of whisk of his tail and walked quietly away, holding his head sufficiently on one side to keep the reins from catching the feet. I called to him and stood still, he stopped and fed; I walked slowly towards him, he walked slowly away, keeping his eye on me with a malicious twinkle; I ran towards him, he trotted off; and thus passed half an hour. I found it was no use trying to catch him, for he was determined on mischief, and there was no help for it. I returned to the hartebeest and got his head and tail and my gun; the skin I left, as it was more than I could carry in addition. I then returned to my horse, who had made use of his time and had been feeding away at the short green grass. As I came towards him, he moved on as before: fortunately he seemed to know the road that he had come, and returned on his spoor. Now and then he would canter on half a mile or so, stop and feed till I came near, when he would start off again. It was a great trial for my temper, as my load was considerable and the journey before me very long; the burning sun was directly over my head, and its heat consequently intense. I took a pull or two at my flask, and trudged on for upwards of four hours before I came in sight of my friend's house, this tantalizing rascal in front of me the whole time. I then went to the stream near, and finding a still, quiet pool, cooled myself with a dip in its clear water.

On the following day I got a long halter with a bowling-knot at the end, and cantered this same horse over my journey of yesterday, as I thought it possible that I might find the skin of the hartebeest fit to take away. As I came near, however, I gave up this hope, for I saw a vulture sailing over my head in the same direction in which I was going; I looked up, and saw another and another. When I came near the carcase, I saw a regular inquest sitting there, a dozen vultures at least, most of them gorged to repletion, while others were fighting for bits of the skin. Seeing that there was nothing left for my share, I withdrew.

During the shooting trip with the Boers, I awoke before daybreak, and as I felt very cold and not inclined to sleep, I got up, and taking my gun, walked to a little ravine, out of which a clear murmuring stream flashed in the moonlight and ran close past our outspan. A little distance up this kloof the fog was dense and thick, the blue and pink streaks of the morning light were beginning to illumine the peaks of the Draakensberg, but all immediately around us still acknowledged the supremacy of the pale moonlight. I wanted to see the sun rise in this lonely region, and watch the changing effects which its arrival would produce on the mountains and plains around.

Suddenly I heard a hoarse cough, and, on turning, saw indistinctly in the fog a queer little old man standing near and looking at me. I instinctively cocked my gun, as the idea of Bushmen and poisoned arrows flashed across my mind. The old man instantly dropped on his hands, giving another hoarse cough, that evidently told a tale of consumptive lungs; he snatched up something beside him, which seemed to leap on his shoulders, and then he scampered off up the ravine on all fours. Before half this performance was completed, I had discovered my mistake, the little old man turned into an ursine baboon, with an infant ditto, who had come down the kloof to drink. The "old man's" cough was answered by a dozen others, at present hidden in the fogs; soon, however,

> "Uprose the sun, the mists were curl'd
> Back from the solitary world
> Which lay around;"

and I obtained a view of the range of mountains gilded by the morning sun.

A large party of the old gentleman's family were sitting up the ravine, and were evidently holding a debate as to the cause of my intrusion. I watched them through my glass, and was much amused at their grotesque and almost human movements. Some of the old ladies had their olive-branches in their laps, and appeared to be "doing their hair," while a patriarchal-looking old fellow paced backwards and forwards with a fussy sort of look: he was evidently on sentry, and seemed to think himself of no small importance. This estimate of his dignity did not appear to be universally acknowledged, as two or three young baboons sat close behind him watching his proceedings; sometimes with the most grotesque movements and expressions they would stand directly in his path, and hobble away only at the last moment. One daring youngster followed close on the heels of the patriarch during the whole length of his beat, and gave a sharp tug at his tail as he was about to turn. The old fellow seemed to treat it with the greatest indifference, scarcely turning round at the insult. Master Impudence was about repeating the performance, when the pater, showing that he was not such a fool as he looked, suddenly sprung round, and catching the young one before he could escape, gave him two or three such cuffs, that I could hear the screams that resulted therefrom. The venerable gentleman then chucked the delinquent over his shoulder, and continued his promenade with the greatest coolness: this old baboon evidently was acquainted with the practical details of Solomon's proverb. A crowd gathered round the naughty child, who, childlike, seeing commiseration, shrieked all the louder. I even fancied I could see the angry glances of the mamma, as she took her dear little pet in her arms and removed it from a repetition of such brutal treatment.

The habits of these animals are almost human, and their interior and domestic arrangements much to be admired. My friend M——, before mentioned in connection with my first acquaintance with elephants, possessed a most interesting young baboon, whose fun and tricks frequently afforded me amusement. The baboon used to be allowed to run loose, and accompany us in our quiet walks, and would follow like a dog. It was difficult to restrain his mercurial temperament; at one moment he would jump on one of our backs, holding on by our coats, and then bolt away, as though he never meant to return. His great delight, however, seemed to lie in bullying and frightening the Kaffir women. Did he, with his eagle glance, discover one of these, he would rush at her, with fierce expression and threatening barks. Away she would run, dropping her basket or hoe. He would soon catch her, and, holding on to a leg, would move his eyebrows about, and stare at her, as though he were the veriest vampire on earth. Sometimes this scene would be viewed from the kraal near, and a mangy, spectre-looking Kaffir cur would be hied on to the rescue. Now the tables were turned, and Jacko would have to scuttle away for his life to some tree, amongst the branches of which he would spring with wonderful agility, until with a rapid twinkle of the eye he discovered that he was high enough to be safe from the gnashing teeth of the infuriated dog below. Instantly becoming calm, he gazed upwards and around, with a quiet and contemplative air, as though he had sought this elevated position for the sole purpose of meditating on the weakness of baboon and animal nature generally, but more particularly on the foibles of excited Kaffir curs.

I was much amused in watching this creature's revenge on a crow that had frequently robbed him of tit-bits which by accident had gone beyond the reach of his chain. He watched this bird flying round him, settling, and walking nearer, and again flying; so he left his meal, and laid himself down, as though the wished-for food was entirely beneath his notice. The crow settled near, and carefully watched the proceedings. First he inspected the chopped potatoes and meat, and then the sleepy baboon. Again the tempting morsels attracted his hungry appetite, and after one or two retreats, he at last came fairly up to the tin dish,—not a move from the baboon. Crow gobbled down a bit, and looked suspiciously round,—still all was safe. Again a mouthful was bolted; then, as if satisfied that it had entirely mistaken the character of the hairy little creature about whom he had been suspicious, but who was really at heart a very generous fellow, the bird dived its beak well amongst the good things. An attentive observer might now see the hair on the back of the baboon rising up in a very curious way, while his body seemed to be slightly writhing. Suddenly, with one spring, he was upon the bird, who had scarcely time to open its wings. With a chorus of triumphant barks he held the crow by the neck, while he swung it about at arm's length, so that any expostulating "caw" that might have been uttered was strangled before it could be circulated, like a disloyal article in a continental newspaper. No one could say of this bird that it carried out the corvine principle, and—

"—— died as slow,
As the morning mists down the hill that go."

For the whole business was over in half a minute, after which several feathers were pulled out, and the carrion then flung away, as a scare and warning to all other hungry crows. The baboon then finished his dinner with a very satisfied air.

His literary taste was the cause of his being a chained prisoner, as, rambling one day into a hut near, he drank a bottle of ink, ate a box of wafers, and was found by the owner studying the watch-making practised by "Dent, London." When we consider that this baboon was not two years old at the time, and several young gentlemen of my acquaintance are ten and eleven, it may fairly be expected that when he arrives at their years, he may be able to rival them in many of their practices.

* * * * * *

Upon the return march from Bushman's River, I was nearly having to pass the night in the open country, without dinner, supper, or blankets. Finding the slow pace of the waggons very disagreeable, and the road dull and uninteresting, I proposed to a Lieutenant G——, of the party, to join me in a little detour in the surrounding country. We left the road, and riding at right angles to the line of its direction, continued our journey in a supposed parallel direction to the road, after a dive into the plain of about three miles. Now it so happened that when we left, the road pointed nearly south, but shortly after it turned to the east; thus, when we fancied that we were moving in a parallel direction, we were in fact going directly away from it. We rode on quietly, taking a bread-and-cheese luncheon from our pockets, and seeing only a few ourebis, that were, however, very wild; until our attention was drawn to a moving object by the side of a grassy watercourse. Watching this object carefully, we soon saw it was a leopard, and rode towards it quietly, so as not to cause an alarm, if possible, until we were near it. When within about sixty yards, the animal saw us, and crouched down in the grass. Having my favourite gun, the left barrel of which threw a bullet with the precision of a rifle, I fired at the leopard as I saw it crouching; it scarcely moved, and the bullet threw up no dust, convincing me by this one circumstance that I had hit the animal.

We rode up to where it lay, and I was about dismounting and walking up to the spot, when, just as my foot was out of the stirrup, the leopard jumped up, gave a snarl, and bounded off, apparently safe and sound. Both our horses reared and turned round, and, before I could arrange matters, and bring my second barrel to bear, the leopard looked beautifully small at the distance of three hundred yards. I pitched a bullet, however, just over him, with, of course, no result.

As the sun was nearly setting, we now changed our direction at right angles to the old one, thinking by this that we were steering directly for the road; we were, however, in reality, only now going parallel to it, and at nearly twenty miles' distance. We rode on and on, our horses beginning to show signs of fatigue, we having been in the saddle about six hours, with only half an hour's rest. They had, however, a longer journey before them than we imagined. We soon were overtaken by the darkness, and had to fix on particular stars near the horizon as guides; these sometimes were lost sight of as we went down a kloof. The riding was rather rough, as big pointed stones two or three feet high were pleasantly mixed up with the long grass, about five feet in its growth. It was too dark to see these and avoid them, and more than once horses and riders came floundering down in one heap. Once or twice we were in doubt whether we should camp for the night, or still try to reach the road. We had a consultation about our position, and where we ought to ride to reach the road. After some discussion, we discovered the real cause of our failure, and therefore rode more to the right than we had before done. At length, we crossed a road, and my companion at once said we were all right, and proposed cantering on. I was not quite so certain about being right, but was almost overruled; so I dismounted, and, kneeling down on the ground, examined for spoor. Knowing that a gun and waggon horsed, with about half a dozen other waggons with each a span of oxen, could not pass without leaving sign, I crawled along for some distance, but could not trace more than two fresh waggon-wheels. I therefore determined that this was the wrong road, and that we must ride yet farther to hit the one that our people had followed. I was very nearly giving in, as G—— argued very powerfully; but he at last consented to go on a mile or two, and if we did not come to any other road, to return to the present one. We rode about four miles, when another beaten track, which they here compliment with the title of a road, was crossed; on dismounting, I found that waggons, oxen, horses, and nailed boots, had all passed on that day. We followed this road, and in about two hours reached the Mooi river; on the opposite side of which our camp for the night had been formed. It was about $1\frac{1}{2}$ A.M. when we reached the waggons, hungry and tired, our horses, however, being wonderfully fresh, although we had been nearly fourteen hours in the saddle. The road that we first crossed would have taken us twenty-five miles before we could have seen a house, and we should have reached the river fifteen miles from our camp.

CHAPTER VIII.

The Bivouac—Hotman's story—Terrible misfortune—Both sides of the story—How to find water—Kemp's story—Death of Mabili—Single Elephants to be avoided—Hendrich and the Leopard—A struggle for life—A weary night—A poisonous companion—The rescue—Savage hermits—The "Trek-boken."

ONE evening the Boers wished me to tell them something about England, but by a little tact I changed the subject to their own adventures, and at length persuaded one of these men to relate what had happened to himself. I listened to his words with great interest, for the locality was good for a tale of thrilling adventure. The only noises that disturbed the stillness of the silvery moonlight night, were the language of the Kaffirs, with its low harmonious expressions, the crackling of the bivouac-fire as fresh fuel was added, and the distant shriek of the jackal, and laugh of the hyæna, which seemed in this demon-like language to hold communion with the restless spirits who dwelt in the wild regions around us.

" Water is a fine thing, and none know its value who have not suffered for want of it," said Hotman, one of our party.

" Tell us your story about the elephants," asked another.

" I was shooting," said Hotman, "some years back near the Pongola, and had had very good sport; the season was very dry, and we had been for two days with very little water, and that was rather brackish. The vlei being nearly exhausted, and the oxen having sore feet,

I determined to go out and have a look for some water, and if I found any, to lead the waggons to it at once. I climbed up a tree near the outspan, and thought that I saw a line of bushes some distance off that showed like the presence of water. Taking with me Karl, a Hottentot,—who was worth his weight in gold, spoored and rode well, a steady hand with elephants, and seldom got drunk or told lies, all great recommendations for a Totty,—we started away to the bushy place which I had seen, leaving my other Hottentot and three Kaffirs with the waggons.

"All my horses had died of the sickness, and several of the oxen were very bad with the same disease. I gave directions that my Kaffirs were not to leave the waggons until I returned, as elephants were near them, and I wished them to keep a fire burning night and day, as a protection. Enough water was in the vlei to last two or three days, with care. We had scooped out a hole, and to obtain water, dipped the small tin cans in it till we got a pailful, which we gave then to the oxen. I had ordered the Kaffirs to drive the oxen far away, and to make them fast when they came near, so that the vlei might not be trampled in, and the water consequently spoiled.

"Karl and I trudged on for some miles to a little 'kop,' where we hoped to get a better view round. There was still an appearance of water in the direction where I had first expected, and we made towards it; we arrived there about sundown, and found not a drop—a few stunted bushes were all that could be seen. We lighted a fire, and had a little beltong meat dried in the sun for supper. The day had been very hot, and I was thirsty already, but was obliged to manage without drinking. I knew that I should lose my oxen if I did not find water on the morrow.

"During the night several animals came round the light of our fire, and once I saw a lion: I shouted, and he went away.

"Early in the morning we were off again, taking a sweep round towards the waggons. I thought that we were certain of finding water this day; so, although very thirsty, I was not at all alarmed. We walked until long past mid-day, without getting a glimpse of any likely-looking place. The dry salt meat that I had eaten caused me to suffer very much from thirst; the heat of the day was also very great. I kept a bullet in my mouth and bit it; but this soon ceased to be of any use, and my tongue was rattling in my mouth like a stone. I felt growing savage, gave up the idea of water for the oxen, and thought only of myself.

"We had to sleep out another night, as I was so much exhausted I could not walk fast. Karl suffered nearly as much as I did; but I think that a Hottentot is by nature more seasoned than a white man, and endures privations better.

"On the following morning I could not swallow anything,—thus took no breakfast. I was looking forward with joy to the prospect of even a mouthful of the brackish water that was at the vlei, which I trusted was not yet all exhausted. We neared the place where the waggon was left just as it was getting light. I fired my gun to let my Kaffirs know that I was coming, but received no answer, nor could I see anything of the white waggon-top. We began to think that we must have mistaken our bearings; but upon getting nearer, we saw an object that looked like the waggon lying on its side: no one was near it, and there was no sign of a fire. What could be the matter? We walked up quickly to the spot, but first went to the vlei, for a little water. Here the catastrophe was explained. Instead of water, a thick mud-paste covered the ground; large circular holes, nearly a foot deep, and two feet in diameter, were, as it seemed, dug all over it; one or two large flat places looked as if the vlei had been rolled with the trunks of trees; these had been baked with the sun, and were nearly hard and dry,—not so much as a drop of water.

"A troop of bull-elephants had rolled in the mud and trodden all the water away.

"Not content with that, they had either through rage or curiosity upset the waggon, broken one wheel off, and scattered everything about. My Hottentot and Kaffirs no doubt had bolted on the first appearance of the elephants, without so much as firing a shot to try and drive them away. The oxen had also fled; and there we were, with a few biscuits, beltong, powder, shot, and guns, a hundred miles from help. This distance would have been 'nix' (nothing) if we could only have procured water; but I knew of none within forty miles, and we had now been forty-eight hours without quenching our thirst.

"I lay down on the ground in despair. The ivory I had collected was scattered all about; I thought I never should convey half of it to my home.

"Home! How was *I* ever to reach home?

"I said to Karl, 'You are stronger than I am, you go on,

you may get to water soon, but I am so weak I must stop here and die.'

"'Ne, bas' (no, sir), said Karl; 'let us try on the other side.'

"I thought, if I could only shoot a buck, I would not hesitate a moment about drinking his blood; in this idea a hope dawned upon me, and I struggled on.

"Towards the middle of the day Karl pointed out a moving object some distance from us. We stopped to look at it, when Karl exclaimed, 'Wasser soon, bas.'

"'Why, how?' I asked.

"'That is reitbok,' he said: 'where reitbok is, there are reits (reeds); where reits, there wasser.'

"I saw his reasoning, and that it was not likely that a reitbok would be very far from water.

"This hope gave me fresh strength to go on: we followed the slight traces of this buck, and soon came to a regular beaten track that the buck had made in going to and returning from water. We soon came to the vlei: there was not much water, but still it was worth more than gold to me; I drank as I never drank before.

"We stopped beside it all night, and I began to feel hungry, and to want something more than the dry beltong; when, just at daybreak, a reitbok came to drink; Karl was going to shoot him, but I would not let him, explaining that it appeared as though Providence had sent the buck yesterday to save us from dying of thirst.

"'Perhaps He sent him to-day to save us from dying of hunger too, bas,' was Karl's irreverent answer. He was, however, allowed to retreat unharmed.

"After four days' travelling on foot, I came to fresh waggon-spoor; we followed it up, when I found it was Eus and Maritz returning from a shooting-journey. They had some spare oxen, which they lent me; I returned with this help, mended my waggon, and had my revenge on the herd of elephants, killing three of them before I left."

"Well," said Kemp, "when I go into a country where there is not much water, I always take my baboon."

"You don't drink him, do you?"

"No, but I make him show me water."

"How do you do that?"

"In this way:—When water gets scarce, I give the Bavian none: if he does not seem thirsty, I rub a little salt on his tongue; I then take him out with a long string or chain. At first it was difficult to make him understand what was wanted, for he always wished to go back to the waggons. Now, however, he is well trained.

"When I get him out some distance, I let him go; he runs along a bit, scratches himself, shows his teeth at me, takes a smell up-wind, looks all round, picks up a bit of grass, smells or eats it, stands up for another sniff, canters on, and so on. Wherever the nearest water is, there he is sure to go." This anecdote was corroborated by others present.

I think a tame baboon to point water is a new phrase to our non-travelled sporting friends.

"These elephants must have been very angry," said Kemp. "One never knows in what temper to find them: they are on one day quiet, and seem scarcely to object to being shot at, while on another they will not allow you to come within a quarter of a mile of them without charging you. I have been very careful how I approached elephants, ever since my Kaffir was killed by them last year, near the Um Volozie." Another story was here called for, and Kemp told us the following:—Whilst up the country shooting, he came on the fresh spoor of a very large bull-elephant: the traces were quite fresh, the game having passed early that morning. His Kaffir, who was named Mabili, was a capital shot, very cool when near large and dangerous game, and brave as a lion. This man was walking beside the Dutchman, who rode a small pony.

It had been arranged between these two, that Mabili was to be entitled to half the game if he put the first bullet into the elephant. This was to give him a greater interest in the hunting, and make him keep a sharp lookout. If, however, he only assisted at the death of an elephant, he was to receive whatever the Boer thought that he deserved.

They followed the spoor of the elephant through an open park-like country, a few scattered bushes and trees being the only cover.

They had proceeded about four miles on the traces, when the elephant was seen standing under a large tree. I will describe the scene as nearly in the Dutchman's manner as I can remember:—

" He swung his trunk a little every now and then, or I could not have distinguished him from a large rock, he stood so still. We made our plan immediately. I was to leave my horse where we were, and stalk with my Kaffir up to the elephant, for he seemed so quiet that I had no fear that I should not surprise him, surprise being half the battle with an elephant. Mabili had a single-barrelled heavy rifle of mine, that threw a three-ounce bullet, while I was armed with the gun I have with me now (a double-barrelled, eight to the pound). We took advantage of every tree and bush on the ground to conceal our approach, and we arrived to within fifty yards apparently unnoticed. Just as we were going to fire, the hitherto sleepy-looking brute turned quickly round with ears extended, gave a tremendously shrill trumpet, and charged straight at us. We both fired at him, and both hit him; but he never even shook his head, and continued dashing along after us. I turned and ran towards my horse, but had little hope of reaching him, as the distance was great. I therefore dodged sharp to the right, in the direction of a big tree that I had noticed near. I did not know what had become of Mabili, but, on looking round, saw that he had turned in the opposite direction; he was quite right to do this, as it generally puzzles an elephant when those he may be chasing separate. It seemed, however, as if the animal had got its eye well on poor Mabili, as it turned after him, and soon was close on him. I feared that there was no chance for my poor Kaffir, but shouted as loud as I could and fired, that I might take off the elephant's attention. It was useless; in the next instant he had caught Mabili with his trunk, with which he seemed to press him to the ground, dropping on his knees at the same time so as to thrust his tusks into him. I thought I heard a faint shriek, but, instantly getting on my horse, I galloped up to the scene, and sent a couple of bullets into the savage monster.

SINGLE ELEPHANTS TO BE AVOIDED.

He had taken up the mangled body of poor Mabili, and was slowly walking away with it, held by his trunk; when I wounded him, he dropped the body, and, giving one of his shrill trumpets, came at me. I did not care much for him now, as I could gallop away from him easily, and, loading quickly, repeated the dose. Six double shots did I give that fellow all about the shoulder before he showed any sign of their hurting him; he then seemed a little weak, and sent a good deal of blood out of his trunk. I was determined to kill that elephant, if I followed him for a week. Upon giving him three more shots, he swung his trunk about a little and fell.

"I now looked for the remains of my Kaffir, and found him crushed to pieces; his death must have been quick, as a tusk had gone quite through him, breaking in his chest.

"We buried him next day under the tree near which we had first seen the elephant. This man was the best hunting Kaffir I ever had. Always take care how you go near single bull-elephants—they are always very savage: but of all things mind cow-elephants without tusks; they are not common, but if you do come across a '*poes-kop*' like this, '*pas-op*' (take care)."

Many other tales were told at the time, in which I took great interest. The place was a good one in which to listen to such stirring relations, and they were told without any wish of boasting or display, but merely related as by no means unusual occurrences to those present. Another story was told, which I remember, from the visible proof that was given me of the relator's veracity.

The relator of the story, who was called Hendrick, was a short dark man, but had plenty of sinews, and a look of determination about the eye and lip, evidently showing that upon occasion he could make good his words by deeds. He was asked to tell me the story, and did not appear at all unwilling to comply with the request:—

"When I was a youngster about seventeen, I was staying at the house of a neighbour, who had suffered from the visits of a leopard, which had killed nearly twenty chickens during two nights. No one at the house was much of a shot, and they did not like meddling with this fellow. Now, for reasons of my own, I wanted to shoot him."

"Tell the truth, Hendrick; you wanted to show the pretty Katrine you were a man," said one of the party.

"Well, I did wish it," said Hendrick; "so I started one morning quite early, without telling any one what I was going to do; and mounting my pony, I rode to a kloof about four miles off, where I knew the chicken-killer would most probably be found. My gun was only a single-barrelled, but I did not care much for that.

"I went down the ravine on foot, and looked all about for spoor. When I had walked some distance in the kloof and amongst some trees, I found the remains of a buck partly eaten. I saw that it had been seized by the neck, and therefore knew that a leopard had killed it, a hyæna or wolf generally seizing by the flank. I looked carefully all round, but could see nothing of the leopard; but at last I happened to look up in the trees, and there he was leaning over a large branch and eyeing me most viciously. When he saw that I had discovered him, he sprung quickly to the ground, and darted away through the long grass. I had just time to fire at him as he went, and saw by the twist of his body that I had wounded him; but he jumped along like a cat, and as though not much damaged. I ran up the ravine to my horse, and galloped after the leopard, which I could see going along very fast. He was making for a much larger ravine, where some tall trees showed their tops above the banks.

"Leaving my horse outside, I went into the ravine on the spoor, which I had great difficulty in following, as the briers and wait-a-bit thorns were troublesome to push through.

"After a little way I saw some blood, and could now get on better; my gun had a good charge of powder in it, and I held it ready for a shot, and felt that my knife was loose in the sheath. I did not much like the work, now I was really at it; but it would never do to go back and say I had not looked to see if my leopard were dead.

"I sat still a little while to collect my pluck and listen for any sign: not discerning any noise, I moved on again.

"When I was down nearly at the bottom of the ravine, I suddenly saw close to me the wounded leopard: he did not run away this time, but crouched down and spit at me like a spiteful cat, laying his ears back and showing his teeth. I fired straight at him at once, and must have hit him; but he still did not move for about an instant. Then with a bound he came close to me, and, just as I was drawing my knife, sprung on me, at the same time seizing the arm with which I tried to keep him off, and fixing his claws into my shoulders. The pain was so great that I shrieked out; but there was no one within five miles to help me, and I knew that I must fight the battle myself for my life. My right arm being free, I plunged my long knife into the brute's stomach and ripped him up to the chest, and gave him one or two digs behind the shoulder, which must have found his heart, as he suddenly relaxed his hold and fell down from me. The flesh on my thighs was badly torn, as he had fixed his hind-legs there and scratched me, as I have seen two kittens do to each other at play. This struggle was all over in a few seconds, but I had been knocked down, torn, and my arm broken during the time. I tried to get up, but felt giddy and queer, and fell back on the ground insensible.

"When I again came to myself, and knew all that had happened, it was quite dark, and I found myself very cold. I tried to get up, but came again to the ground, from pain and weakness. I was in great agony, and felt dreadfully thirsty. A little stream ran down the kloof, and I could hear the water rippling along merrily within a few yards, and yet I could not move. I must have bled very much, as my legs were awfully torn as well as my shoulders, and my arm broken. I could not judge at all what time it was, as, where I lay, the trees prevented my getting much of a view of the stars, and there was no moon to judge by. I lay thinking whether I should live or die, and what my friends and Katrine would think had become of me. The only probable chance of any one coming to help me seemed to be that my pony would go home when he found I did not return to him. A Hottentot then might see him, think something was the matter, and perhaps spoor me to where I lay. I was hoping anxiously for daylight, as I would then try and load my gun, and fire some shots, which would probably be heard at a distance. I so frequently went away for a day or so and stopped at my brother's, that I did not think the people at the house would be at all alarmed at my absence during the night. I thought over all that had happened to me, and could not blame myself for having been foolhardy, although I was unlucky, and ought to have killed the leopard dead at once. I never knew how it was that he escaped the second shot, for I aimed straight between the eyes, and rarely missed a steady shot. I felt certain that the leopard was dead,— there was that satisfaction at least, and I hoped I should get credit for my courage. I was very anxious for the arrival of day, as I thought help might come then. I had several times tried to move, but the attempt had caused such pain in the wounds, that I could not stir an inch. I thought I felt close against my shoulder a movement of something or other crawling: I did not notice it at first; but once or twice I felt a slight pressure against my arm, which still had a little sensation left. I could not get up, so lay quiet, and did not worry myself about it.

"A long time seemed to pass before the daylight came; I lay almost fainting and stupid from the pain and cold, but at last determined to try and load my gun. I turned my head with difficulty, and looked down for my weapon and powder-horn. As I looked at my broken arm, which was lying uselessly beside me, I saw a great brown-looking thing lying over it. It was an instant or so before I knew what was there; but then I saw that it was the fat bloated body of a hideous puff-adder, lying close against me, evidently for the sake of the warmth. Why I did not shriek out I don't know, but I never moved. This adder, then, was the thing that I had felt pressing against me for some time, and this poisonous reptile had been my companion for hours.

"I kept my eyes on him, and could see a slight muscular motion in his body every now and then like breathing; the idea came across me that he was drinking the blood of my wounds, and had perhaps already bitten me. I felt that I must watch him, and could not look in any other direction; I dared not attempt another trial to get up, as I might fall back on this brute, and get at once a dose of his poison, and be dead in an hour. At last the joyful sound of voices came upon my ear, and there was shouting; I dared not answer, lest the movement in doing so might enrage the adder. I had the fear that the people might not come down to look for me if they heard nothing, and might go on, leaving me to die where I was. I listened, and could hear people talking, but could not make out the words or to whom the voices belonged, but had no doubt that they were some people come in search of me. I at length was certain that, whoever it was, they were now spooring me up, and at last heard their steps come nearer, as they pushed the branches on one side.

New hope seemed to come into my heart at these sounds, and I breathed more freely.

"As the steps approached, the puff-adder moved; he raised his broad head, not quite two feet from me, and looked in the direction of the new comers; then dropping down, he glided away through the brushwood. I watched him retire, and saw the leopard lying dead within a yard of me. But now that I was comparatively safe, I could no longer bear my situation, and drawing in a long breath, I sent forth a loud cry. The people were immediately around me, and perceived what had happened, with the exception that the puff-adder had been my bed-fellow.

"The party consisted of my brother and three Hottentots. These men had informed him that they feared something had happened to me, from the fact of my pony returning alone in the evening. The whole party had spoored me from the first kloof to where I lay. The Hottentots, finding the blood-spoor of the wounded leopard, feared that I had attacked him again, and that he had killed me.

"They carried me on the boughs of trees, which they fastened together with reims,* and at last managed to convey me home.

"I was three months before I could move out of my bed, and all my friends thought that I should die.

"Look at my arm! look at my shoulder, where the leopard's claws tore me; the wounds were given thirteen years ago; see the scars even now!" Saying which he

* Strips of untanned leather.

bared his arm and shoulder, where the terrible marks were yet apparent.

"When you come across a wounded leopard, you '*pas-op*'" (take care), was Hendrick's moral.

I thought over this story frequently during the night, and impressed on my mind that I would always be careful of leopards; another instance having occurred, in which a bombardier of artillery was much torn by a wounded leopard close beside his barracks at Natal. With the usual bravery, but want of sporting skill, of the British soldier, he went into the bush armed with a sword to finish a leopard that had crawled in badly wounded. The savage animal sprang upon him, seized his hand, and would have killed him, had not a fortunate shot from a civilian, who had followed the soldier, laid the leopard low. The loss of the use of his hand was the only damage this man suffered, fortunately for him.

These Dutchmen seemed to think that the black rhinoceros was the most formidable customer in South Africa. The lion, which is considered in England so far to exceed all other animals as dangerous game, did not seem to be held in greater awe than either the rhinoceros or a solitary old bull-buffalo. The latter is sometimes sent from a herd by a combination of young bulls, who, disliking his monopoly of the ladies, combine, and turn him out; he then seeks some deep ravine, and buries himself amongst the bushes. He is always sly and vindictive, and will suddenly rush out upon an intruder. One of these brutes once sprang upon a gallant friend of mine, tumbling horse and rider over with a charge that came and was past in an instant.

The Boers gave very interesting accounts of the enormous herds of game in the interior. They acknowledged that a large herd of elaud such as we had seen was a fine sight, but said that the whole face of the country covered for miles with a densely-packed body of blesbok, bontebok, springbok, and wildebeest, was a still finer one. They said in that the great "trek-boken," or journey of the springbok, the numbers were inconceivable; that they destroyed all the grass, leaving the plain like a vast cattle-fold; that hundreds died from being in the rear, and not getting anything to eat, while those in front were fat, but from this very cause became at last lazy, and gradually fell in the rear, to become thin in their turn, and again move to the front.

CHAPTER IX.

Bush-shooting—Silent walking—How to cock a gun—How to sit down—Delights of the bush—How to obtain honey—The honey-bird—The grey monkey—Ball better than shot—Variety of bush game—Hardening bullets—The alligator—The Pouw—Boldness of the eagle—The Osprey.

SILENCE and quietness are the two important acquirements for success in bush-shooting, and a sharp look-out must also be kept on the surrounding forest: the hunter must move like a ghost, and have his eyes everywhere. Few understand what the term quiet walking means until they become expert bush-rangers.

My careful follower, Inyovu, will now enter the bush with me in search of buck. We are not armed for elephants (that is, our guns are of too small a calibre), so we keep a look-out for their fresh foot-prints, or other traces, and immediately take care to avoid the animals. Inyovu has a gun to carry, more for his own satisfaction than use, as he is a miserable shot, and requires a longer time to aim than an artilleryman would take to lay a mortar. From his professor-like skill, however, in silent walking, he could, when sent out alone, often shoot and bring home one of the three sort of bush-buck that frequented this region. When he accompanied me, it was entirely for the purpose of carrying anything that I might shoot.

The part chosen for this sport was generally the most open in the bush, and the least crowded with underwood.

In time I had my separate beats, and used to draw them as regularly as hounds draw their respective covers. Dress is a most important part in these excursions: the trousers of the country, made of untanned leather, and termed crackers, are very good; a long jacket of dark blue or green is better, but a dark dull red is even more killing; the *veld-schoens* (shoes) worn by the Dutch are certainly far superior to any other boot or shoe I ever saw; they are comfortable, soft, and silent, not unlike the mocassin. Having entered a few yards in the path chosen, which should be one well worn by the elephants, it is advisable to wait a few minutes and listen, to be certain that all is going on right: the stealthy advance then commences.

The first thing to be done is to look where the foot that you are going to advance can be placed. If any dried sticks or leaves are in the way, the greatest care must be taken, for the cracking or crushing of either would alarm the bush for miles. This may seem giving too much importance to the matter; but the case is thus: the animals that live here trust to their sense of hearing and smelling more than to their sight; a slight collateral circumstance, if I may so term it, also alarms their naturally suspicious nature. A buck may be forty yards from you unseen; your tread is heard; he takes the alarm, and bounds off, giving, as he goes, that warning whistle that every bush-hunter detests. Others on his line of retreat take up the panic, and, for I may say a mile at least, the crack caused by your incautious tread is, as it were, telegraphed. This watchfulness of the bucks, &c., easily accounts for the *absence* of game complained of by every tyro in bush-shooting. We will suppose that our advance has been conducted without a cracking or crushing of leaves or sticks, and we come to a branch which has been broken by elephants, and lies across the path. Here we have a very tough customer. If the branch is too low to creep under, we must move cautiously over it, stepping carefully between the small branches, and keeping our balance steadily on each leg in succession—the slightest blunder here would be serious. Another branch merely bent across the path, and a few feet from the ground, is slowly raised with one hand, while you pass under it; the next man behind receives it, passes, and, if the last of the party, allows it to regain its original position. As this latter proceeding cannot be done without a slight rustling of leaves, it is better to stand for two or three minutes to allow any suspicion that may have been raised to be forgotten by the animals near. We now take a peep round, and get a better view by stooping low down, the underwood and branches not being so thickly leaved close to the ground. Ah! something moved in that deep shadow; now for the Kaffir's eyes; a signal with the finger, and Inyovu is on his knees, head low, and looking at the suspicious object, which is about fifty yards distant, partly hidden by the intervening stumps, and indistinct in the gloom of the bush. Inyovu, more by the movement of his lips and the expression of his countenance than by words, indicates it as *imponze* (buck). The gun, which for bush-work I always loaded with ball, as more rapid in its killing powers, is now brought to full cock, but not simply in the usual manner, for the click would be instantly responded to by the darting off of the victim. The cock must be held tight with the thumb while the trigger is pulled back; the cock then raised to the full, and trigger released: this is all done silently. The piece is now slowly raised, and the best place chosen between the branches for the path of the bullet, as a little twig will turn a ball. During this examination and preparation the buck is silently stealing away, lifting his legs high and slowly; a nice open space is seen clear of brambles, and the previous silence is broken, first by the report of the gun, and, secondly, by a " bah!" from the moving animal: a rush is made to the spot, and a red bush-buck, about the size of a roe-deer, but stouter, becomes the reward of the previous precautions. The usual operations are performed on him, and a slight rest is taken. For two people to sit down in the bush would be a very simple thing, and liable to no mistake, we should imagine; but it is not so. Inyovu won't sit beside me on the old log, but, facing me, takes his position. " Why did you move, Inyovu?" " Must not sit side by side in the bush; we only see half round. Sit face to face; you see one half, and I the other; then no animal approaches without being seen." After this caution, I never again made such a cockney blunder with Kaffirs. Two or three powerful doses of snuff act like a glass of grog on my dark friend, and I find the stimulating effect of a pinch on myself; the day is intensely hot, and but little wind is stirring. Inyovu remarks that we must not go further down this path: I heard a buck just blow the alarm, and he must have " got our wind." The wind has changed a little, as, throwing some sand in the air, he watched the light particles float away in the direction that the path turned. It now became a question of how much meat was required, whether another buck was to pay tribute on that day. Three Kaffirs and four dogs to feed daily, besides a most infallible appetite on the part of myself, consumed a large quantity of flesh. If more venison were required, our first buck would be concealed in the fork of a tree, or other convenient place, to wait until called for; and the same stealthy work carried on until a sufficiency was obtained, when we would retrace our steps for those bucks that we had left hidden two or three days. A week can be passed in this way very pleasantly, for the charm of the bush never wears away; the mystery is always the same. The hot winds that sometimes blow on the flat or open country are scarcely felt under the sheltering branches; the heat of the sun is, in the bush, only occasionally annoying, while the scent of the wild flowers gives a most delicious perfume to the air. The brilliant plumage of the birds flashes occasionally across the path, and the busy, playful, little grey monkey amuses you with his threatening grimaces. The exercise also of the faculties that this sort of amusement necessarily entails, I believe, must lead to a higher state of health in both body and mind than is likely to result from the acquaintance of strong tobacco and brandy-and-water, that are sometimes the early companions of "Nothing-to-do" gentlemen, who are condemned to pass a certain number of days in the far south-east of Africa. A tropical forest is a nosegay of sweet-scented flowers; and as the traveller crushes a blossoming plant, or his horse disturbs the position of the creeper-hung branches; his course may long be traced by the extra perfume which these African weeds then send forth. Frequently, during my pursuit of wounded game, I have stopped, and turned my attention from the blood-stained footprints, which stir the savage half of man's nature, and have become almost romantic, whilst regarding the grace and beauty of some vegetable gem, adorned with flowers of dazzling brilliancy and leaves of luxuriant growth.

My savage companions could not sympathize in the more refined feelings thus brought out. They could see but a "muti" (tree or plant), and, as it was neither fit for food or physic, they were frequently disposed to consider me weak for examining a plant that, although as dirt to the savage, would still have obtained the prize at our best botanic fêtes. These barbarians could see nothing either to wonder at or to gratify them in a simple flower, and, like many a white man, they considered that, as it was not useful or good either for eating, drinking, or physicing, it must necessarily be beneath the notice of a wise man.

The wild honey that was found in the bush was very delicious. It was taken from the owners in the coolest manner; coolness, in fact, being the best defence.

While walking with my Kaffir, he would suddenly look up with a very knowing expression, and the usual "ether," indicative of a satisfactory discovery; this discovery perhaps being nothing more than a common bee. It would be alarmed, and its line of flight watched; we would follow the direction that it took, and then look out for another bee; and so on until we were led up to the hive, which was generally situated in a hollow tree. The Kaffir then, gently inserting his arm, seizes hold of a large piece of the comb, and quietly withdraws his hand; he then walks quietly away a few yards with his prize. The bees, of course, fly all round him, and settle on his face and shoulders; he does not attempt to drive them off, but waits until they leave him. He then pouches the honey, wax, and eggs, and goes again to the hive to repeat the performance. If any of the bees get a squeeze with the hand or arm, they give a peculiar buzz, which seems to intimate to all other bees that they are to attack the intruders. Once on taking a bees'-nest, I was severely stung; they came and settled round my eyes, and I could with difficulty beat them off, and make my escape: it was all owing to my having squeezed a bee by accident as I was getting out the honey. Their stings, however, are not so severe as the English bee, as I suffered but little from these numerous stings. The middle of the day is generally chosen for taking a bees'-nest, as fewer are then at home.

Sometimes the position of a beehive is discovered by the aid of a honey-bird. This little creature appears to have sense beyond its feathered brethren; it apparently calls the traveller, and indicates that it wishes him to follow it, uttering perpetually a peculiar note, and flying from tree to tree, until it reaches the vicinity of the hive, when it gives a grand chorus of chirps. This useful little creature is, of course, rewarded with a share of the honey, and has the pickings from the hollow tree besides.

One frequently met numbers of the little grey monkeys in the bush. These mercurial little creatures are very amusing, and I often thought that they must have great fun with the elephants, the old-fashioned staid character of the latter being just the sort of butt that monkeys would choose upon which to play their practical jokes. A monkey can jump on and off an elephant's back with very little fear of consequences, thanks to his wonderful activity; or can pull a tail or an ear, with but little chance of meeting punishment from the powerful trunk. I consider these monkeys as the regular and acknowledged harlequins of the bush, and never could bear the idea of shooting at one. I frequently had disputes with my Kaffirs on this subject, as they would get into a great state of excitement if there were a good chance of knocking over a monkey; the skin, when converted into long strips, being a very fashionable article to wear round the waist or ankles.

I made a very good double shot on one occasion, by which I killed a buck and doe of the black bush-buck. I obtained a snap shot at the buck as he was bounding over a bush, and dropped him; the lady came back to peep at what had detained her good man, and suffered for her curiosity. I was much in want of meat at the time for my Kaffirs and dogs, or would have spared her.

In both these instances I found the advantage of using a bullet in place of shot, both animals dropping dead at once. If shot is used, at least half the bucks wounded escape for the time, and die miserably in some dark part of the forest, a feast for wolves and jackals. With a bullet-wound they rarely travel far, if hit anywhere about the shoulder.

Really one never tires of the forest-life, there is pleasure in even walking through its paths, made as they are by the African elephantine M'Adam, and merely looking at the trees and shrubs, each and every one of which would be a gem in England. It is a conservatory on a Brobdignagian scale. Then, to a sportsman, there is the excitement: At which shall we have the first shot, a buck or an elephant, a buffalo or a guinea-fowl? or shall we walk the whole day and see nothing but a poisonous snake, wriggling away in the dead leaves? There is always something here to be seen that is interesting from viewing it in its natural state. The manis is frequently found in the bush; lots of little creatures, like weasels, and birds of most brilliant plumage. There may be no accounting for taste, but I would rather walk through an African forest than either up Cheapside, or even Regent Street: the one is all real and true, the other artificial and in great part false, if we are to believe the chemical tests by which most of our groceries have so lately been exposed.

Twice in the Natal bush, and once across the Umganie, I killed three bucks in one day. When across the Umganie, I shot the first as he was in the open ground, and knocked him over with a bullet as he was running; the other two I killed in the bush. Monyoni's brother was with me, and it was hard work carrying the venison home. A curious thing happened with one of the bucks that I killed on this same day. It heard us coming, but did not know exactly where we were, and jumped into the path about ten yards in front of me. I gave it a raking shot, to which it fell, but got up again, and was going away on three legs, when I dropped it with a bullet in the neck. I was much surprised that it rose after being struck with the first bullet, which ought to have gone right through it, and to have come out in the buck's chest. I looked for the two bullet-holes, and saw but one. Upon opening it, the mystery was solved,—the bullet had broken against a bone, and was in a dozen pieces. For this fracturing I accounted by my attempt to harden the bullets for elephant-shooting by adding tin to the lead, and the tin, being the lighter metal, had floated to the surface of the lead, and some of my first bullets had been cast of nearly pure tin, instead of the right composition, and therefore were as brittle as glass. The right hardness is when the teeth can only just leave the least mark on the bullet: this gives about one-eighth tin as the right mixture.

My two Kaffirs returning with me one day to the Umganie Drift, we found the tide up, and the water consequently too deep to get across: it was about five feet in the deepest part. *This* would not have prevented us from wading, as there was not much current running, and no sea on; but as great numbers of hungry sharks were on one side, and alligators on the other, we did not like to venture, the breadth being nearly two hundred yards. The alligator is a very unpleasant customer if you are in the water. An accident happened at the Drift, about two miles from the mouth of the Umganie, to an Englishman, a very worthy settler. He lived in a little cottage across the river, and was returning one evening with a supply of fresh meat, which he carried with his clothes over his head: the water was about breast-high. Suddenly, when about the middle of the river, he was seized round the waist by the jaws of an alligator. He dropped his meat, and caught hold of the animal's head, calling at the same time to a Kaffir who was near. It was either the shout or the seizing that frightened the creature, for it let go its hold, and the poor man reached the opposite side of the river, where he fainted. The wounds he had received were very severe; he was three months before he could move about, and never again seemed the same man that he was before this mangling. I often saw an old Kaffir, near the Umganie, who had nearly the whole fleshy part of the thigh torn off by an alligator as he was one day crossing the river. My days and evenings of patient watching were not rewarded by a shot at this rapacious brute.

The alligator often devours its prey as it comes to drink. Slowly approaching some unsuspecting animal, it seizes it by the nose, and drags it under water; the weight of the alligator prevents the animal from raising its head; it is in consequence soon suffocated, and is dragged to a convenient retired place until required, or sufficiently high to suit the Epicurean taste of this scaly monster.

Besides the animals that I have already particularly

THE POUW.

mentioned, very good sport could be had with wild fowl of different kinds,—partridges, guinea-fowl, pheasants, and bustard. The large description of the latter, called by the colonists the *pouw*, is a magnificent bird, and is considered a great delicacy for the table. They have been shot weighing about twenty or thirty pounds. They walk about the newly-burnt grass picking up the fried worms and other animals brought to light by the fire. These birds being very difficult to approach, I generally rode round and round them, commencing my circle from a long distance, and gradually narrowing it, taking care, however, not to look at the birds. They are so keen-sighted, that, were you to look fixedly at them, even when distant, they would immediately fly away; whereas, if they consider that you do not see them, they will crouch down their heads and remain perfectly still, letting you circle up to them. Having always one barrel loaded with ball and the other with buck-shot for this work, I was ready to take a long shot with the bullet, if there was any appearance of the birds taking an early flight. If, however, no signs of impatience were shown, and the *pouw* tried the hiding dodge, the plan was to get within eighty or one hundred yards, dismount, and run in towards the birds: they could not rise very quickly, and a dose of buck-shot, as they opened their wings, was generally effective in stopping them.

Upon wounding a young *pouw* one day, as I was riding home, I was opposed by a rival sporting gentleman, in the shape of an eagle. The *pouw* rose nearly under my horse's feet, but, as I was cantering, he got some distance off before I could pull up and fire; the dropping of both hind-legs told a tale of mortal wounds, and he sailed steadily down to a little clump of bushes. His unfortunate condition had not escaped the all-observant eye of a hungry eagle, who was sailing about over me; nearly closing his wings, he dashed after the *pouw*, caught him before he reached the ground, and flew away with him. To see one's dinner thus walked off with was too much to bear quietly. I therefore galloped after the robber, who soon came to the ground, finding that the weight of his burden did not assist his aërial performances. I reached to within a hundred yards of him, when he again rose; taking a steady aim at him, I fired, and sent the bullet sufficiently close to astonish him, as he instantly dropped my property, and made off, leaving me in quiet possession.

There are a great many varieties of the eagle and hawk tribe in South Africa; some specimens are very small, others magnificent fellows. The wild, shrill scream of the osprey, or sea-eagle, always struck me as being very characteristic of this bird; there is a defiant and bold sort of sound in his voice, heard so plainly, while he, thousands of feet high, is almost, if not quite, invisible to the eye. Then coming down suddenly, like a bolt from heaven, he pounces on some victim, whom he clutches in his talons, and again soars aloft with a triumphant piercing shriek. I obtained a fine fresh mullet, on one occasion, from one of these feathered fishermen, whom I saw passing high over-head with his prize. I sent a bullet whistling by his ear, which made him drop the fish; it came down with a loud bang on the grass, and was still alive when I picked it up. The osprey sailed round two or three times, as though regretting the loss of such a good supper, and retraced his aërial course for another victim.

CHAPTER X.

A shooting-party in the bush—Elephant "sign"—The elephants heard—Caution in the bush—Approach to a wary elephant—The better part of valour—Traces of the wounded elephant—Sic vos non vobis—Acute ear of elephants—The elephants' signals—More of them—Tree'd—Teaching the young idea—A family picture—Chaffed by monkeys—A sharp lookout—The disadvantage of "crackers"—A Kaffir coward—Capricious temper of elephants—Elephants in the "open"—An awkward position—Sharp practice.

ON one of those beautiful mornings that are met with in or near the tropics, a light westerly wind blowing, we started for some small pools of water, distant about three miles from the town of D'Urban. The party consisted of myself and two Kaffirs. I had on a small straw hat, well browned, a dark blue flannel shirt, and a pair of the untanned leather breeches of the country, denominated crackers. The "*veld schoens*" (field shoes), similar to those worn by the Dutch boers, are much better than boots, as they are comfortable, soft, easy, and very silent. A long dark green jacket, fitting loosely, and covered with pockets, was my only other article of raiment. This was my favourite costume for the bush, and one that I had found particularly difficult to be distinguished when surrounded by the thick underwood and gloom of the overhanging trees.

My two Kaffirs had each a powder-horn and bullet-pouch hung over their shoulders, a necklace of charmed woods, and a small piece of buckskin of about a foot in

Missing Page

Missing Page

One's senses become wonderfully acute when much employed at this sort of work, but still they are far inferior to those of the animals which are being pursued.

You move with great caution, and apparently very quietly through the dark avenues that the elephant has made for you; yet, upon getting a peep at the branches of a far-distant tree, twenty or thirty monkeys are to be seen watching you, and skipping about from branch to branch, as though in derision of your unskilful attempt at a surprise. The single note repeatedly and slowly uttered by some hermit-like bird, suddenly ceases as you come within a hundred yards of him, and he flits away under the arches of the forest, his brilliant plumage glittering in the sun. These, and many other facts, intimate that man's faculties are dull and imperfect, in comparison with those of the animals which live in these mysterious regions.

When you know that the giant of the forest is not inferior in either the sense of smell or hearing to any animal in creation, and has, besides, intelligence enough to know that you are his enemy, and also for what you have come, it becomes a matter of great care how, when, and where to approach him.

"They must never know you are coming, and have time to make a plan," was the advice of a famous elephant-hunter. I carried it out on all possible occasions.

We continued our advance till we were within a hundred yards of the elephant that we had first heard. We sat down and listened for some minutes to discover if any others were near, as it would have been injudicious to make an attack on this one, and thereby stand a chance of having our retreat cut off by any other elephant that might be nearer. We discovered no others very close, but the snapping of branches in the distance occasionally showed that our purposed victim was not without company. Throwing up some sand, we found the wind was favourable for our advance, although the eddies that are always met in the bush rendered it advisable to move on with as much quickness as was consistent with silence.

Our advance, although conducted with the same stealth that marks the movement of a cat towards its prey, was still not sufficiently inaudible to escape the refined senses of the elephant. He ceased feeding, and remained for some minutes like a statue. A novice would have laughed had he been told that a wild elephant of twelve feet high was within a few yards of him; the only indication the animal gave of his presence was a slight blowing through the trunk as the unsavoury flavour of my warm Kaffirs was wafted to his sensitive olfactories, or as a dried stick cracked under his spungy feet. The density of the underwood, which was caused by the festoons of wild vine and creepers, prevented our seeing more than a yard or two in many parts; and though the branches directly over us were shaken by the movement of the monster's body, yet we could make out nothing but a dark mass of bush: to have fired thus, therefore, would have been folly. Monyosi had frequently eaten little bits of his charmed wood: I dared not speak to ask him its specific, but I afterwards learnt it was infallible as a preventive against injury from wild beasts. My own man, Inyovu, was as pale as a black man could be, and his whole frame appeared to suffer much from cold. I dare say, had I counted my own pulse, I should have found it quicker than usual.

The elephant's patience was the first to be exhausted: with a half-growl, half-trumpet, he forced himself through the tangled brushwood towards us. He came in sight so close to me, that the muzzle of my rifle was considerably elevated when I fired. With a turn and rush that a harlequin might have envied, I soon got over a hundred yards, the line to run having been determined on previous to firing. It would not have been wise to stay and look if one were being pursued; run first, and look afterwards, was the approved plan. It is a poor sort of courage, that fears taking precautions, lest its truth should be questioned.

There was a crash somewhere behind me as I ran, but I could not tell in which direction; seeing, therefore, that I was likely to come against others of the herd if I continued my retreat, I took up a position with my Kaffirs beside a large thick tree, and proceeded to load my rifle, which I did not accomplish without a reproof from Monyosi for ramming down the charge whilst the butt of the gun was on the ground.

We could now hear the troop of elephants rapidly retreating through the forest. The loud crashing of the thick branches showed the alarming sound of a rifle had caused a headlong rush to be made, that sounded like a rolling fire of musketry.

We did not give them much time to get away, but followed at once to the spot from which I had fired. I had no hope that my elephant would be dead; I knew the tough constitution of these animals too well. I was disappointed, however, at finding no blood, none appearing for the first few yards; I began to think that, by some strange chance, I had missed him. We soon, however, saw two or three drops of blood, and then more; at length it lay about as though poured from a pail. Both my Kaffirs were delighted, and exclaimed that we *must* get him. I had not much hope of so satisfactory a result, having made many a weary journey without success after other elephants quite as badly wounded as this. Monyosi followed the spoor with great accuracy; he had taken the dimensions of the feet of the wounded animal, and could therefore recognize the prints on every doubtful occasion.

We had followed about two miles in this way, when we heard a loud crash in advance of us. Approaching carefully in the direction, I caught a glimpse of an elephant some forty yards distant, standing in a little open space. Aiming at his shoulder, I at once gave him the benefit of my heavy rifle. I stooped under the smoke to see if he had fallen, but saw him rush away. I was turning round to join my Kaffirs, who had fallen back a few yards, when the bushes almost close to me were violently shaken, and the elephant that I had first wounded shuffled out into the path up which we had just come. He was not ten yards from me, and my only chance of escaping detection was by remaining perfectly still. He did not seem to notice me, but to have been attracted by the rich flavour of my

Kaffirs. He heard their rapid retreat, and charged after them; of which movement I immediately took advantage, and slipped off in a contrary direction. My rifle was soon loaded, and I was then more ready for another encounter.

I was anxious to discover what had become of my Kaffirs,—not that I had much fear for them, each could be trusted alone; but I wanted to have the benefit of their advice as to our proceedings.

I dared not stay where I then was, however, as several of the herd were now trumpeting furiously, and kept slowly approaching the spot from whence I had fired. They had evidently recovered from their first fright, and had determined to drive away their persecutors. I therefore retreated a couple of hundred yards, and gave three slow whistles, my usual bush-signal, which was instantly answered a short distance from me.

Upon consulting, neither of the Kaffirs would hear of again approaching the troop, saying that the elephants knew of our presence now, and were too savage. I began to think so, and therefore reluctantly withdrew to the outside of the forest.

On the next day Monyosi followed the spoor of the two that I had wounded, but failed in coming up with them.

About a week after this adventure, two Kaffirs, who I knew never did shoot, came to me with a pair of elephant's tusks to sell: they said that they had found them in the bush; but, upon noticing that I was anxious to know where this discovery was made, they denied having found them themselves, but said another Kaffir had done so. From what I afterwards ascertained, I am certain that those teeth belonged to one of the elephants I had wounded on the day which I have just mentioned.

Soon after this affair, the herd left the Berea bush, and moved several miles up the coast. I then again took up the bush-buck shooting, at which capital sport could now be had, as the elephants had made so many paths, and trodden down so much of the underwood, that one's progress could be made with less noise, and in consequence seven or eight fair chances at buck could be had in a day.

One or two more accounts of the giant game of Africa may perhaps be excused.

I have before spoken of the acuteness of the elephant's hearing, and I had a very good proof of it on the occasion that I will now mention.

As I was making my rounds one afternoon on horseback, I heard the crack of a broken branch some distance up a path that led to a flagstaff on the top of the Berea. I knew at once that the noise was caused by some elephants browsing; I therefore left my horse outside the bush, that I might proceed quite quietly, and walked up this road for half a mile to an open space of about an acre, from which I had a fine view all round. I soon discovered that a large herd of elephants were in the hollow just below the rising ground on which I was standing, and they appeared to be working up to the position from which I was looking out for them. I was well to leeward of the herd, and had taken up my position with praiseworthy silence, and at about sixty yards from the edge of the dense cover. I kept at this distance to avoid any eddies of wind that might otherwise have carried to the elephants the knowledge of my presence: there was a breeze blowing, so I did not fear the animals getting my wind. I had waited patiently for more than half an hour, watching for a shot, and could see several of the top branches of the trees shaken by the elephants which were feeding; some were within thirty yards of the edge of the bush, while several others were scattered about at different distances. I did not feel inclined to enter the bush, as it was so dense, therefore very dangerous; and I hoped to have a good view of the game in the open. Suddenly, and without any apparent reason, an elephant, which was feeding at about two hundred yards from me, gave a trumpet of alarm. This warning-note I had frequently heard, and had often been surprised at the code of signals that these sagacious animals seemed to have. I knew that this note had not been blown without good cause; the well-trained herd instantly ceased feeding, and remained without the slightest noise for nearly a minute, when they all appeared to have made themselves acquainted with the cause of alarm, as they walked away rapidly in the bush, blowing through their trunks, and making the branches crack in their passage. I could not make out for what all this was done, but listened carefully for some time, and heard nothing that should have caused alarm.

After waiting some minutes, I was about to return to my horse, when I heard voices, and soon after saw two men of the Cape corps, who were half-drunk and riding up the road at a slow trot. They asked me " if this was the way to Pietermaritzburg?" Feeling very angry at being thus disturbed, I told them to listen to the elephants which were getting ready to charge; they stopped for an instant, when, hearing the snapping of the branches caused by the elephants' retreat, which was still audible, they muttered an oath in Dutch, turned their horses round, and dashed down the road, too late, however, for my satisfaction, as they had effectually spoiled my chance of a shot in the open.

These men must have been heard by the elephants when nearly half a mile distant, and fully five minutes before I could note the slightest sound of their approach.

I had been to lunch on wild honey one morning in the Berea with my Kaffir Inyovu, when he suddenly called my attention to the sound of a broken branch at some distance: we both knew that the noise was caused by elephants. I wiped my honeyed hands and walked through the forest; we shortly came on the fresh spoor of some cow-elephants, which were attended by their calves. The traces were very recent, as some branches and grass that the animals had placed their feet upon, had not yet ceased springing up to regain the original position.

There was very little wind blowing, but what there was unfortunately blew from us to the position which the elephants occupied. There was no help for it, so I determined to approach them under these unfavourable conditions. About fifty yards from where I guessed the elephants were standing, the underwood was very thick. I pushed on carefully and quietly, but soon found that these sagacious creatures knew all about my approach. They shook the branches, grumbled, and trumpeted, as though they really meant mischief. I certainly was not game to go in at them here, as I could not tell in some places, had an elephant been within five feet of me.

About twenty paces from this dense part, I had noticed, in passing, a large tree and an open space around it: from the branches of the tree the wild vine hung in thick clusters. I thought that if I mounted into this tree I might have a view of some stray elephant, and therefore be able to approach him with more certainty and get a safer shot at him. I walked back, and placing my gun against the stem of the tree, caught hold of the vine and hauled myself up into the branches; I purposed looking round first, and then getting my guns up. No sooner was I up aloft, than Inyovu, who seemed to think it rather lonely being left down, placed his gun beside mine, and followed me into the tree.

As I could not see any elephants by carefully scanning the surrounding bush, I was thinking about descending when a rustling amongst the underwood at a few yards' distance attracted my attention.

Suddenly a cow-elephant made her appearance. she was not very large, but I at once saw that she was destitute of teeth, and was of the class that the Boers had told me were the most savage in a herd. She stuck her ears out on each side of her head, and twisted her trunk about as though smelling every breath of air. She then came a few yards forwards, and gave a little scream; this seemed to be a sort of call, that was immediately answered by a small bull-elephant, which came shuffling along with an old-fashioned look of intelligence, and ran in front of his mamma. He stood a little while with an air of wisdom, as though to intimate, that although young and small, he was still quite up to everything, and could teach his mother many a "neat plant :"—he looked a most precocious young elephant. Presently he advanced a few yards, and swung his trunk about over the footprints of the Kaffir, whose naked feet, I imagine, left a better scent than my "*veld schoens.*" Young elephant then screwed up his trunk, and twisted it in the air, with an expression as much as to say, "Now, really, this is a dreadfully bad smell." During all this time we remained perfectly still in the tree, and the elephants, trusting but little to their sight, and not expecting their enemies to be up aloft, had not noticed us.

The young one was evidently much admired by his mamma, and continued following our footsteps to the end of our walk, and to where we had stood for a short time, and then returned: there he was at fault, and could not make things out at all.

I had remained perfectly still during this performance, as I did not wish the elephants to know that I was up the tree. Had they gone near the guns, I should at once have tried the effect of an English yell, with a second shout from my Kaffir; but Inyovu, beginning to be alarmed, tried to get higher up the tree. I felt convinced that we were quite safe, as the branch on which we were standing was at least twenty-five feet from the ground, and was also very stout.

The noise that my Kaffir made in mounting higher seemed to puzzle the elephants; they twisted round, flapped their ears about, and turned the muzzle of their trunks in every direction. My attention had been so taken up with the two elephants that I have mentioned, that I had not noticed a large bull which had approached from the other side to watch proceedings. A slight noise that he made drew my attention to him, when, on viewing his gigantic ivories, I became ambitious, and could not resist the temptation of trying to get to my guns to obtain a shot. I caught hold of the wild vine, and was swinging myself down, when the noise that I necessarily made seemed to alarm the elephants. The old lady gave two or three grunts, which recalled her hopeful child, and they all waddled off in the most absurd manner. It was a very pretty family picture.

The elephant has always seemed to me a most grotesque animal; the old-fashioned appearance of the young ones, and the awkward gait of all, with that absurd look as though their skins were second-hand and did not fit; the action of the hind-legs, like an old man's strut with a pair of breeches on that are far too big, tend to make them look ridiculous; and yet, withal, they walk about as though they considered themselves the complete mould of fashion.

I reached the ground only just in time to see the elephants' hind quarters twist about behind a bush, waited a few minutes below the tree to see if either of the three would return; but hearing nothing, I got my two guns up the tree with the help of my Kaffir, and patiently waited there, in the hope that the elephants would return for another inspection. Had I been fortunate enough to have taken my guns up with me at first, I could have easily dropped one of these elephants dead, as their backbones were within twenty yards of me, and a heavy bullet driven down near the vertebræ would have humbled the proudest elephant in Africa.

I had not the slightest idea when I first ascended the tree that any elephant would have come out into this open in search of me; and climbing up a bit of vine being difficult while holding a gun, I waited until I should see some black backs that might indicate the position of the elephants before I hauled up my artillery; thus, however, I lost this splendid chance.

After sitting patiently for upwards of an hour, and hearing nothing more of the animals or even a sound of their presence, I gave up the idea of waiting for them, and was making preparations for a descent, when I saw the top branches of some small trees a few yards distant begin to shake very violently. I cocked my gun, and was quite ready for a bull-elephant, when I saw, to my great disappointment, that the disturbance was caused by two or three little grey monkeys, that were jumping about, and had evidently come to have a joke with me. They looked up into our tree with a very severe sort of critical expression; made several faces and two or three short bows; scratched their sides vigorously, and jumped from bough to bough until out of sight.

To show the attention that is sometimes paid to trifling

matters in bush-ranging, I will give another day's sport with Monyosi in the Berea.

We had gone in after elephants, and were on their spoor of the previous night. There had been a great deal of listening and peeping, as the day was so warm that we expected the elephants would be clustered together in some shady glen, and would not move until we were right upon them. As we were seated, listening, Monyosi suddenly looked up attentively at a tree near us, and seemed to think that all was not as it should be. I asked him what was wrong, when he said he did not know, but that a bird had flown to a tree near us, stayed a little while, and had then gone away. By the manner in which it had hopped about, he could see that it was alarmed at something; and it would not have flown towards us, had its flight been occasioned by our noise. I thought the cause a slight one; but still, it is the dust, not the rock, that indicates the wind's direction. Monyosi did not seem easy, but proposed that we should proceed in the direction from whence the bird had approached us. We did so, and after one hundred yards sat down to listen. Presently a very slight crack of a branch or bit of stick caused our guns to be raised to full cock, and we to peep about between the branches for a sight at whatever it might be. The game was very cunning, and for full two minutes there was not a move on either side; our patience, however, was the greater, as we soon heard two or three light steps from the suspicious quarter. I saw a smile on Monyosi's face; he uncocked his gun, and gave a low whistle, which was responded to by another in the bush a few yards distant. Soon after, a young English lad, born and bred in the colony, and two Kaffirs, all three armed with guns, came quietly up to us. I knew the boy, and he informed me that he was after the elephants, but, hearing our approach, could not make us out; he thought that he caught a glimpse of something rather red, which was really my untanned leather breeches, and that he fancied it was a red-buck; but the glance was so slight, that he could not be quite certain. He consoled me, however, by saying "he should not have fired at me unless he knew that the elephants were a long way off." We had stood listening one to the other for about three minutes, and the bird that flew past had given the alarm to Monyosi.

How would some of my friends compete in war singly with black men like this? But fancy one hundred such against perhaps twenty young soldiers inexperienced in the colonial cunning, and laughing contemptuously at the black niggers to whom they are going to give a licking! Many bleached skulls, that do not require one to have the science of Professor Owen to know that they were once tenanted by a spirit recognized in this world as a white man, might tell what was the result of carelessness, and underrating the enemy, and perhaps a little overrating one's own skill.

We joined the party which we had met in the bush, and together followed the spoor. I now witnessed one of the rare cases of downright cowardice in a Kaffir. One of this English lad's Kaffirs was a very good hand after buck, but did not aspire to anything more. As we neared the elephants, and heard their rumbling, this black cur shook as though he had an ague, and said he would not go any further. The English boy told him if he went away he would only have one shot at him, but that he generally drove a bullet pretty straight. This argument the Kaffir seemed to consider a very convincing one, as he kept on with us. The elephants were on the move when we came upon them, and a young bull was quietly walking up a path directly towards us, with a branch held in his trunk. My white companion recommended me not to fire; but, seeing the elephant's shoulder, I sent my $2\frac{1}{2}$-ounce bullet into it. I turned and ran, but found, after a dozen yards, that the coward Kaffir was in my way. He did not know exactly what to do, and was not moving at that rapid pace which I always considered advisable after wounding an elephant in this dense forest. A bundle of charmed woods was hung round this Kaffir's neck, thick enough to have saved the whole Zulu nation for evermore from savage elephants or hungry lions. Feeling indisposed to jog on behind him, I caught hold of this necklace, which was the only article of attire that he wore, and dragged him back, at the same time slipping in front of him. As I passed him, he turned round with horror depicted in his face, and wildness in his eyes. He just called out, "*Bulula, bulula!*" (Shoot, shoot!) and then came after me: he thought my hand had been the elephant's trunk, and that he was nearly a gone Kaffir. I managed to get a long thorn deep into my knee during my run, which caused such pain that I could not proceed on the spoor. I went a little way, and saw plenty of blood, but gave up the search to the English lad and his two Kaffirs, whilst I with difficulty reached home. I never heard what was the result of the pursuit,—whether they found and killed, or lost. I was lame for nearly three weeks afterwards, as the thorn was poisonous.

The temper of the elephant seems to fluctuate in even a greater degree than that of man. Sometimes a herd are unapproachable from savageness, at others they are the greatest "curs" in creation. I had received so many warnings from the elephants frequenting the Natal bush—elephants, as I before remarked, particularly savage, from knowing the strength of their jungle, that I used every precaution in approaching them, and always acted as though a fierce and determined charge were to follow the report of my gun. I believe that I frequently ran a hundred yards after firing, when there was no occasion for doing so; but I am convinced that on one or two occasions this little exercise saved me from feeling the weight of an elephant's foot.

Being across the Umganie with Monyosi and his dog one day in search of buck, I found the elephants in very bad "fettle." We had been sitting under a tree in a little open glade in the centre of the bush, and Monyosi was relating some of his adventures while in the Pongola country, elephant-shooting, he having lately returned from this trip.

In the centre of this glade there was a pond of water that the elephants frequently used for a bath, or to drink from. We had seen no fresh traces of either buffalo or other large game for some days, and in consequence we supposed they had journeyed up the coast for a change.

I had brought a small double-barrelled gun, instead of

the heavy rifle that I should have used had I expected elephants; whilst Monyosi had his old ship's musket.

Suddenly there was a great cracking in the bush, and we both jumped on our feet; the branches seemed all alive, shaking and cracking as though a hurricane were blowing.

We eagerly watched for an explanation, although, both being pretty well up to "sign," we guessed that the disturbance was caused by elephants.

At about fifty yards from us the first giant broke cover; he came out very quickly, gave a grumble, aud ran down to the water, giving a shrill scream as he reached it. This was apparently a signal to others that all was right, as they came out of the bush immediately: at least forty elephants were in "the open" at one time; some were large fellows, whilst others were only babies by comparison. Two or three of them, on coming to the water, lay down in the mud and rolled, whilst a big bull-elephant sent the water from his trunk in streams over his body.

We watched them a minute or so, to see what they would do, when Monyosi by accident let go his dog, he having with difficulty held him tight since the appearance of the herd. The cur immediately ran down and barked at the elephants, whereupon they turned round and rushed towards the bush which they had just left. I aimed at a large bull, taking the spot between the eye and the ear as my target: I heard the bullet strike, and then gave him a second shot on the shoulder. The distance was about seventy yards, and my gun a fourteen-bore. This latter circumstance was of course a great drawback, still, however, I expected some notice to be taken of the two wounds; but the elephant never shook his head. Coiling up his trunk, he charged straight into the forest, followed by the whole herd, crushing and smashing all before them, like a parcel of runaway railway-engines. Monyosi told me afterwards that it was fortunate none of the herd had charged us, as there was so little cover that we might very probably have got the worst of a hand-to-trunk fight. This Kaffir always pleased me very much by the manner in which he spoored; I could safely trust him on the spoor, and he would follow with the accuracy of a bloodhound. Several of the men whom I employed would often go wrong, and lose the footmarks of some particular animal in a herd, and thereby cause considerable delay.

On one occasion I was in a very awkward position with a troop of elephants.

I had left my horse to graze, and was walking round the bush, near some deserted Kaffir gardens. I was searching for buck, and had no idea of elephants being near. A fine black bush-buck gave me a chance, and I fired at him; he bolted away into the bush, and I followed. There was only one elephant-path, and it was so overgrown and blocked up that I could with difficulty force my way along it. I kept a good look-out for the buck's spoor, which I followed for about a quarter of a mile into the bush, when I suddenly heard an elephant move close to me. I lay down on the ground to try and get a glimpse of him, and soon saw a whole string of elephants moving along very quickly, distant about sixty yards. I knew at once, by their way of moving, that they

were after me, either from curiosity or rage. My shot at the buck had made them acquainted with my presence. They seemed to be moving round so as to cross my footsteps, and thus to block up the only path by which I could retreat. I feared also, that, when they caught my scent, they would hunt me up.

Only a few days previous I had found the skeleton of a Kaffir in the bush with the ribs smashed, evidently the work of some powerful pressure or blow; and Inyovu seemed to think that it had been done by an elephant's foot.

I did not like the look of things, but there was very little time in which to make up my mind; so turning, I ran as well as I could down the path up which I had just come, hoping thus to get along in front of the elephants and before they could cross my spoor. I could hear them crushing through the bush nearly in front of me, and was afraid that I was already blocked in, but they were still some yards distant; the branches struck me some smart whacks on the face, and one or two thorns buried themselves in my legs. I won the race, however, though only by a few yards, as the elephants were close to the path as I passed them: they heard and smelt me, and gave tremendous shrill screams. I kept on, and was soon clear of the bush, but did not cease looking behind me until on my pony's back. This sort of work certainly keeps one up to the mark, and may be decidedly called sharp practice.

CHAPTER XI.

Journey to the Zulu country—Hunger the best sauce—A popular song—An unexpected guest—Panda's regiments—His pet vultures—An ingenious scarecrow—Another reit-buck—The telescope—A lesson in spooring—A trial of nerves—Intruding leopards—A Kaffir feast and concert—Baked, blinded, and poisoned—Peshauna, a Kaffir belle—Kaffir love-tale—An abduction and a rescue—None but the brave deserve the fair.

HAVING received intelligence of a very good game country, between the Imvoti and Tugela rivers, which was seldom visited, either by the traders who went into the Zulu country or by any hunters, I determined to make an expedition into this part, which was about seventy miles from Port Natal. To accomplish my trip with comfort, I provided myself with a pack-ox that was able to carry about a hundredweight; this animal I loaded with some spiced beef, as a stand-by in case of getting no game, some brandy, biscuits, salt, powder, tobacco, and a few beads; the latter as presents for the Kaffirs. I started my ox, with two of my Kaffirs and one of my horses, to get a day's journey in advance, reserving my second horse to ride after the cavalcade. I made all inquiries as to the style of place, but found it a rare occurrence for two people's stories to agree. Some said there was no game at all there, excepting a few bucks; one or two Kaffirs had heard that elands and buffaloes were often found in the country near the Imvoti river; others said there was not a single head of anything to be found. Putting all these accounts down at their proper value, I determined to inspect the place and judge for myself; for I generally found that the ignorant or indolent reported that there was nothing in a country in which a sportsman would find plenty. I started across the Umganie at peep of day, and made a journey of nearly forty miles, when I came up with my Kaffirs. They had been joined by my old friend Matuan, who told me that he was going in the same direction to buy cattle, he having obtained some money by the sale of Indian corn, which he grew in great quantities. I had a small tent amongst the packs on my ox, just big enough to crawl into; it was about seven feet long and three high, and made a comfortable little kennel. I noticed a Dutchman's house about a mile off; but as I had everything I wanted, and the night was fine and moonlight, I preferred camping under the trees where I then was. We lighted a fire and sat round it. A tin mug full of brandy-and-water being served out to my black companions, they became very talkative. Inyovu, who was armed with one of my guns, had managed to shoot a red bush-buck on the journey, and we were busy lodging the venison in our hungry maws. The appetite one gets at this out-of-door work is perfectly wonderful; being in the open air all day and all night, I suppose, causes a man to become very much, in habit, like some of the four-footed *carnivora*. In the eating way there is no doubt about it; the meat disappears in heaps; enough to feed an Irish family, here only serves as a meal for one. Scarcely is it finished, when an infallible appetite is again crying out for a supply. I had, unfortunately, forgotten my plates and dishes; I was also without a fork; neither, however, were missed by the Kaffirs; so I was forced to imitate their proceedings. A long strip being cut off the buck, it was laid on the red-hot embers, and was turned occasionally until cooked; a wisp of grass was then put in requisition to hold one end of the meat, while the hot ashes were shaken and knocked off, with a graceful swing of the left hand the other end was caught in the mouth, and held hard until a mouthful was separated with the knife; the remainder was kept hot until one was ready for a second mouthful. This was certainly not a very elegant way of dining, but still it was most delightfully simple. The Kaffirs seemed to like the flavour that the wood gave to the meat. Not having a taste that way myself, I made use of an iron ramrod to keep the meat from the ashes; I strung the slices on the ramrod, one end of which I stuck into the ground, and allowed it to bend over the fire at an angle of forty-five degrees, cutting off the bits of meat as they were done. After each of us had eaten as much as would have choked three beings in civilized society, the Kaffirs commenced a song. It was a very popular one in this part, commencing, "*Eno baba gofile*," with a splendid chorus of "*E, yu, yu, yu; E, yu, yu, yu.*" It was surprising that no accident happened to any of them, as they shouted at the top of their voices for nearly an hour with a fierce and determined action. Even after my wolf-like repast, the noise was too much for me, and I was about begging them to drop the curtain on their performance, when they suddenly stopped. I looked up and saw the white eyes of a strange Kaffir a few yards from the fire. I saw that my party expected me to speak, so gave the usual salutation, "*Saca bona,*" which was responded to by him. I then asked him to come and sit down and tell us the news, and offered him my snuff-gourd. He soon told me that he was the head man of a neighbouring kraal, that he had heard my Kaffirs singing; and, in fact, he thought a good thing was going on, and he might as well have a slice of it. We handed him the bones of the buck to pick, which were all that were left; he cleaned them most completely, scarcely leaving a mouthful for my two dogs, which had been anxious observers of our operations. My Kaffirs were asking all sorts of questions from the new comer. I found great satisfaction from understanding the language, and before I retired for the night had made out the following as having been the early career of our guest:—

His name was Eondema, and he was one of Panda's officers. Panda being the great Zulu chief across the Tugela, he mentioned Panda's name with great awe, as if it were not quite safe even here to speak of it aloud. Eondema was a very fast runner, and had therefore been in Panda's light infantry regiment called the *Impofarns* (Elands).

"Panda," said he, "is a great chief, has many thousands of cattle, and thousands of warriors. His hosts are like the grass, or a flight of locusts; you might cut them down, or tread on them, but thousands would still come on, and victory must be theirs." He had many regiments, which he called by the names of animals, or by their qualities. These were—the *Injlovus*, or Elephants, all men of great height and strength. They were armed with a very heavy spear for stabbing, and their shields were made of ox-hides, and were stained black. "*Ma mee!*" They were strong! exclaimed Eondema. Then there were the *Ingulubi*, or Wild-pigs; the *Inyarti*, or Buffaloes; the *Imvubu*, or Hippopotami; the *Impofarn*, &c. All these regiments were armed with spears and shields. They imitated the actions and noises of the animals from which they took their names, and were obliged in their battles to bring back their own or their enemy's shield and assagy. When they attacked, they rushed on at a charge in line. One or two assagies, used for throwing, were lighter than those used for stabbing, and were thrown at the enemy when within about forty yards.

The regiment was divided into divisions, the right division throwing their spears to their left half-face, and the left division to their right half-face. This arrangement was intended to dazzle the enemy, and make the shower of spears more difficult to avoid. Eondema belonged to the *Impofarn* regiment, and, being ambitious, he was always either shooting elephants (being fortunate enough to possess an old musket) or bartering cattle. Eondema's herds attracted the attention of the chief, and a jealous eye was cast upon them; but they could not well be taken from him without his having committed some crime. Nothing was, however, easier than to find a stick with which to beat him. As it is with others, so it was with Panda. Eondema, there was little doubt, had, by his witchcraft, caused an old cow of his chief's to die. Fortunately for him, a friend intimated (at great personal risk) that a party had received orders to assagy him during the following night. A hasty retreat across the Tugela (the English boundary) saved him, at the loss, however, of cattle and wives. Being a sharp fellow, he soon again made money, *alias* cattle, and was at this time head man of the kraal near which I stopped on this night.

There does not seem to be any very great regard for human life amongst the Kaffir chiefs, should they find their authority, supremacy, or selfishness in question.

A story that has been told me—for the truth of which I beg I may not be held responsible—may give an idea of the light manner in which life is regarded, particularly in the old and infirm. Although this story may, or may not, be a fact, still an anecdote on a country's peculiarities, even if it is embellished, generally gives an idea of the people's habits.

Panda keeps, it is said, some pet vultures, and if his supply of beef is short, and he does not like killing an ox, he pats his darling birds on the head, asking them if they are not very hungry. Then calling one of his soldiers, he directs him to go and knock old Father So-and-So on the head, and drag him into the bush for his vultures, as they are very hungry. A fit meal for a vulture—a tough old Kaffir!

I went to sleep after Eondema's story, but could occasionally hear the voices of the party. They seemed to find eating the only thing necessary; they did not drink or sleep. On the following day I was amused at seeing an ingenious plan that the Kaffirs used to frighten the birds from their corn-gardens. These were sometimes of great extent, ten and twenty acres being in cultivation together. Several descriptions of birds, in large flocks, invaded them, and would have done great damage in carrying off the corn, but for the precautions taken. In the centre, or most elevated spot of the garden, a kind of platform was erected, on which were two or three boys and girls. From this stage three ropes (manufactured by the Kaffirs) were tied to the extreme ends of the garden, and sufficiently low to be amongst the thick stalks and stems of the Indian corn. These long lines were connected to each other on an enlarged plan of a spider's web. When a flock of birds was seen to settle in any part of the field, two or three of the youngsters caught hold of the line that led over the spot, and shook it violently, shouting at the same time: the noise made by the rope frightened them away on the wing at once.

A white stranger was a very rare visitor in this part. As I had turned off the high road to the Zulu country, I could hear the great fact of an "*Umlungo*" arriving, shouted from hill to hill, and kraal to kraal; the Kaffirs generally all turned out to see me, passing remarks on myself, gun, and horses, in the coolest manner. When they found that I could speak to them in their own tongue, and was on a shooting trip, they had a much higher opinion of me than if I had been a trader. On the next night I took up my quarters at the kraal of a sporting Kaffir, who was called Inkau; he had a gun and was a mighty Nimrod, having shot elephants, buffaloes, hippopotami, and nearly all the large game.

He was supplied with powder by a Dutchman at Natal, for the purpose of shooting elephants, half the ivory falling to the said Dutchman's share. He informed me that buffaloes and elands were not farther off than we could walk while it took the sun to go from "there to there,"—pointing to two clouds in the sky. I was now pleased that I had not paid any attention to the croakers who had assured me there was no game whatever about here. Elephants were not far off either, and bucks so plentiful that they would often destroy the mealeas (as the Indian corn is here called), if it were not regularly watched. Inkau very graphically described the manner in which a buffalo was to be shot:—"You must get close to him, and shoot *so*," said he, standing steady as a rock and aiming with his gun. "If you do like this, you won't kill him;" at the same time giving effect to his explanations by shaking himself, and holding his gun as if in a great fright. Inkau's description was correct.

As it was still nearly an hour to sundown, I went with two or three Kaffirs to a neighbouring ravine, in which a reit-buck was generally found. Inkau, like nearly every Kaffir whom I have seen, could only shoot well at a stationary object; this reit-buck, therefore, by keeping a sharp look-out, had managed to escape so many times from Inkau's erring bullet, that at last he gave up firing at him as a waste of powder. On our nearing the long reeds, the buck sprang out, and cantered quietly up the hill; the Kaffirs shouted to me to fire, but I waited until his outline stood out in bold relief against the sky, when I lodged an ounce of lead in his shoulder, which had the effect on him of an irresistible invitation to that night's supper; his steaks were most excellent eating, and I thenceforth stood high in Inkau's estimation.

A reit-buck, as he falls, weighs something over a hundred pounds, and in Inkau's kraal, at the feast, there were about thirty people, men, women, and children. Yet such were the performances in gastronomy, that there was after dinner scarcely a sufficient quantity of the reit-buck remaining to supply me with a breakfast on the following morning. There was such a scarcity of corn in this kraal, that I had difficulty in getting even a mouthful for my horses; they suffered consequently in condition, and the one I rode on the first day, was too weak for me to get anything like a gallop out of him. I started quite early in the morning with Inkau, to a spot which he told me elands frequented. We reached a commanding position, where I pulled out my telescope for an inspection. My companion had never seen such an implement before, and could not comprehend what I was doing; so that when at last I rested it on the saddle, and got him to look through it, his delight and astonishment knew no bounds. Good sight is much valued by the Kaffirs, and the possession of a telescope would raise a man to as high a position of envy there as that of a Koh-i-noor its fortunate owner in England. No game appeared in sight, so Inkau proposed that we should make for some high table-land a few miles distant. I led my horse and walked beside Inkau, who rarely saw a clump of bushes or a distant peak, but what he had to tell me that he shot something *there* so many moons ago, indicating by his fingers the number.

A LESSON IN SPOORING.

He was a determined sportsman, and seemed to love hunting for the sake of sport alone. He did not care what work he went through, and was certainly a most gentlemanly Kaffir, as he never asked for a present, or any reward for all his trouble, and seemed unexpectedly pleased when I presented him, on leaving, with the value of a blanket, some powder, and a box of lucifer-matches. On passing near a deep woody ravine, he told me that he would go down in it and beat the bush for a buffalo, and that I might wait up at the top, where I should probably get a shot, as any game that might be in the ravine would come out on that side, and make for the dense bush by the river. I did as he requested, and heard him coolly beating the bushes in the hollow beneath. Presently something came rushing towards me; I was all ready for a buffalo, but saw only a bush-pig, which I allowed to pass unhurt, fearing that the report of my gun would alarm the country, and that my Kaffir would not consider this pig a sufficient excuse. Soon after, Inkau came out of the bush, and said, "No buffalo there to-day," and walked quietly on. When he crossed the spoor of the bush-pig, he suddenly stopped, and looking down, said, "A buffalo has passed here this morning!" I was amused at what I thought was his mistake, and allowed him to make one or two more remarks about it; I then told him that it was a bush-pig. "No! a buffalo," he positively asserted. The grass was long but green, and no sand could be seen, or any ground that could take an impression. I said that a bush-pig had passed there just now. "I know it," he answered; "look here,"—pointing to where the grass was trodden down, and was still springing slowly up again,—"that is wild pig, but that"—pointing to some other marks that were on the same track—"is buffalo. Besides, a wild pig does not eat the tops of grass." As he gave this last conclusive argument, he picked a handful of grass, and showed me the tops eaten off. I saw that I had fallen several degrees in his estimation by such great want of observation. The matter being settled beyond a doubt, he followed instantly on the trail, which led down to the river. Inkau moved at a run, so I mounted to keep up with him. We soon came to a part of the bush too thick for a horse to go through; I therefore dismounted, off-saddled, and turned my nag out to graze, and then entered the bush. As we neared the game, which we knew we were doing by the freshness of the spoor, Inkau slackened his pace; he was steady as a rock, and was evidently well supplied with nerves. He asked me whether I felt at all afraid, as he would go on alone if I did. I answered him by holding out my gun at arm's length, when he, seeing it quite steady, complimented me, but cautioned me by saying that the buffaloes here were very dangerous. I did not think this was such sharp work as the elephant-hunting about Natal, in the thick bush, as although the buffalo is very savage and cunning, a small tree will save you from him, whereas an elephant must be fenced off with rather a big one. The usual careful approach being made, the danger in this sport is not very great. Accidents happen to men who move carelessly, either thinking that they are not near game, or anxious to show that they are not afraid. An incautious person is sure, sooner or later, to meet with a mishap, if he goes much after dangerous animals. A true sportsman need not trouble himself about what people think. Some may take a delight in being able to say that they have walked in a bush, and fired at elephants and buffaloes, without any of the precautions that I have named as necessary; I should recommend them not to do so often. We shot this buffalo, but I will give details in another part. I was afraid that some of the *carnivora* might feast on him, so we determined to return to my horse, and make the best of our way back to the kraal. A large party instantly set off with assagies to bring in the meat, while I had some dinner and a glass of brandy-and-water. I then strolled out to a neighbouring kloof, and poked about the bushes in search of game. Hearing some guinea-fowl calling, I drew my bullets, and put buck-shot into both barrels. This is a plan I rarely practised, as it is better always to retain a bullet in one barrel; in the present case the neglect of this might have led to a serious affair. Having crept down to where I thought I heard the guinea-fowl, I saw a couple of creatures moving in the long grass. I could not see what they were; but thinking that they must be bucks, I crept down towards them until well within shot; I then stood up, and ran forward. When within a few yards of the objects, I was brought to a stand-still, by seeing a leopard jump up: he gave a snarl at me, and then bounded off, followed by a second one. They went away just like two cats, leaping lightly over everything in their course. My finger was on the trigger to fire, but remembering the Dutchman Hendrick's advice, I thought it wiser to let them alone. I saw them go over a rocky hill some distance off, and was quite willing to let them thus retreat.

I returned up the ravine, and killed two guinea-fowl at one shot, as they were running furiously along a path. I thought my old buffalo might not be so tender as a guinea-fowl, in which supposition I was correct. A Kaffir girl plucked one of the birds for me, and I thought it particularly good, although it had not the addition of bread sauce or gravy. As it was getting dark the Kaffirs returned, almost weighed down by the immense weight of meat. Never had there been such luxurious times in their land; meat without reserve; snuff in plenty; and a round of brandy-and-water for the principal men. One or two large earthen vessels were placed on the fire, and huge pieces of the buffalo were put into them to stew. During the cooking, all the men assembled in the largest hut, which was circular, and like all the others. It was about twenty feet in diameter, about seven feet high, and in shape like a beehive. A large place in the centre was hollowed out for the fire; no chimney was considered necessary, a little hole that was in the thatch being more for look than use; the smoke from the fire was thick and blinding. The Kaffirs sat, like so many dogs, watching the meat stewing, at the same time trying little tit-bits of about half a pound or so, just as whetters to their appetites. They soon began a song, which was an extempore laudation of me: there was a great repetition of the same words, but very good time was kept, and a great deal of exercise gone through. The arms were held something in the attitude that a prizefighter would assume, and the body violently jerked up and down. Every now and then one of the party would give a signal, when they all would stop, and a man, with a very high tenor voice, shout a few words; at the termination of these a chorus would join in amidst yells and shrill whistles. Throughout, however, they kept a sort of regularity, and, although barbarous in the extreme, it was music of its kind. They did not seem to understand why I preferred to remain outside in the cold, and repeatedly asked me to come inside the hut; so not to appear exclusive, I took off my coat and waistcoat, and joined the festive scene, by which I appeared to give great satisfaction. In a quarter of an hour, however, I had had quite enough of it; I was baked nearly to a cinder, blinded with the smoke, and poisoned with the smell. A Kaffir, after his bath, is not the most sweetly perfumed animal in the world; but when five-and-twenty hot men assemble in one hut, and sit round a fire, it becomes too much to get over even with the aid of powerful snuff. I therefore pitched my tent outside, and, concealing myself between its folds, was soon asleep. The moon was still high when I awoke, and, not feeling inclined to sleep again, I took my gun, and wandered out in the cool night-air. Not a sound indicated the presence of human beings; the country all round could be as plainly seen as during the daylight, the night was so clear and bright. Several mysterious sounds occasionally could be heard both far and near; the hyæna's laugh was frequently audible, and twice I most distinctly heard the deep growl of a lion, sounding as though he were on a range of hills some three or four miles off: there was no mistaking his voice when once heard. I stopped out for nearly an hour, enjoying the beauty of the moonlight, and the wildness of the noises that alone disturbed the night: not a breath of wind was stirring. I could see indistinctly dark forms moving about on the opposite hills, an occasional shriek from which indicated some prowling jackals or hyænas on the look-out for prey. I soon began to feel very cold, and returned to creep again under the folds of my tent.

The following day was spent in an unsuccessful trip after elephants that Inkau had heard were near the Imvoti; we saw nothing of them, and returned home tired and hungry.

Amongst the members of this kraal was a very nice-looking Kaffir woman. The women can be handsome, although perhaps admiration for them is an *acquired taste*. Well, Peshauna (the girl's name) was the best-looking of Inkau's wives, and was placed as head woman of Inkau's kraal; she did but little work, and was highly dressed, in the extreme of the fashion, not in crinoline or embroidery, but in beads and brass. Round her head she had a broad band of light-blue and white beads; a pendent string of the latter hanging in a graceful curve over her eyelids, giving them the sleepy, indolent look assumed by so many of our fair sex. Round her neck in numbers, strings of beads were negligently hung, and a little apron of fringe about a foot long was fastened round her waist; this was neatly ornamented with beads of red, white, and blue; her wrists were also decorated with bracelets made of beads and brass, while her ankles were encircled with a fringe made from monkey's hair. This was the full-dress costume of Peshauna. To these adornments the most affable and agreeable manners were added, quite divested of that *hauteur* and assumption so often practised by acknowledged belles; she had a most graceful way of taking her snuff; and stuck through her ears were two very long mimosa thorns for the purpose of combing her woolly locks. I think all must agree in placing her on record as a most charming and divine nymph! She was, alas, another's! Twenty cows had been paid for her, and five men assagied, before she became the property of my gallant friend Inkau. It took at least a pint of gin before I could work him up to tell his story, which he did in words something like the following; his action and expression, however, had so much to do with the beauty of the story, that it loses fearfully in retailing:—

"I had long heard people talk of Peshauna being a beauty, but did not think much about it until I went buffalo-shooting near her father's kraal. I stopped there one night and saw her. *Ma mee!* she was *muthle kakulu!*" (the superlative of beautiful). "I talked to her a great deal, and I thought that she would soon like me. I went out next day, and shot a young buffalo. I managed to get help enough to bring it to the kraal, and I gave it all to Peshauna. Her father had asked many cows for her, but somehow no one had yet offered enough. When I heard this, I felt very frightened lest some one should carry her off before I could manage to buy her. My two wives I had always thought would have been enough for me, and I had given so many cows for them, that I really had not twenty left. I considered how I could manage, and hoped that fourteen cows paid, and seven more in ten moons, would be as good as twenty now. But Ama Sheman, her father, would not have this, and told me that a young chief named Boy would give the twenty cows at once. I was very angry at this, and asked Ama Sheman to wait a little, which he agreed to do for four months, as he said he would sooner see her my *umfazi* [wife] than Boy's. I went home, and was always after elephants. I got very rash, and was nearly killed by them once or twice, for my gun was not big enough. At last I killed a large bull-elephant, and got eight cows as my share. I started off at once to tell Ama Sheman that my cows were ready. He did not seem pleased to see me, but told me he should like to see my cows. He was an old *chingana* [rogue], and wanted to see which had the finest lot of cattle, Boy or I, as Boy had now offered twenty cows as well as myself. Mine were the finest, so it was agreed that I was to take Peshauna as my *umfazi*. When this was settled, I went out to try and shoot a buffalo for our marriage-feast. I did kill a large one before the sun was up high, and I returned with it to the kraal. As I came near, I heard the women and children screaming. I ran up, and found that Boy had watched all the men out of the kraal, had then walked quietly in with three of his people, and caught my dear Peshauna, and, before she had suspected anything, carried her off. Ama Sheman went out to try and stop them, but he was knocked on the head with a knob-kerry, and lay as if dead. They got off well from the kraal, and were out of sight when I returned, for they did not think I should be back so soon. I shouted for the men, who soon came in. We got our assagies, and I had my gun. Ama Sheman came all alive again, and eight of us started in chase. We went fast, and soon sighted the four rascals. As we came near them, they seemed surprised, and did not know what to do. They soon let Peshauna loose, and ran for their lives. We gained on them, and I threw away my gun, that I might run quicker. They had a river to cross, which was deep; they were wrong to try and get across; they ought to have fought on this side. Before they had gone over half the water, we had assagied two of them. They soon sank, and were eaten up by the alligators. The other two got over. We all jumped into the water, and swam after them. One of our young men, a very fast runner, went past me, and neared Boy; as he did, he shouted to him not to run like a dog, but to stop and fight. Boy took no notice until the man was close to him, when he suddenly stopped, turned round, and threw an assagy, which went through our fast runner, and killed him. It was Boy's last achievement, for I was on him like a leopard, and my assagy going into his heart was pleasant music to me. The other Kaffir was killed by Ama Sheman. We hid their bodies, as we did not wish a war with their kraal. We all kept the story quiet, and they did not for some time discover what had become of Boy and his party. The hyænas and vultures soon picked their bones."

I complimented Inkau on his bravery, and told him that I thought his wife Peshauna was well worth the price he had paid, and the danger he had incurred, for her possession; and when she came again into the kraal, I looked upon her wild beauty with additional interest.

CHAPTER XII.

A Kaffir hunt—A battue—Fire-making—A luuch *al fresco*—Troublesome invaders—Flight of locusts—Crows outwitted—Alligator shot—A lion-chase—Strength of the lion—A slight mistake—Snuff-manufacturing—A proposal of marriage—Kaffir kindliness.

ONE morning, Inkau told me that some large buck were in plenty not far from his kraal, and he thought that, with my help, he and his people might be able to have some very good sport. Being most anxious to witness a grand battue amongst the Kaffirs, I urged him to get all the men together who felt disposed for the expedition; and about a hundred assembled, all armed with either spears or knob-kerries.

I determined to be an observer of the proceedings rather than an actor, and not to shoot at anything unless I saw it must otherwise escape, and, by thus leaving the Kaffirs entirely alone, to watch their particular devices.

The country was open, and of that park-like description so common in Africa; the covers being about ten acres in extent. These were, at a given signal, surrounded by men, whose assagies or kerries were held in readiness for throwing. Two or three Kaffirs, who were told off as beaters, would then go inside and beat the bushes and grass.

Some of these woods had been drawn blanks, when, on entering a thick patch of reeds and bush, a "Tally" was given by a beater, which was responded to by a grand flourish of assagies from the ring of men without. A couple of the wild bush-pigs broke out of the cover, and had scarcely shown themselves for a second when an avalanche of spears and sticks came down upon them. The swine immediately presented the appearance of ruffled porcupines, as the assagies were sticking in numbers into their hides, and pointing in all directions. Still they made a bold rush for their lives: it was of no use, however; for twenty stabbing-spears were driven deep into them, and piggy was soon made pork. The savages seemed to take great delight in the single act of drawing blood, several spears being thrust into the pigs long after they had ceased to move. I thought it a piece of wonderful forbearance when I found that four men received directions to take the pork home. I fully expected to see the pigs eaten then and there; delays in these things the Kaffirs seem to consider as dangerous; and having an appetite always in readiness, they find but little difficulty in accommodating themselves to time and place.

Our next find was a couple of black bush-buck, male and female. They broke out of the cover gallantly, and the ram, lowering his horns, charged straight at the line of Kaffirs. A shower of missiles which were hurled at him failed in checking his career, and he dashed forward, leaving his partner on the ground. The Kaffirs quickly cleared the road, and allowed him to rush through, giving a grand volley of assagies as he passed; half a dozen remained in him, and his fate was then decided. He stopped once or twice, and tried with his mouth to pull out an assagy that was sticking in his shoulder, but could not manage it. The Kaffirs, by keeping wide on each side, had run on ahead, and were now gradually inclosing the gallant stag again, delivering their assagies as they approached him. The buck seemed undecided where to charge; he was once or twice driven back by the yells of the Kaffirs and the rattling and shaking of their oxhide shields; he soon fell under the blows and stabs that were freely given to him.

The idea of dining off these two bucks was too great a temptation for my black companions to resist; they were now bent on eating, and I saw preparations made for lighting a fire, for which neither lucifer nor flint-and-steel were used.

Two dry sticks, one being of hard and the other of soft wood, were the materials used. The soft stick was laid on the ground, and held firmly down by one Kaffir, whilst another employed himself in scooping out a little hole in the centre of it with the point of his assagy; into this little hollow the end of the hard wood was placed and held vertically. These two men sat face to face, one taking the vertical stick between the palms of his hands, and making it twist about very quickly, while the other Kaffir held the lower stick firmly in its place; the friction caused by the end of one piece of wood revolving on the other soon made the two pieces smoke. When the Kaffir who twisted became tired, the respective duties were exchanged. These operations having continued about a couple of minutes, sparks began to appear, and, when they became numerous, were gathered into some dry grass, which was then swung round at arm's length until a blaze was established; and a roaring fire was gladdening the hearts of the Kaffirs with the anticipation of a glorious feast in about ten minutes from the time that the operation was first commenced.

I joined the party as usual on these occasions, and did great credit to an Englishman's eating powers. I was much amused at the cool manner in which Inkau treated some of the men present, who seemed to be considered amongst the lower class of Kaffirs. He cut up the bucks with his own hands, thereby securing the best and most choice bits for himself and me; while every now and then he would look round the circle of black and expecting faces, and chuck the common pieces, or tough bits, to these poor wretches, who snatched them up, and after half-cooking them, bolted piece after piece, like hungry curs.

These two bucks, although each weighed about 120 pounds, were only sufficient for a light luncheon for the Kaffirs; although to me the men seemed to be crammed like boa-constrictors. They showed a great disinclination to move after their repast, although they complained that they were still *lambile* (hungry). An immense quantity of snuff was consumed, the tears coursing each other down the cheeks of many of the party, from the strength and rapidity of the doses. Seeing so great a disinclination on the part of the Kaffirs to use any exertion now that they were full of meat, I went by myself to have a look for a sea-cow, as the colonists call the hippopotamus, the Kaffir name for which is "imvubu." I was told that they were to be found in the Imvoti river, and they were not very frequently disturbed in this part. The Kaffirs near the river frequently suffered very much from the depredations of this game, corn-gardens being sometimes nearly destroyed and trodden down by the sea-cow during one night. Other animals also persecuted these unfortunate people. A herd of elephants might quietly walk through their fences some night, with the same ease as though the barricades were cobwebs, crush to the ground the nearly ripe crop, and leave the whole Kaffir village with but a poor chance of obtaining a winter supply of corn. These Kaffirs were rarely possessed of a gun, and did not like to venture too near these savage intruders; and the shouting and beating of shields did not always produce the desired effect on the elephants. Sometimes a venturesome Kaffir would get himself smashed by attempting to drive away a savage troop, and this would act as a warning to other Kaffirs; and they therefore frequently preferred being pillaged to being squashed. Sometimes a party of bucks will get the habit of sneaking into the corn of a night, when it is green and young, and will enjoy a good feed at the expense of the kraal's crop of mealeas.

The worst visitation, however, is a flight of locusts; and no idea can be formed of the destruction which these creatures will accomplish in even a couple of hours. I saw several heavy flights during my residence at Natal, the heaviest of which came upon the country at the back of the Berea, and extended about four miles inland. I can only compare its appearance to that of a heavy fall of snow, where each flake is represented by a locust. My horse would scarcely face them, and I was often nearly blinded by a great brute coming into my eye with a flop. I did not practise the same refined cruelty on this delinquent that a gentleman of South-African reputation told me he had one day done when a locust flew into his eye. Although blinded momentarily in one eye, he still kept the other on the rascal, who sought escape by diving amongst the crowd on the ground. After dismounting and capturing it, he passed a large pin through its body, and placed it in his waistcoat-pocket. Whenever the damaged eye smarted, he pulled the locust out of his pocket, and passed the pin through it in a fresh place: so hard-lived was this poor wretch, that I was assured the eye became quite well before the locust died.

Birds also frequently annoy the Kaffir gardens; and these people's power of defence against them is so limited, that it is absurd to see the importance they will sometimes place upon their destruction.

I once won the heart of an old Kaffir and all his wives, by killing two birds that had persecuted him for a considerable time.

He came from a great distance to request my aid, and I rode out with him and shot two crows that had made a regular joke of him for several weeks. These two birds had established their quarters near his kraal, and were going to build a nest in a large tree. The Kaffir would soon have destroyed their eggs, but in the mean time the birds took every opportunity of stealing any mealeas that might be put out to dry, or bits of meat that might be left in the sun, and were for a moment unwatched; his gardens, also, were examined occasionally for seed. When the old Kaffir rushed out at the birds with his knob-kerries, they would fly away quickly, giving an ironical sort of "caw," and settling high up in the tree, look down upon him and continue their jokes. I witnessed this proceeding on first arriving at the kraal, and laughed immoderately at the old women's expressions, as they shook their fists with rage at the birds, and told me the crows were so cunning, that they would not walk into a trap, and that they always served the man in the same manner in which I had seen them behave. I walked quietly down to the tree on which the birds were perched, they little suspecting the new dodge that was going to be practised on them: they gave some very jocular caws as I came near them, and eyed me with a sort of supercilious bend of the head. The excitement of all the Kaffirs was intense, as they looked on from a distance to witness the effect of my attack.

I walked round the tree until both birds were nearly in a line, they meanwhile watching all my proceedings most carefully, and I have no doubt flattering themselves that they were not going to be humbugged by me. Suddenly a charge of shot rattled through the branches, and down the crows both dropped, fluttering, to the ground.

A yell of delight from the expecting Kaffirs was the result of the success, as they rushed down towards their formerly triumphant, but now humbled enemies. Half a dozen hands eagerly seized on each bird, and in a few seconds their bodies were torn into the smallest pieces and scattered to the winds, whilst a shower of thanks and great praise fell to my share.

AN ALLIGATOR SHOT.

I walked quietly up the banks of the Imvoti for nearly three miles, but saw no signs of Hippo himself, although the spoor was very plentiful. The day was very hot, and, seeking a shady tree, whose branches overhung the stream, I sought shelter from the sun's rays and rest for my legs. I was soon interested in watching a colony of the pretty little yellow orioles, which were building their nests in the trees near the river. They had selected those branches that were pliant and overhung the stream, a little additional weight on which would have lowered them into the water; they were thus secure from the depredations of birdsnesting monkeys, whose egg-hunting attempts might have resulted in a ducking. These birds seemed to be excellent weavers, and knit the grass in the most ingenious way. Their nests were made in the shape of a glass retort, the necks pointing downwards.

Upon casting my eyes on the water below the tree near which I was sitting, I saw a small black snout just above the water: it was perfectly still, not a ripple showing that it possessed life. Watching it attentively for a few moments, I saw it begin slowly to rise, and then recognized the head of an alligator: aiming between the eyes, I lodged a bullet there, which struck with a crash. The alligator sank instantly, but I could see that the water was agitated, as though the monster were having a tussle for his life among the mud and reeds below the surface. I kept a sharp look-out at different shallow parts near the pool, but could not see him rise anywhere. After waiting for some time, I returned to Inkau's kraal, which I reached just before dark. A party went the next day on my trail and examined the river, and found the scaly monster floating and quite dead in the pool where I had left him.

On the following morning, a Kaffir came to Inkau in breathless haste to say that the evening before one of his cows had been killed, as it was returning home, by a lion, that had paid no attention to the shouting of the boy who attended the cattle, but had carried her away right before his eyes. Inkau was the great Nimrod of these parts, and at once agreed to go in search of the lion. He went into his kraal and brought out a very large necklace of charmed medicine, which he fastened round his neck, and with powder-horn, belt, and musket, and a very large snuff-gourd, he announced himself ready to depart. I thought my horses might be safer where they were, than if I took one to ride to the kraal of the strange Kaffir, who was named Maqueto. I therefore directed my own Kaffirs to look after them, and to watch them from place to place as they grazed.

A walk of nearly twelve miles up the river brought us to the scene of the lion's depredation on the previous night. All the women and children kept close in their kraals, and shouted to us, "*Hambani gathle*" (Go on well); while some men, who did not seem at all inclined to leave the protection of their palisades, complimented us as we passed, and said, "*Inkosi wena*" (You are chiefs). Inkau did not make a boast of his courage, although he said, "*Abantu saba naye*" (The people are afraid of him, *i. e.* the lion). Inkau looked at the print of the lion's foot, and pronounced him very big; he then followed quietly on, while Maqueto was now for making his adieu; but Inkau seemed indignant, and asked him why he left us. Maqueto said he had no gun. Inkau pointed to his assagies, which, however, Maqueto explained, were as nothing for attacking a lion. The controversy was getting warm, when I interfered, and said that we should not want Maqueto's company, but should be better without it.

We then went on with the spoor, which took us over some freshly-burned ground, and down towards a deep kloof, with high square rocks sticking up round the edges. We found that the lion had scarcely allowed the cow's body to drag on the ground, but had apparently carried it along quite easily, and as though of no weight. The Zulu breed of cattle are smaller than the English, the cows not being even so large as an Alderney; still it was a good weight to jog along with in his mouth. We went down the kloof with great care, listening after each dozen steps; but there was not a sound to be heard, no crunching of cow's bones, or other indication of the lion's presence. We soon came to the remains of the cow, very little, however, being left; for a lion had dined first, wolves and jackals afterwards, and vultures had then cleared up the scraps. I proposed to Inkau that we should lie in wait for the cow-slayer's return, and, if necessary, sleep on the ground; but to this he seemed to have a great objection, as, like most Kaffirs, he disliked to work all night if he could avoid it. We cautiously walked through the long grass, and examined the kloof to the extreme end: as we came back, and got near the remains of the carcass, we threw some stones into a bush that we had not passed near. Just as we did so, something jumped out of the bush, and rushed through the long grass. I could only see a brown back occasionally showing over the long Tambokie grass, but fired where the movement was. Inkau instantly bolted like a shot, while I followed him with equal rapidity, and we stopped behind a tree at about sixty yards from where I had fired. I loaded, and was then all ready for any creature that might charge.

I asked Inkau at what animal I had fired. He said, " Don't you know?" I told him that I was not certain, but fancied it might be the lion. He acknowledged that he saw so little of the animal that he really could not say: thus we had fired at a something, but neither of us, although by no means novices, could tell what this was.

We were most particular in our approach to the spot, and threw several stones in advance, but saw nothing until we came right on the body of a hyæna lying dead. The shot had been a very lucky one, for, aiming well forward at the moving grass, I had struck the hyæna with the bullet under the ear, and it had passed through the skull, dropping him dead in his track. We looked round the top of the kloof for spoor by which to trace the lion; none was to be found, and we had to return without even the satisfaction of a shot.

I won an old lady's heart by a present of tobacco on my return to Inkau's kraal. She had been frequently looking at me very attentively, and paid me some neat compliments; had she been young, and more like Peshauna, I should have been flattered; but unfortunately her appearance was not one that would be at all likely to inspire the tender passion. Her face was thin and wrinkled, while her whole body looked as though it were covered with a skin that had been originally intended for a very much larger person. She had also suffered from sickness, as was shown by the scars all over her body,—signs of the cupping and bleeding that had been performed on her by some Kaffir doctor, with an assagy in lieu of a lancet. Still she did not seem to be much displeased with herself,—a circumstance for which I can only account by the absence of looking-glasses in this village.

I did not feel much inclined to move after my long walk this day, so I took a seat near the door of the hut, and watched the old lady turn my tobacco into snuff. She first cut it up into little bits with an assagy, and brought two large stones to the hut; into the lower stone, which had a well-worn hollow, she put all the bits of tobacco, and with the other, which was nearly circular, and about the size of an ostrich-egg, she commenced grinding the tobacco: it seemed very hard work, as she pressed heavily on the stone during the operation. After a time she added some water, which made the mess into a sort of paste, something like a child's dirt-pie. After a great deal of grinding and scraping, the composition began really to look like a snuff-powder. She then got a wooden spoon nearly full of white wood-ashes, and mixed them with the tobacco. More grinding seemed to amalgamate the two compositions, when she tried a pinch herself, and pronounced that it wanted drying in the sun, and would then be good.

A PROPOSAL OF MARRIAGE.

During the whole time that she was at work she was uttering disjointed remarks to me, and at length proposed, in the most shameless and barefaced manner, that I should marry her daughter. I requested to know which of the damsels then present was the proposed bride, and was shown a young lady about twelve years old, who had very much the appearance of a picked Cochin-China fowl. I concealed my laughter, and told the old lady that when this lassy became taller, and very fat, I might then think more seriously of her proposition; but as at present I had not six cows (the required price) handy, I could not entertain the subject. The old lady told me she would get the skin and bone adorned with fat by the time I came on another visit; and, for all I know, this black charmer may be now waiting in disappointed plumpness. I stayed seven days at this kraal: after the third day I had no bread or biscuit, but merely roasted Indian corn and meat, with the *amasi* and *ubisi* (sour and sweet milk). I therefore felt the want of bread, butter, and a bed, and bidding my shooting companion farewell, I distributed beads and tobacco to the women and some lucifers to the men, and then took my departure.

I should wish to testify to the manner in which I, a perfect stranger, unknown by name or reputation to these savages, was treated during this visit. They were kind, civil, and really hospitable. It was pleasing to see a young Kaffir girl come each evening with a bowl of milk and some corn, and, putting them down quietly beside me, look with her wild black eyes into my face, and musically say, "*Ar ko inkosi*" (Yours, chief).

A clever and good missionary was settled near here, and all the Kaffirs spoke very highly of him. His good influence might have done something in turning these Kaffirs' minds in the right direction, but all their civility and good feeling appeared as though natural and not by tuition. I do not look to the cause, I merely state what was really the case. They might have murdered me, and concealed the fact with sufficient cunning to prevent its discovery; but their only idea seemed to be that of simple honest-dealing.

CHAPTER XIII.

The Natal Kaffirs—Pseudo-Christianity—Ideas of a future state—The Kaffir prophets—Black lawyers—A wife's true value—Husband and wife—White savage *versus* black—Injustice towards the Kaffirs—Nobody wrong—Necessity of an army—Mr. Holden's opinion—Severity sometimes necessary—Real character of the Kaffir.

THE Kaffirs about Natal are a fine honest set of men; they will outwit you in a bargain like Englishmen, if they can; but this all seems to be fair, and in the way of trade. If I went to a kraal for some milk or anything, they would at once ask me what I would give them for it, and if I offered a certain amount of snuff or money, they would wrangle for more; but if I explained to them that I came as a guest, they nearly always gave freely what I wanted. The less they had been accustomed to white traders, the more generously disposed they seemed. I never felt that I incurred the slightest risk in going singly anywhere amongst these people. They seem to have a very wholesome dread of an Englishman's power, and so consider it policy to make him a friend. They were peaceably disposed, in spite of our bad government, and seemed willing to listen to the missionaries, many of whom were located in the district. The labours of these teachers were, however great, unsatisfactory; for whilst they taught by word what was right, many other white men taught by deeds what was wrong; the simple-minded savage was therefore sadly puzzled, and was often, I thought, inclined to look upon us as a set of humbugs, from this difficulty of separating the bad from the good. "Are your laws and your God so good, that you send teachers to benefit us, and yet you cannot get your own men to obey them?" was the question of a young Kaffir to me, after he had seen a drunken Englishman in the streets of Pietermaritzberg during the day.

It too frequently happens, that in our eagerness to civilize the savage, as we term it, we but impart to him the vile qualities that are common amongst the white men. The natural equilibrum of the savage mind is thus upset, and only those instructions are retained that agree with the man's own inclination. I once met a Kaffir whose clothes gave evidence of his having lived near white men. When asked to do some work for me, he refused, stating as his reason, that the black man was as good as the white, and he did not think, therefore, one ought to work for the other. He was sitting down at the time drinking and smoking. Upon investigating this case, I found that a missionary, endeavouring to instil religious principles into this savage, and give him a motive for becoming a Christian, had assured him that in the sight of the Creator there was no difference between a black and a white man. This fact was enough for our friend, he jumped at the offer of baptism, answered to the name of Lazarus, professed belief in everything, and sat down with the comfortable idea of being as good as the best white man that he had ever seen. This man, of course, would do more harm than good amongst his fellows; they could discover the false reasoning, but would conclude that it had been taught by the missionary, and would reject, in consequence, all religious instruction. All these Kaffirs seemed to have a capacity for appreciating the beauties of their country, wild and graceful as it is to the English eye, which gazes with delight on the sweet-scented evergreens and graceful vines. The glories of the European conservatory are here but a common tree or an overgrown weed. Amongst scenes like these, the men I employed as aids in hunting had received their instruction. The heavens and the stars were their wonders and puzzles, spooring, throwing the assagy, and tending the cattle, their courses of study; the wild animals that they frequently encountered had infused into them a dash of their own savage natures; their barters and ambitions were limited to a few cattle, a blanket, and a gun.

Every man of whom I inquired, appeared to believe in a future state, and that his position in that state would depend upon his deeds in the present one. His ideas on the subject were as wild and uncultivated as his country. Still he had a belief that by doing certain things he propitiated the spirit that ruled over the future. May not these simple but earnest proceedings of the good savage, joined to an ever-present wish to do right, obtain for him from above (when weighed in the scale of mercy) the position of the man intrusted with one talent? That he does not do what is right according to our Christian notions, is often the result of imperfect instruction, and the want of proper example. But he is in a less dangerous position than the civilized being who has received his ten talents in the shape of education, and yet wilfully neglects to use them in the right way. In judging these Kaffirs, if there appeared any indication of the good, or what could be admired in their thoughts or deeds, I placed it on record in my memory, with just the same impartiality that I did when anything equally bad was shown.

It is too frequently the custom, not only when judging the savage, but also our own kindred,

> "That for some vicious mode of nature in them,

Or

> By the o'ergrowth of some complexion,
> * * * * *
> These men,—
> Carrying, I say, the stamp of one defect ;
> Being nature's livery, or fortune's star,—
> Their virtues else (be they as pure as grace,
> As infinite as man may undergo)
> Shall in the general censure take corruption
> From that particular fault : The dram of base
> Doth all the noble substance often dout,
> To his own scandal."

Some of the Kaffir prophets are most wonderfully eloquent and clear. They will talk for an hour or two without being at a loss for a word, and, strong in argument, they can bring many examples to make good their case. They are very gentlemanly in their language, and I do not think that they use as much personal abuse as do many gifted orators in civilized countries. An Englishman ought not to underrate their talents in this particular, or he will probably be worsted in an encounter of words. A proof of this lawyer-like talent was exhibited by a great chief near Natal; he was met, however, with equal skill by the officer who went to him as ambassador. There is no greater crime amongst savages than for a simple man to accumulate cattle in large quantities, as it is thought an attempt to rival his chief. When this is the case, a cause for slaughter and appropriation is soon discovered; the other parties are equally on the alert to watch for suspicious demonstrations against them. If they suppose that anything is intended, they leave their cattle, and make a rush into the district under English control: they are *there* safe, and cannot be pursued by the army of the indignant chief, as it would be a breach of frontier rules. The chief to whom I refer had upon one occasion crossed the boundary after a renegade; so we sent an ambassador to him to remind him of his conduct, and demand an apology. On the matter being discussed, the Kaffir remarked that it was very hard that we did not allow him to punish his traitors by following and slaying them. " If," said he, " your own men mutinied, murdered your officers, and ran into my country, you, I know, would want to follow and punish them, while I am not allowed to do so." It was true enough that, should this have happened, we certainly should have followed and captured the mutineers. So the ambassador had but one answer, which was, " The Englishman's laws are so just and good that all men, black or white, run to them instead of away from them." A Kaffir is very grasping in bargains; he will always ask much more than he purposes taking, and will argue and talk for a considerable time before he can be beaten down. If some easy person once pays a high price for an article, it is afterwards very difficult to obtain the same sort of thing for a lower, and the market is at once spoiled. A man of mine wounded by accident an old Kaffir woman in the leg; the headman of the kraal at once demanded from me a cow as compensation, as accidents are not recognized by Kaffirs. He brought his dinner and snuff-box to my hut early, and sat talking until late, for three days, gradually lessening his demands, until two sticks of Cavendish tobacco eventually satisfied him. Had I given in to his exorbitant demand, the price would have been an established one, and an old Kaffir woman could not have been wounded under the penalty of a cow. The Kaffir notation is different from ours; they calculate so many elephants' tusks = so much money; so much money = one cow; six cows = one wife; this being the highest currency amongst them. It may strike many of my readers (in case I have them) as odd, that a wife should be valued at such a price. Their family arrangements, however, are different from ours: whereas our first expense is generally the least, with them it is the greatest, and the only one; all that takes place afterwards being interest on their original investment. If a Kaffir has a large family, especially of girls, they are soon made useful in the cultivation of his gardens, and, when at a "coming-out" age, are sold at their fair valuation in cattle. The honeymoon over, Mrs. Matuan, or Eondema, is set to work at once at turning over the Indian-corn garden, or making baskets to hold milk, &c. The master of the house, in the mean while, has a look at his cattle while they are feeding, milks the cows on their return at night, and then lies in his hut smoking dakka, a very intoxicating root, something between tobacco and opium. Thus, an investment in wives is a very common custom amongst rich Kaffirs. I made a great mistake on one occasion when I intended to give the Kaffir Monyosi a reproof. On going to his kraal, on a warm beautiful day, to ask him to come out and shoot, he told me that he was very lazy, and wanted to stay in his hut and smoke. I told him to come out and shoot, and show himself to be a man, and not stop in his hut all day like a woman (thinking of our English customs). He gave a knowing sort of grin, and said, "The *men* stop in all day; the *women* go out and work!" A Kaffir's riches consist in either wives or cattle, some of the great chiefs having a hundred wives, and many thousand head of cattle.

Travellers vary in their accounts of the nature of the South-African savage. Each should speak according to his experience, but at the same time he should judge fairly, and with all due allowance for the ignorant state of these people.

The frontier Kaffirs, I have before said, are confirmed rascals; but I doubt whether we have not made them so ourselves; and we are pursuing a plan to form the Natal Kaffirs on the same model. Let us see whether other writers differ from me in their conclusions with regard to the savages. Captain Harris, in his "Wild Sports of Southern Africa," says : "How truly it has been remarked by Captain Owen, that the state of those countries which have had little or no intercourse with civilized nations is a direct refutation of the theory of poets and philosophers, who would represent the ignorance of the savage as virtuous simplicity,—his miserable poverty as frugality and temperance,—and his stupid indolence as laudable contempt for wealth. Widely differing, indeed, were the facts which came under our observation; *and doubtless it will ever be found that uncultivated man is a compound of treachery, cunning, debauchery, gluttony, and idleness."* Here the hinge appears to turn upon the term uncultivated man; and I am convinced that there are very many in the most civilized countries of Europe who as well deserve the term, without any of the excuses, as the savages of Africa,—at least, as those about Natal, of whom I now speak. Was the treatment I received at the kraal of Inkau, alone and at their mercy, either a compound of "treachery," "cunning," or "debauchery"? The gluttony and idleness I care not to defend; but these are not very grievous crimes to lay to the charge of able-bodied men who can taste meat scarcely once a week.

I doubt whether I should have been treated as well in many of the manufacturing districts of England as I was here in Africa. In the former place, the only notice a stranger may get is having "arf a brick eaved at him," or being "pinned by a bull pup."

Imagine the feelings of a Highland chieftain and his clan upon being quietly told that they must move away from their mountains and their country, but must not grumble, because the government has made a grant of land of five acres per man for his people on the Plumstead marshes, or some other place equally unsuited to their taste; the only reason assigned for this act being that their ancestors' land, hallowed by victories and associations, is now required for a cotton-spinning manufactory. Would these otherwise loyal subjects become rebels, think you?

Now let us see if the treatment of the Kaffirs of Natal is very different from this.. It must be borne in mind that the poor heathen, in addition to his natural *amor patriæ*, believes firmly that the spirits of his fathers are watching over him from the hills that they have during life inhabited; and that if he quits those hills, he, in a measure, withdraws from their care. The Journal of the Bishop of Cape Town, dated June 9th, 1850, states: " I have heard to-day from a lady who lives in the neighbourhood, that the chief, Umnini, of whom I have before spoken, removed from his lands on the Bluff (Natal) last Friday. He came to bid her farewell before he left; for they had been kind neighbours to each other. It was not without sorrow that he quitted his birthplace, where he has resided all his life, and withstood in his fastnesses the victorious troops of Tshaka, who conquered the whole country, and brought into subjection all the native chiefs, except this one and another. But now we want his land; it is important for our growing settlement at D'Urban that it should be in our possession; therefore he must go. He is weak and we are strong." Although it is not sacrilege to suppose a bishop might be mistaken, still we will ask which of the two following is the more probable case:—

That the Lord Bishop of Cape Town knew perfectly well what he was writing about, had good information of the facts he mentioned, and merely forbore from using stronger language on account of his holy character; or, that he was quite wrong altogether, and was mistaken with regard to the affair?

Might it not have been Umnini's own wish that caused him to quit the land on which he had dwelt for half a century? *Could* it not have been that he at last came to consider the soil that had drunk the blood of his warriors who died in defending it from the attacks of the savage Tshaka, as desecrated by the act instead of hallowed? Or did he not consider that *though hundreds of moons* had shone upon him and his fathers in this place, future moons ought hereafter to shine upon him in a less fertile soil; and therefore, agreeing to the white man's wishes, he *willingly* quitted his home for the price of a few head of cattle and went forth a wanderer?

As to our strength and the Kaffirs' weakness—oh, no! those things never happen here; if they did, some might ask, with the innocence of the child in the show, which was the uncultivated savage famous for " a compound of treachery and cunning," and which the Christian. The same ambiguous answer might naturally be returned, " that we had paid our money and might take our choice."

These proceedings are all very well, if we look merely to this world as all and everything; but when we think of the next, the reflection is hardly so satisfactory.

But who is wrong? Surely it is not the soldier, who merely goes to see that the orders given to him are carried out. The Colonial Government will say it is not they that are to blame, as land must be had. And it certainly is not the English Government that should bear the onus.

It appears that amongst many of the officials of South Africa, there is a practice of adhering to the letter of the law, instead of the spirit; that is in strict accordance with the character shown by the soldier, who did not save a woman from drowning when he was close beside her, because he had been taught not to act without orders, and there was nothing in the Articles of War about drowning women.

Let it not be supposed for a moment that I agree with those who are ever crying, "Do away with the soldiers," or "Spare the poor savage from punishment." When we have to deal with the ferocious savage, whether he is so naturally or has been made so by the mistaken policy of our forefathers, it is nothing but the strong arm and the firm hand that can and will ever keep him in subjection or prevent him from being a murderer and confirmed thief.

Soldiers may be an evil, but so are doctors; and whenever the disease war breaks out, it must be vigorously attacked by the physicians, in the shape of soldiers; and the more ably and the better these soldiers attack the disease, the sooner will it be stopped, and the less frequent will be its recurrence. It would be as ridiculous and short-sighted a policy to send away all the doctors, hoping thereby to stop sickness, as to weaken our force anywhere in any country, by withdrawing or reducing its army, in the hope of better maintaining peace.

The savage invariably considers that forbearance in war is caused by fear, and he is more ready and eager for battle after kindness and mercy have been shown him than he would be after a severe lesson. The Kaffir, when he really is a savage, is a most ferocious one; and although the distance that separates England from the Cape is so great, that events taking place there are scarcely discernible; still, they would cause a great stir did they happen nearer. Twelve hundred men, the number slain by these savages in the last war, would look a large body in Hyde Park. The same policy that punishes and subdues the aroused and vindictive Kaffir, ought to encourage and sympathize with him when he is quietly and peaceably disposed.

Since penning the preceding pages, I have read a work on Natal and the eastern frontier of the Cape Colony, by the Rev. William Holden, who was living at D'Urban during my pilgrimage in the same neighbourhood. As he was an excellent Kaffir linguist, and was always spoken of by Kaffirs and white men with respect and affection, it is gratifying to find that his fifteen years of experience bring him to the same conclusions, with regard to the treatment of the Kaffirs, at which I may be considered to have jumped hastily after only three years' investigation. I will quote from page 215 of his work :—

" But let not those who are invested with a little brief authority use it in playing all sorts of fantastic tricks, or something worse. A Kaffir has a sharp sense of justice, and whilst he will respect and reverence the officer who will give him just punishment for his misdeeds, he will abhor the man who does him wanton wrong, and may be tempted to settle accounts in his own way.

" The Kaffirs must be treated like children. If a man has a large family, and leaves them without restraint or control, his children become a plague to himself and a scourge to the community. The Kaffirs are children of a larger growth, and must be treated accordingly; *children* in knowledge, ignorant of the relationships of civilized society, and strangers to many of the motives which influence the conduct of the white man. But they are *men* in physical and mental powers; *men* in the arts and usages of their nation, and the laws of their country; and the great difficulty in governing them is, to treat them as men-children, teaching them that to submit and to obey are essential to their own welfare as well as to that of others.

" Some kind-hearted Christians will say, 'This is much too severe;' but my firm conviction, after many years' experience, is, that it is not merely the best, but also the only way to save the native races from ruin and annihilation; and that, had the Kaffirs on the frontier of the old colony been treated with more apparent severity after the first war, a second outbreak would not have taken place. Who, I would ask, is their best friend, the man who would save them by apparent severity, or the man who would destroy them by mistaken kindness? I presume the former. Besides, it should not be forgotten that what appears to be severe to us is not so to them, since many of them have lived under the iron rule of cruel capricious despots, with no security for life or property, and are consequently unable to appreciate or understand our excess of civilized kindness; being strangers to those refined feelings which operate in the breast of the Christian. The result of too mild a policy is, that in a few years they are changed from crouching, terror-stricken vassals, to bold, lawless, independent barbarians."

These latter remarks may appear out of place in a book of rough sketches of sport, but the Kaffirs were to me such trusty allies, faithful servants, and kind instructors in many things, that, as a small token of gratitude for their services, I cannot refrain from making known the rough and thorny path that they are made to tread.

CHAPTER XIV.

A buffalo hunt—A sudden meeting—A Kaffir's advice—Buffalo killed—An African race-course—The start—The run—The charge—Won at last—Unpleasant neighbours—The single spur—Light-coloured Kaffirs—Know thyself—Neglected education—Black and white—Too knowing by half—The fool's argument.

MONYOSI, his brother, and my Kaffir Inyovu, were with me across the Umganie one morning, when we came upon the fresh spoor of a single buffalo. The spoor was very neatly taken up by Monyosi, who noticed it on some very hard and difficult ground, where it would have been totally invisible to unskilled eyes. The professor marked it, and, after following for nearly two hundred yards, brought us to several other foot-prints, all of that morning's date; there seemed to be about a dozen in the herd.

We found that these buffaloes had entered the forest by one of the old elephant-tracks, and had kept straight on as though wishing to bury themselves in the most retired glens. They had neither stopped to browse or graze, but passed all the feeding-places with temperance and self-denial.

We quickly followed on their traces, and were rewarded, after journeying two or three miles, by finding the signs very recent: we were then only a minute or so behind the herd. We waited a short time to listen, and soon heard a slight rustling of the branches to our left, which showed us that the buffaloes were moving about. We turned back a little, and arranged so that we should approach them from the leeward side. Monyosi seemed to be more careful and cautious in his approach to these buffaloes than I had ever seen him with elephants. This, I afterwards learnt, was caused by his having been knocked heels over head and nearly killed by a wounded buffalo, some months before I made his acquaintance. I allowed Monyosi to lead, taking care to follow close to his elbow; the two other Kaffirs bringing up the rear of the cavalcade.

We were expecting to come upon the buffaloes at every turn, and each muscle of Monyosi's well formed figure was seen as though strung in readiness for a spring to the right or left. I looked round to see if the two Kaffirs were following close, and upon again turning my head, saw Monyosi bringing his gun up to his shoulder. Kaffirs generally fire very slowly, and I had time to notice that a buffalo was standing looking at us about five paces distant, to take a quick aim at his forehead, and fire at the same instant with Monyosi.

None of us waited to see what was the result of our fire, but each bolted as hard as his legs could carry him in the particular direction that the path nearest him might lead. I turned round and made play down that by which we had approached, but fancying that I heard the branches crashing behind me, I dodged short to the right up a convenient cross path. This proceeding was only just in time, as I saw, on looking round, that two buffaloes had charged down the same path that I had first followed; one of them was evidently disposed to be mischievous, as he stopped and turned after me. Dropping my gun, I caught at some wild vine and quickly scrambled up a tree, and sought protection amidst its elevated branches. My position was now quite safe, and I could laugh at my savage adversary. So he also seemed to think, as he took but one look at me and trotted away.

Of the Kaffirs I had seen nothing since we fired: they had disappeared most miraculously. I gave the usual whistle, and was answered at some distance by them. They came to the tree on which I was perched, looked at me, my gun, and the buffalo's foot-prints; everything was instantly explained to them; they shook their heads, covered their mouths with their hands, and gave a long *w-o-w*. After asking one or two questions, Monyosi advised me not to run again towards the direction in which a buffalo's head pointed, but to dart to the right or left.

We found plenty of blood on the trail, and hoped to come up with our wounded friend. His hardened old constitution did not seem to have suffered much as yet; for four miles at least were passed over without our at all appearing to gain on this old die-hard.

We had entered directly into the bush, and had consequently to retrace all our steps to get clear again; it was nearly dark now, and twilight is scarcely a reality near the tropics, darkness following so immediately on daylight. The Kaffirs proposed our stopping on the trail, but I was unfortunately very hungry, and had a very great desire for a bottle of Bass and a beefsteak, which I knew awaited me at home; I therefore gave up the idea of a leaf bed, and voted for a return. We came along very quickly, and reached the edge of the bush after the moon had risen some time, and had given her light in exchange for that of the sun; she did not equal it, but she certainly made it as much like day as it is possible for night to be; we could see everything, out of the shades of the forest, quite as distinctly as by daylight. A large herd of wild pigs had come out to have a peep at the open glade in which we were; they loomed large in the distance, and we mistook them for buffaloes; upon getting near enough for a shot, they were discovered to be bush-pigs. We shot a couple before they knew of our approach.

On the occasion that I mentioned of buffalo-shooting, while on my trip up the country with the Kaffir Inkau, he led on quietly and steadily, and at length stopped, and slowly raising his arm, pointed in the direction of a large tree. I followed his point, and saw a fine old buffalo standing with his ears moving about, and his snout in the air. I brought both barrels to the full-cock, by the "artful dodge," without noise, and gave the contents to him right and left behind the shoulder, when he sprang forward, and dashed wildly through the forest. After rushing a hundred yards or so, at full speed, he dropped dead.

I went across the Umlass for a week's shooting with a Kaffir named M'untu; near his kraal there was some undulating ground sprinkled with bush, which was said to be visited occasionally by buffalo. Having one of my horses fit to go, I was anxious for a gallop after these wide-awake fellows. Starting at peep of day, I found a herd of ten or twelve grazing near a ravine; they saw or heard me from a considerable distance, and sneaked into the ravine.

It is curious how soon a white man's approach causes alarm to the wild animals of Africa. Whilst a Kaffir can pass about almost unnoticed, the former is at once a cause of terror.

I entered the ravine, and by shouting and firing a shot scattered the herd of buffaloes in a few minutes; I did not get close to them in the ravine, but saw them topping the ridge outside.

I was soon after them: the country was undulating, with a little bush here and there. I yelled at the troop as they galloped along huddled together, and turned them from a thick patch of bush, for which they were making, into a large flat open plain with short springy turf. Here is the Epsom of Africa; a lawn of twenty-five miles, flat as a billiard-table is the course, the match is p.p., the parties are a stout little thirteen hands high pony with eleven stone on his back, and a bull-buffalo sixteen hands high with a feather weight. Now what are the odds—who will bet two to one on the buffalo? No takers! An even bet I name the winner. What is the opinion of the jackal, I wonder, who is peeping over the shoulders of his young family from out of the hole that has been his residence since the ant-bear who built it was killed last year by a leopard? What will the Bushman lay against the *inthumba* (buffalo) being dropped in the first two miles? This fellow does not care much which is the winner, he only wishes to see one or the other killed. From his hiding-place in the rock's crannies, he watches the race with great excitement. If the buffalo is killed, he is sure to fall in for a share of the meat. If the white man breaks his neck in some of the jackals' holes or game-pits, it will be hard lines if this own brother to the baboons does not manage to have a good ride that very night on the saddle that the *umlungo* (white man) lately occupied.

Now they are all ready for the start,—great excitement in the crowd. Jackals shuffle and shriek; even the hyæna, that has hitherto appeared asleep, wakes up and gives an hysterical laugh; the vultures and eagles, from the top of their grand stand high up in the clouds, have a capital view, wheeling slowly round, in readiness either to gorge the flesh of the buffalo or pollute that of the white hunter. The hoofs of the horse striking on the ground act the part of starting-bell; the hunter's approach is thus discovered; the buffalo whirls his tail, and the Umlungo bends in his saddle; and "They're off!" would be the remark were any there to make it. But no, not a living soul is seen; all is earth, sky, and wild animals. One white man is the only thing bearing God's image that is now within ten miles, and he is employed in fulfilling the ordinance that " over every beast of the field shalt thou have dominion." The Bushman, on the distant rocky mountain, sees the race plainly without the aid of a telescope, and watches intently what is so intelligible to his experienced eyes, but what would be to some of our highly scientific savans' visions like two indistinct specks. The light weight takes the lead at a rattling pace, and leaves the eleven stone far behind; he trusts to his speed, but still thinks it may be necessary to keep those rocky mountains under his lee, in which to retreat, as a sort of nest-egg. Away they go; flowering geraniums and

THE RUN.

candelabra-shaped amaryllis are trodden down as though the veriest weeds on earth. "Cluck, cluck—click, click—*nhlpr-nh!*" Why is the Bushman so excited? Ah! he knows all about it; the buffalo has turned a little, and is now making for some old game-pits, with a sharp stake in the middle of each. Now, what a chance!—both buffalo and horse may be engulphed—all three perhaps killed! What a glorious finale this would be! Fancy the jollification of buffalo beef to commence with, and a second course of horseflesh, while between the mouthfuls a knife might be driven in spite between the ribs of the broken-necked white man, whose body would be lying by! What would be a feast of turtle and venison compared to this? In England you don't know how to live and feast like a Bushman. Unfortunately, and bad luck for "Cluck-click," neither buffalo nor horse has yet broken his neck. There is no one looking on to see how the horse goes,—no one to give another fifty for him,—no one to see how he crossed that old watercourse; and yet how boldly the man rides. He is not riding in this style merely to sell the animal: he does not look round to see if any of the swells of the field are watching him, and then for applause, or money in prospect, cram his horse at a stiff rail, at which his craven heart would not dare even to look were no man near. No! it must really be that the heart and soul of this desert rider are in his sport, and that he feels—

> "There is rapture to vault on the champing steed.
> And bound away with the eagle's speed,
> With the death-fraught firelock in his hand,
> The only law of the desert land."

A streak of blood on the black hide of the buffalo, and foam from his mouth, tell a tale that he has not run thus far even without being distressed in more ways than one. Now they are near the Bushman's box, who sits like a judge to see them come in. Hi! hi! here they come! there they go! Bang, bang! the buffalo stumbles; he got the second barrel in the ribs. The horse begins to reel in his gallop a little, but, being well held together by his rider, he has at least another mile still in him; now the hunter rides nearly alongside the bull, and it is neck and neck. What a change! tables turned! Truly it is so; the hunter is the hunted. The buffalo, with head low, is charging; the rider, steering his horse with firm hand, and a watchful eye on the *inthumba*, suddenly wheels, and, dropping apparently off his horse, steadily aims at his riderless competitor; two little white puffs of smoke may be seen, and a thousand echoing guns are heard, like a volley, from the surrounding mountains. The buffalo has had enough; he quietly drops on his knees, lays his head on the ground, doubles his hind-legs under him, and reposes at full length on the plain, to rise no more. The race is run; the Derby won by the thirteen hands and eleven stone. The prize is valueless as regards money; the flesh is given to Kaffirs who are sent after it; the head and horn are too heavy to carry—but the tail is the prize. This trophy, years afterwards, may be looked at by some Nimrod of sparrows—questions asked about it; and in response to the information that it is the tail of an angry old buffalo that was taken after a long run, and when the owner had been shot whilst charging, this hero may then inform you that he thinks that sort of sport must be rather good fun, and it is just the style of thing to suit him. The prize is of no value save to the winner. Who can paint the feelings that he enjoys, however, as he sits and contemplates this poor old dried bit of skin and hair, and looks back on the beginning and end of the run in which his hand, without aid, won it? Can it be that a single mind only enters thoroughly into a scene like that which I have feebly described, and that the memory has drunk so deeply of the details, stirring to itself, but valueless to others, that the mere look of the prize suffices to recal the scene.

Is it not a greater proof of sense and of the power of intellect than arguing whether Brown's conduct was right in submitting to be told that he was anything but what he should be; or in calculating what ought to be the fair odds if the Middleham colt gives 7 lb. to the b. f. by Sir Sutton,—or—or—— Well, we will suppose it is a mad corner; it may be a treat to some, as sense and intellect are so very common, to have a little madness now and then. I for one am content to be thus afflicted every day of my life, as long as I am not confined in Hanwell, or prevented from roaming in thought over lands blessed with the sun and air pure from heaven, in place of bronchitial fogs, foul sewers, and gloomy skies. We will suppose that the eleven stone told, and the horse was beaten; no matter, we have not lost our money or our honour. We need not take a trip to the continent as it nears the settling day at the Corner; we have only to jog quietly back to the kraal or the camp: a day's rest, and all one's losses are regained, and disappointments recovered. Hurrah for the desert!

* * * * * *

While riding about near some kraals, not far from M'untu Umculu's, I saw a very fine herd of Zulu cattle; they are beautiful little creatures, looking more as though they were a cross between an antelope and a cow than merely common cattle. I approached them to have a nearer look, when they seemed equally disposed to stare at me. We stood thus for about a minute, when two or three young bulls came forward quite close to me; others followed, the first advanced, more came in front of them, and I found that I was getting regularly hemmed in by these curious gentlemen. I therefore turned tail, and walked quietly away; they followed me rapidly, coming in the most impertinent manner with their horns within a foot or two of my legs. I shouted at them, but it merely seemed to raise their anger, as they stamped furiously; they were evidently unaccustomed to receive white men with courtesy. I saw they were working themselves up for mischief, so dropped the spur into the horse and rode for it, when they came after me at once, leaping and prancing with their tails erect. I really began to think it was no joke, and that I should have had to put a bullet through one of their heads as an example. As, however, such a proceeding would very likely have embroiled me with the Kaffirs, I rode on. I saw an old Kaffir in a mealie garden at a short distance, so rode towards him and shouted; he rushed down to meet me, and waving his skin cloak, gave some tremendously shrill whistles. He looked like a demon forbidding the advance of his imps. The effect was magical; the half-wild cattle stopped, and I jumped off my frightened horse to ask the old Kaffir how it all was. He said that the bulls did not know much about white men and horses, and perhaps thought that I was some wild animal come to destroy their young. I must own I looked rather a rough customer, and my clothes were not in the best condition—but still this was too bad. I have, however, seen in our most public thoroughfares, men who might easily be mistaken by an unfashionable herd of cattle for "wild animals come to destroy their calves." I mention dropping the "*spur*," which may require explanation. One only of these weapons is used in the colony and this single spur is buckled on the left heel, as, in dismounting and mounting so frequently as is here necessary, the right spur becomes inconvenient, and may scratch the horse's back in throwing the leg over. The reason given is, that it *is* inconvenient, and also that if one side of the horse is made to go, most probably the other will go also.

While staying at this kraal, I was visited by a Kaffir who had all the features of a European; he told me that his mother was as his forefinger, and then, pointing to his little finger, said *that* mother was a white woman, that she came out of the sea, and had been the wife of a chief. I was much interested in all this, as the white woman of whom he spoke, was without doubt one of those unfortunates who were saved from the wrecks of the *Grosvenor* and another ship, who had seen all their male relatives and ship-friends murdered, and were then forced to become the wives of the Kaffir chiefs or principal men. The descendants of these mixed people can even now be traced in some of the light coloured Kaffirs of the Amaponda, the Umzimvubu, and Umzimculu; and it is not improbable that a small rivulet of the blood of the Howards may be even now flowing in oblivion under the dark hide of a naked assagy-throwing, snuff-taking heathen of Africa. Some things that this Kaffir told me were strange and curious. Memory here serves as a library. It is a book of reference much in use, and one that is therefore nearer perfection than can be conceived by those whose ivory tablets or ledgers daily record events.

South Africa is an excellent country in which to obtain a knowledge of ourselves; solitude being so common and unavoidable a contingency that we soon become perfectly reconciled to our own society, and learn to argue and reason as though with another person. If we are worsted in this encounter, we have the same satisfaction that Dr. Johnson had, knowing that we supply our adversary's arguments as well as our own. An excellent and good understanding here exists between our outer and inner selves, and each individual knows his own respective worth.

It is a land in which one's value as a man is decided, in the unerring scale of trial, to an ounce. It is pleasant to know one's true position, if only for a short time, and even if much lower than we have been accustomed to consider our due. It prevents us from making many mistakes, and deters us from undertaking many things that we could only blunder through did we attempt.

The very slight knowledge that the bustle of civilized society permits us to gain of ourselves, causes us sometimes to commit grievous errors, that may render us ridiculous to the reasoning bystander. We may pride and plume ourselves on merits and qualities that we do not really possess, but that only exist in idea, caused by the flattering of our *friends,* or some chance of fortune. We then have a way of reposing, with a self-satisfied and complacent air, on imaginary laurels that we never have culled, and, did we but really know ourselves, might be perfectly certain we never should.

An Englishman has such a just appreciation of what is true and genuine, that I am sure he would be delighted at having his perfections thus correctly made known to him. Even supposing he has for tens of years previously hugged himself with too favourable an idea of them, there may still be a sufficient time left for him to cram this real knowledge of himself. Even if he get but a smattering, still it will prepare him in a measure, and therefore make the shock less at that great trial at which we must all, sooner or later, have our merits weighed, and in which good fortune and riches will be considered as only additional trusts for which we shall have to account satisfactorily.

So frequently have some of my most certain axioms turned out myths, that I have long since come to the conclusion that I *know* absolutely nothing at all.

I have been put down so completely by naked Kaffirs

and dirty Hottentots on the subject of South-African spooring, &c., of which I might otherwise easily have fancied I knew something, from having lived the gipsy-like life of a savage for upwards of two years, and during that time having been occupied night and day in the pursuit of wild animals, and gathering information from the natives—that I frequently now listen attentively and patiently to criticisms on the sporting proceedings of such men as Sir Cornwallis Harris and Gordon Cumming, oracularly delivered by gentlemen whose experiences have been gathered from watching the deer in Greenwich Park, or from knocking over a cock-pheasant in the well-preserved covers of their private manors. For I always remembered that these people *might* know more on the subject than the sporting giants whom they are attempting to vilify.

Well do I remember on one occasion being the butt of at least a dozen Kaffirs, for no other reason than because I could not tell whether a buffalo had galloped or only walked over some hard and grassy ground, that retained less impression than a dry turnpike-road. How amusing it was to see them sitting down on purpose to quiz me, pointing to each footmark, that to my dull perception was little more than the scratch of a penknife, and then asking if I could not now see the pace at which the animal had moved. I was compelled to acknowledge myself a dunce, and to explain to them that my education in early youth had been in this particular science dreadfully neglected. They would then show and explain to me how I was to judge of these things in future, with a kindness and simplicity that were very beautiful.

This proceeding is nearly a type of what takes place in civilization, where it frequently happens that a man is politely sneered at because he is unacquainted with the slang or local joke of some particular clique, or does not submissively follow the habits and fashions of the reigning set. Human nature, whether black, red, or white, is very much alike all over the world; each to the unseasoned eye has its special peculiarities and prominent points of ridicule, and I doubt whether a Zulu chief and *umfazi*, with their scanty attire of strips of skins and bead and feather ornaments, would produce more ridicule were they to walk up Regent-street, than would an English gentleman fashionably attired, or a lady with looped and festooned dress and embroidered under-garment, at the court of Kaffirland.

In every land and in every society, men are found who think they raise themselves, or show that they have unlimited penetration, by trying to cast disbelief on the statements of others, and thus endeavour to prove that they themselves are very wise men. Now, I would sooner be what is vulgarly called humbugged half a dozen times, by some man relating to me a falsehood, after assuring me he was merely telling the truth, than I would once cast disbelief on a true statement. In the first case, the sin is on the relater; and we merely believed him to be a truth-teller when he was in reality a liar. But in the second case we expose our ignorance, by often thinking that impossible which really exists, or we insult an honest man by doubting his honesty, and injure ourselves by shutting our ears to the reception of facts.

On the morning after my tree interview with the elephant, I happened to mention to an English *gentleman* of the sort that I have described, what a curious scene I had witnessed on the previous day. It was against my established rule, however, to relate anything connected with sporting matters to persons whom I casually met, but on this occasion my usual caution had left me. I was plainly told by this gentleman that he did not believe me. I was not angry; but as this was a person who might be described as so knowing that he actually believed nothing at all, I gave him plenty of opportunities to commit himself.

There is an old saying, that "a bet is a fool's argument." It is, however, frequently the only argument that will convince some people, and it proved so with the person whom I have mentioned. I offered to make him a bet that I could prove that the elephants *did* come to me under the tree, and in fact that everything had happened just as I had stated it. He tried to escape from this trial, but I plainly told him, that if he did not accept the offer, it would be an acknowledgment that he was wrong. The bet was made, and I was to give my proof.

I called in two witnesses, and then related what had happened with the elephants on the previous day, taking care to give every detail. I then sent for a white man, who I knew spoke the Kaffir language very well, to act as interpreter, and also sent for my Kaffir Inyovu, who was up the tree with me. On their arrival, Inyovu was requested to state what had happened in the bush on the previous day. He at first said that he wished me as his chief to speak; but upon my requesting him to give his own account, he spoke nearly word for word what I had previously said. I then requested that any two Kaffirs might be sent on our spoor, and the tree examined that we had ascended on the day before; but my doubting gentleman hauled down his colours, although with a very bad grace, and acknowledged that he now believed the whole account.

The money I intended returning to him, after I had proved my adventure to have been true, but unfortunately was unable to do so, because it was never paid to me.

I recommend this ordeal to others who may be annoyed by such mosquito sort of gentry; it may not be quite right on principle, but is very decisive and convincing. I know one gentleman, however, who avoids this fiery trial, by asserting that he makes it a rule never to bet. For him it is a most useful rule, as he is so invariably obstinate, and at the same time wrong, that were he to fall into ungenerous hands, his obstinacy or his money would soon melt away; and I am disposed to think that the latter would be the sooner lost.

CHAPTER XV.

Kaffir killed by a snake—Medicine necklaces—Narrow escape—Puff-adders—Adventure with a black snake—Snakes distressed by their own poison—Poison-spitting snake—A day's sport—Boa-constrictor killed—Its mode of attack—Size of the slain snake—Secretary-bird.

ONE morning Inyovu, in great distress, came to tell me that his father had been bitten by a very poisonous snake, and he was afraid that he would not live. As his kraal was only ten miles distant, I determined to ride over, and see what aid I could give; taking with me some *eau de luce* and a sharp penknife, in case it was requisite. Upon arriving at the huts, all appeared calm and tranquil, and I hoped that the man had recovered. I was, however, coolly informed that he had been dead some time. Inquiring into the matter, I found that the snake was a large black one, called by the Kaffirs *M'namba Umkulu*, or great puff-adder; it did not resemble the ordinary puff-adder in colour, size, or character, being larger, quite black, and having none of the peculiar puffing which the puff-adder always shows when he is irritated. The larger snake is as highly poisonous as the common puff-adder, and quite as much dreaded. The man was bitten in the leg, above the knee, and not having his snake-charm with him at the time, of course could not hope to be saved. These charms are of peculiar kinds of wood, and are worn round the neck, and strung like beads; the bits of wood being of all shapes, and about the size of large beans. Each separate piece has its *spécialité;* one is to cure laziness, others the bites of snakes, others diseases of cattle, and also to enable the wearer to escape from the dangerous game which he may be hunting. These pieces of wood were eaten by the Kaffirs whenever they were ill or in danger; it appeared as though a kind of homœopathic dose only was necessary, as but a very small portion was taken as a remedy. I but once took of this medicine, and I must bear witness to its efficacy in my case.

I suffered very much one day from the heat, and feeling a great lassitude coming over me, I told Monyosi that I could not go any further into the bush, giving him my reason. He at once said that he had some medicine, especially for this complaint, from which he very frequently suffered. (I strongly suspect that his only complaint was laziness.) He offered me a piece, which I accepted on condition that he should also eat a bit. It tasted something like rhubarb, but was also very bitter, and hot. In a few minutes, strange to say, I felt quite recovered, and walked many hours in the bush without distress.

Inyovu's father, from what I could gather, must have lived about three hours between the period of the bite and his death; this would not give a person much time to be "shriven." I saw his body, and it did not seem to be much swollen or altered. The number of poisonous snakes in this district was a great drawback to the delight of the sport; for when walking through long grass one was never certain that some horrid serpent was not ready to give a bite that would speedily terminate one's career. Although this dread gradually wore off, it was occasionally refreshed in the memory by some narrow escape from being bitten.

For example, I once shot a coran across the Umganie, and as it fell amongst some long grass and bushes, I could not find it, and for some time pushed the grass about with my ramrod. Suddenly a something, that looked like a broad dead leaf, rose up almost under my hand from amongst the brushwood that I had turned over. It was about a foot from me, and only attracted my attention by a sort of waving motion, as it was a good deal concealed by the grass, and upon looking at it, I perceived it was a hideous cobra, with its hood extended. I stood like a statue, and the snake dropped down and glided away. Why it did not bite me I know not, as I must have struck it unintentionally with my ramrod. These things are over in a few seconds, but one travels over a long space of time during their occurrence, and the impressions which they leave are most vivid.

When it slid away I first truly realized the danger in which I had been, and jumped from the spot as though the ground had been red-hot. I feared also that I might have been bitten unconsciously, and was thus anything but happy for several hours. I searched no more for my wounded coran in that place!

I was in the habit of bathing morning and evening in the Natal Bay, and selected some old piles, the remains of a pier, as the most convenient place from which to jump, as the water became deep just beyond the last of them. An old pile-driving machine stood on the sands close by, and it had a low square platform which was an excellent substitute for a dressing-room. One warm evening I had undressed as usual, and was walking over the deep sand to the plank from which I took my accustomed header, when I noticed the sand began to heave about a yard in front of me, and the broad ace-of-clubs shaped head of a puff-adder rise up in a threatening attitude. I should not have been more astonished had I seen a whale in the same place, as no cover for a snake was near, and it seemed such a very unlikely locality. I jumped back immediately, and looked about for a stick or stone; before I could find either, however, the adder had shaken the sand from his back, and quietly glided under the little platform on which all my clothes were lying. I gave up the idea of bathing that night, and began to think how I was to regain my raiment. I kept a watchful eye on the lower part of the platform, and creeping up to it, made a sudden grab at my clothes and bolted away. I took care to shake each article very carefully before putting it on, but more particularly my boots, for on my first arrival in the colony, a kind friend informed me that boots were a favourite resting-place for snakes. And to assist the idea he had inserted a hair brush into one of them, and, just as I was pulling it on, shouted for me to "look out for the snake." I arranged a grand attack on the snake's residence the following day, when two full-grown and five young puff-adders were killed. It was very fortunate that none of these adders had ever taken a fancy to locate themselves in the leg of my trousers, or the arm of my coat, for the sake of warmth, during the time that I was cooling myself in the water. This family must have been under the driving-machine for some weeks, and I have no doubt they admired the very regular attention that I daily paid to my ablutions. I fear that the stamping always necessary in drawing on a boot after bathing, must have sadly annoyed the young fry. I never liked going near this place afterwards, and was obliged in consequence to invest some capital in a square board upon which to perform my toilet.

I had another escape from a snake near the Sea-cow Lake, about six miles from Natal. I had been looking for a duiker, which I was anxious to shoot for the purpose of concocting a bowl of soup, this particular animal being celebrated for that purpose. As I was slowly walking through the grass, something just in advance of me moved and the grass shook. I stepped back, preparing for a shot, as I expected a buck to spring up. Instead of a duiker, I saw the broad head of a black snake, of a most poisonous species, rise up little more than a yard from me, and draw his head back as though about to strike. I felt a disinclination to raise the gun to my shoulder to fire at him, thinking that he might then spring at me, so taking a quick aim from the hip, I fired, and nearly blew his head off. He tumbled over, and, with one twist, expired. I approached carefully, and found him to be a very large black snake, about seven feet long, and nearly as thick as my arm. I took him home, and on dissection saw that his poison-fangs were three quarters of an inch long, and the bag above them was full of poison. A bite from this fellow would have settled my account with this world in about three hours.

It is a very difficult thing to recommend a cure for a poisonous snake's bite. One of the most simple and classic is to suck the part. When a person is alone, this is of course only possible if he is bitten in the hands, arms, or low down in the legs. Cutting out the bitten part is considered the best remedy, but this requires a tolerable amount of nerve and determination. Some say that running about most perseveringly will keep off the stupor that generally follows the reception of this powerful poison into the blood. Happily, having no personal experience in snake-bites, I cannot speak with certainty about their cure.

I am under the impression that the poisonous snakes are much troubled, at certain seasons of the year, by the poison-bladder becoming surcharged, and that thus, being anxious to rid themselves of this poison by biting something soft, and thereby pressing it out, they naturally seize the first thing which their instinct tells them will not injure their poisonous fangs. Two instances that occurred at Natal appear to bear out this theory. A Hottentot was crossing the Mooi river drift, another man following a short distance in the rear. The last man saw a snake dart out from some rocks, seize the first Hottentot by the leg, and glide back again; the bitten man died within a very short time of receiving the bite. There is at the present time a man in the Royal Arsenal at Woolwich, who, when far up the country with his master, and walking near the waggons, perceived a puff-adder spring at his face. He suddenly lowered his head, and the snake wound itself round his wide-awake hat. The man knocked the hat off, and the snake was immediately shot by a looker-on. The puff-adder always springs backwards, and can make extraordinary leaps. There is a very fine specimen now to be seen in the Zoological Gardens, Regent's Park.

I have heard from both Dutchmen and Kaffirs that there is a snake which spits out its poison at any one who may approach, and makes capital shots. Blindness often follows if the victim is struck in the eyes, and a horrible disease of the skin if the face or hands are touched by the poisonous secretion. I am not aware of the appearance or name of this reptile. Besides the venomous snakes that I have mentioned as being common about Natal, there is also a species of boa-constrictor which grows to a considerable size; and although this snake is not dangerous, still it is slaughtered by man whenever met, as it is destructive to birds and small bucks. I shot six of these during my prowlings around the bush and swamps of Natal; the largest was shot when I was in company with an English gentleman who rarely went out shooting and was a prey to despair almost before he had commenced. As the whole of that day's proceedings serve to show that it is well never to give up or to throw away a chance, I will describe them in detail.

We had for nearly four hours continually searched kloofs and ravines, but we had seen no game whatsoever. As we were riding over a little hill, I thought I saw something move on an opposite ridge, a little behind me and on my left hand. I would not look round, but rode steadily away until we had passed over the hill and were quite out of sight of whatever had caught my attention. I then mentioned to my companion that I fancied I had seen something move on the opposite hill, and that I purposed creeping back to have a second look. He voted for *riding* over the hill, but this I would not hear of.

Keeping well down in the grass, I managed to peep through a tree, and there saw a fine reitbok looking after us. He stood up for about a minute as if he were watching to see if we had really gone away, when, seeming to think everything safe, he laid himself down again. I reported what I had seen to my impatient companion, and proposed that we should make a long round, and come upon the buck from the opposite side. We, therefore, left our horses, and crossed the ravine between the two hills on foot, taking care to keep well out of sight. I drew my charge of shot and loaded, so as to have a bullet in each barrel; my friend preferring two heavy doses of buck-shot. All being in readiness, we approached the ground that I had marked as the reitbok's lair, and were within fifty yards of it, when the buck got the alarm and bounded off. I had only a snap shot at him, my friend fired at the same instant, and the buck fell. We ran up, and, to the evident disappointment of one of the party, found that the buck had been killed by a bullet-wound which had passed close to the backbone. There was not a single shot-hole in him besides this one; there could be no mistake, therefore, about the arm which delivered the death-wound. We brought the horses to the spot, mounted the dead buck on my pony, and then took up a fresh line of country in hopes of finding another buck. We went some distance with no luck, when my dog flushed a covey of red-winged partridges. We dismounted, and walked about beating the bushes, when I suddenly noticed that he was pointing at a small clump of bush; he did not stand as though it were a bird, but occasionally drew his head back quickly. I called him away, fearing it might be a poisonous snake or a leopard, and, approaching the bush with caution, peeped through the branches, and saw the thick body of an enormous boa-constrictor moving very slowly away. I instantly sent a bullet through the part of the body that I saw, and sprang back, when the bushes were violently shaken as though the constrictor thought this sudden attack was anything but satisfactory. I now loaded the discharged barrel with a heavy dose of buck-shot, and advanced to the bush. Holding my gun out at arm's length, I pushed the branches gently on one side to get a peep at my antagonist and see how he liked what I had done. The snake was very artful, and waited quite quietly until I stooped a little to get a better view, when he darted out his head, making a sort of lunge at me; he opened his tremendous jaws as he came, and then suddenly drew back. I stepped away quickly to avoid this attack, and gave the boa my charge of buck-shot between the eyes before he got out of sight. Turning his head round, he seized his body with his fangs, gave a wriggle, and died.

His mode of attack gave me an insight into the method by which this species of snake destroys animals. The teeth of boa-constrictors being long, bent, and turned back, something in the fish-hook shape, the snakes dart out in the manner I have just described, and seize hold of their prey.

Then drawing their heads back again, they pull the animal to the ground at once, and, coiling round it, commence the crushing process. This power of squeezing must be enormous. On attempting to skin this animal, the muscles inside had the appearance of strings of rope extending from the head to the tail; these he seemed to have the power of contracting or extending, so that a part that might be three feet long as he coiled himself round your body, could be instantly reduced to about a foot, by this means giving any one in his embrace a very tolerable squeeze. I have before remarked that these snakes are not considered dangerous to man, as they are not poisonous; and if those attacked had a sharp knife, and managed to keep their arms free, Mr. Snake would get the worst of it. If one happened, however, to be asleep, and a boa-constrictor then became familiar, he might so have wound himself round arms and body as to prevent a knife being used. I have no doubt that they have power sufficient to crush any man to death in a very few seconds, did they once get themselves comfortably settled round his ribs; but I never heard of such a case during my residence at Natal, although I made every inquiry from the Kaffirs. Formerly there was a great deal of superstition amongst the Kaffirs with regard to this snake, and a person who killed one had to go through a quarantine of purifying; now, however, the Kaffirs do not seem to care much about them. I saw an old fellow near the Umbilo River pinning a large boa-constrictor to the ground with several assagies to prevent its wriggling; he had about a dozen different ones stuck into its body, and seemed to think a few more would do no harm. He told me that the snake was a great rascal, and had killed a calf of his some time before; that he had long watched for an opportunity of catching it out of its hole, and at last found it so, when a smart race of some yards ended in the Kaffir assagying the veal-eater.

We tried to skin the boa-constrictor that I had shot, but found great difficulty in separating the skin from the muscles, and his odour was strong and disagreeable. Whenever we put in the knife so as to touch his nerves, he made a little sort of jump that was anything but pleasant. We contented ourselves, therefore, with a piece of his skin about six inches long, which remained our only trophy. The colours of this boa were very brilliant, and they had a bloom on them like a ripe plum; he was evidently up to good living, for he had breakfasted that day on a partridge, as was shown by the *post-mortem*. His length was 21 feet, and circumference about 1 ft. 6 in.; he must have weighed about 200 lb.

Our bag on this day was a reitbok, a boa-constrictor, and a brace and a half of partridges. I believe that we should not have obtained either of the larger animals, had it not been for a second examination of the suspicious moving grass in the manner that I have mentioned. Had we stopped at once to look at the object, the buck would have bounded away without a moment's notice, but as it was, he fancied he was unobserved and secure.

I give these details to show on what small hinges success in South African sport may turn.

The Kaffirs reported that a boa-constrictor lived in

some long reeds near the Umganie, and they said it was an enormous animal, and fully fifty feet long. I once saw its spoor on the sand, and judged that it must be nearly thirty feet long. On several occasions I sought interviews with it, but was unsuccessful in finding it at home. It is always better to give all snakes a wide berth, and not to go out of one's way to destroy them, unless they have taken up their residence in or near your house, or their destruction can be accomplished with ease and safety.

Many snakes of South Africa are not poisonous: a very good plan for telling them is to notice the shape of their head; anything approaching the form of the ace of clubs, or a breadth across the forehead as it were, is indicative of venom; while those with the narrow lizard-like heads are harmless.

The secretary bird is one of the greatest destroyers of snakes, and either is proof against their bites or is too active to be bitten. He seizes them generally by the neck, and goes sailing aloft with a long reptile wriggling about in agonies. If the bird finds the snake troublesome during his aerial voyage, he lets it fall a few thousand feet on to the hardest ground, and then quickly following after, takes the snake on another trip. A fine in money is very properly imposed in the Cape colony on the destroyer of one of these birds.

CHAPTER XVI.

An invitation—Terrific storm—Silent eloquence—Mounted Bushmen—The Bushman as an enemy—A Dutch hunter—Gallant Defence—A Cockney traveller—Boer incredulity—British disbelief—Adventure with a Bushman—African rivers—Change of sentiments.

DURING another visit of some months at Pietermaritzburg, where I had some excellent reitbock and ourebi shooting, I accepted an invitation to a friend's residence near the sources of the Umganie. A night passed under the canopy of heaven was never to me a matter much to be feared, if good sport was the result; and these residences on the border of the game country made very good starting points for two or three days' roughing it in the open plains. With my two horses and a Kaffir, I started with a very vague idea as to the position of my friend's residence. I crossed the Umganie near the falls, and struck off to the left of the road that leads to Bushman's River, and after riding about three hours, I made inquiry from some Kaffirs whom I met about the distance I was to go. Their explanation of distance is by the single word *kude;* it expresses how long, from a day's journey to a mile, the *ku* being dwelt on for about ten seconds, means a long way. When it is spoken quickly, the place asked for is close; in the present instance, the *ku—u—u—de* was expressive of several miles. As it was near sunset, I asked where the sun would be when I

arrived at my destination. They told me that if I
"*cachema*" (rode fast or ran), the sun would set before I
had gone more than so far, pointing to about half of a
stick he held in his hand; this explanation gave me as
good an idea of the distance, as though he had told it me
in miles and furlongs. We pushed on as fast as we
could; but as there was no road, and the sun occasionally
hidden by dark clouds, it was difficult to keep exactly
the course, especially as many deep ravines crossed our
intended road. As the sun was going down, there seemed
every sign of a severe storm. Those only who have seen
a tropical thunder-storm can judge what a pleasant
prospect there was before us, for an open plain affords a
poor shelter from its violence. As no sign of a habitation appeared on the line we were pursuing, I struck off to
the right, where a klooff a mile distant offered a prospect of
shelter. On reaching it, some large trees, with the usual
creepers spreading over them, made a fairish shield
against the expected pelting shower. I off-saddled the
horses, making them fast to a tree. I sat upon one of
the saddles, covered with a blanket I usually carried
under it, and made the Kaffir do the same with the other.
The deep gloom and heavy clouds that had advanced from
the horizon over our heads, and sped along as if by
express, caused darkness in a few minutes. The slight
gusts of wind, wild and unmeaning, rustled the leaves
about in an unnatural sort of way, while little whirlwinds
seemed to search out every small track of sand, and raise
it in revolving clouds. The birds flew for shelter in
the klooff, and flitted about from tree to tree, as though

T

anxious and alarmed at the signs of the coming storm. The horses would not eat the grass that was almost tickling their noses, but, with one ear forward and the other back, showed by their restlessness a sense of the approach of the demon of storm. The storm approached *too*—like a demon. From the deep black horizon vivid flashes of lightning dashed with uncounted rapidity, the answering thunder not being in distinct and separate claps, but in one sullen roar; nearer and nearer it came with giant strides, while where I sat, all was still quiet, save the slight complaining sound of an occasional whirlwind among the trees. I could mark the course of the storm, as it came nearer, as easily as that of a troop of horse. First, the dust in dense clouds, with leaves and grass, &c., was driven furiously along; then came the rain (it ought to have had some other name, it was no more like the thing called rain in England than the Atlantic is like a pond), its force laid every thing flat before it—the lightning following with blinding brilliancy. This storm was like a whole host of common thunder-storms in a fury. The klooff that I was in offered me no shelter against these torrents, and I was wet to the skin in about one minute, the water running out of my clothes. I was obliged to shut my eyes and cover them with my hand, to stop the pain caused by the dazzling of the pale blue sparks, which flew from one side of the horizon to the other, and from the heavens to the earth, with messages that no man could read. The whole thing was like the encounter of a vast host, one fleeing, the other pursuing—it came and was gone in half an hour. The moon then appeared with its beautiful silvery light, the furious hurricane having passed on its course to the vast plains and mountains of the mysterious interior. Every insect who possessed " a shrill small horn " now began piping it in rejoicing, the cricket and beetles making the air vibrate with the sharp note they utter; while on the plains in front of me, a couple of antelopes walked out to graze, conscious already that the danger was over. After a severe storm all the animal creation seem on the move, and, although it was long past the bed-time of the feathered inhabitants of the ravine, they began flitting about from tree to tree; while some green parrots that seemed to reside here, and had been caught in the storm, and therefore obliged to seek shelter elsewhere, returned in parties of twos and threes, and were then noisily welcomed by their more fortunate fellows. My Kaffir seemed awed by the lightning and thunder; he ate a little of his "*muti*" (charmed medicine) that was round his neck, and sat immovable. When the storm had passed he looked steadily at me for a few seconds, covering his mouth with his hand in his usual way, shook his head two or three times, and shut his eyes. One must have seen his performance to have judged of his eloquence.

As the night was so brilliant, I determined to push on and try to find my friend's location, for I was unpleasantly moist, and everything was so wet that lighting a fire would have been no easy matter. In Africa we travel by " direction:" " Go out in that direction for two days, and you will come to my house," is about the amount of information you frequently get. I knew which way to steer, so pushed straight on in the hope of seeing some sign of a house. After riding about an hour, I saw two horsemen going up a hill opposite to me, about half a mile distant; they were going on slowly, but I could not make them out well, as they were over the ridge so soon. I galloped on after them, thinking that they must be some one from my friends, sent out in search of me, but upon getting on the hill, the horsemen had passed over. I saw them a few hundred yards in advance, they were looking away from me, and one was pointing out something to the other. Before I could see well who they were, my Kaffir came to my side, and exclaimed, *Ma me, ma me!—bululu bulala!—chingana Bushman.* ("Ma me," is a term of surprise, "shoot, shoot, rascally Bushman!"). To explain this apparently cruel proposition, I must state that the Bushmen about here were looked upon with the most deadly hatred, " every man's hand was against them, and theirs against every man." They were the farmer's greatest enemies—wandering from place to place; they had strongholds in the most inaccessible mountains—active as baboons they retreated to these when no other place was secure. For days and nights they would watch from some secret lookout, the cattle or horses of a Boer or Kaffir. Then having made themselves acquainted with the customs and precautions of their purposed victims, they at length crept down to the kraal containing the cattle or horses, took them quietly out early in the night, and made a rapid retreat before the morning light would enable the robbed to discover their loss; the Bushmen then being some thirty miles distant. Pursuit is often impossible, because every horse is generally taken. Should they be pursued, and see no chance of keeping the cattle, they will then either hamstring them or stick a poisoned arrow into them, and thus prevent the farmer from taking advantage of his speedy pursuit. The Bushman himself being very light, and always having a good horse, easily gets away. If by chance his horse is shot, and he reduced to his own legs, he scrambles like a baboon up the rocks if any are near; if not, he seeks cover behind an ant-hill, or in a wolf-hole, and prepares his poisoned arrows for defence. Armed with a quiver full, with five on each side of his head for immediate use, he cannot be approached with impunity, for at eighty yards the Bushman can strike a buck while running. Should a man be wounded, then—

> "Where it draws blood, no cataplasm so rare,
> Collected from all simples that have virtue
> Under the moon, can save the thing from death."

These ten arrows can be delivered in about twice as many seconds; one would assume the appearance therefore of a fretful porcupine, should he venture near these venomous wretches. Forbearance is by the savage frequently mistaken for fear, and dog-like he then seeks to worry. Lest such should be the case with these men, I sent a bullet a few yards over their heads, and its music was the first intimation they had that their council of two was interrupted. They stayed not to complain, but lying flat on their horses' necks, which thus appeared riderless, dashed away into the blue distance. My Kaffir seemed disappointed at the result; he kept quiet for some time, and then remarked, "If they had been buck, you would have hit them"—it was half an inquiry and half a reproof. He would neither have understood or appreciated any moral reasoning I could have given him against taking the life of a fellow creature, however low in scale of humanity.

The reflection of the moon on some windows directed me to the residence of my friend, where a blazing fire, a change of clothes, a plentiful dinner, and a glass of good brandy and water caused a total revolution in my feelings, and I began to think that happiness was not excluded from the simple wattle-and-daub hut of the solitary resident of South Africa.

This settler had been a frequent sufferer from the depredations of Bushmen, and they had only lately robbed him of horses and cattle. He now kept a dozen dogs always about his premises; these creatures saluted any arrival with noise enough to wake the dead. He hinted that, having found the arm of the law not quite quick or powerful enough to prevent these robberies, he had taken the liberty of protecting himself, and following up the thieves rather quickly. On one occasion he *stopped* four of them from ever repeating their wickedness; how he did this so effectually, I could but guess. He showed me their bows and arrows, and I was supposed to infer that he had, by the power of argument, persuaded them to give up vice, and lead a peaceable life. My friend told me that elands were sometimes in sight of his house, as well as hartebeest, and occasionally quaggas; that all the kloofs contained bucks, pheasants, and guinea-fowl. There was another visitor at the house, a Dutchman, a relation of my host's wife, with whom I now became a great ally, he being a thorough sportsman, and having slain every four-footed animal in Africa. I had frequently heard his name mentioned as a most daring elephant hunter, and was delighted in hearing his accounts given in the plain matter-of-fact way that brought conviction at once. He acknowledged that he had but little love for Englishmen, and still less for the English soldier; he gave a very plain reason for his antipathy. He was used with what he considered great injustice by the government on the frontier of the colony; appeal after appeal remaining unnoticed. At last, angry and disgusted, he sold his lands at a great loss, and started with his wife, children, goods, and cattle to join the emigrant farmers, who were then settling themselves in the Natal district, at that time unoccupied by white men. There he thought with the rest that the laws and regulations of the English would not annoy them, and that after conquering, with a great sacrifice of life and hard fighting, the treacherous Zulu chief, Dingaan, they would be allowed to enjoy the fruits of their victories. Not so, however; a party of English soldiers shortly came up to Natal, and the officer laid down laws for them all. *This* was more than the Dutch could stand. They considered themselves as an independent colony, and owned no allegiance to Her Majesty. A fight was the consequence, in which the Boers besieged the English troops, and were nearly driving them to surrender, when reinforcements were landed and the Dutch defeated. Most of them "trekked" into the interior after this, to avoid the English dominion, and amongst them was the visitor here. He gave me a description of the night attack made by our troops on the Boers' camp at the Congella, and its disastrous result, in which about sixteen of our men were killed and thirty wounded. He stated that, whatever idea our English commander had had, he never could have surprised the Dutch, as *they* had Kaffir and Hottentot spies, who were on the look-out all day and all night; and before the last ox was inspanned at the guns, the Boers had received information that the troops were coming to attack them, and had made their preparations accordingly. The hardships that the troops endured in the camp, rather than surrender, afford one of the numerous examples on record of the wonderful gameness and heroism of the English soldier. Having met with a severe check in the attempted surprise of the Boers' camp, a little handful of men stood a siege for upwards of a month, although they were short of provisions, and had but little hope of being relieved. Had this affair taken place in Europe, each actor in the scene would have been immortalized for his endurance and gallantry. An extract from the despatch of the commander will give some idea of the hardships they underwent:—" Upon inquiring into the state of provisions this day, I found that only three days' issue of meat remained. I therefore directed that such horses as were living might be killed, and made into beltong. We had hitherto been issuing biscuit dust, alternating with biscuit and rice, at half allowance. The horseflesh, of which there was but little, we commenced using on the 22nd, and, by a rigid exactness in the issues, I calculated that we might certainly hold out, although without meat, for nearly a month longer." The party were at length rescued by a detachment landed from the *Southampton* frigate, who drove the Boers back and eventually made terms with them. The Boer gave me the whole account in detail, but it might only weary the reader were I to write it. He praised the courage of the English, but said that they were not slim (cunning) enough for the Kaffirs and Boers.

The Boers have generally a question to ask, or a story to relate. They gave me one or two very interesting accounts of the interior, and I was at last asked to tell an adventure of some kind. I did not think that I was likely to amuse my hearers much; for if I related some of my African adventures and experiences they would have thought them as ridiculous as I did the following. When returning from a rough voyage of seventy-eight days from the Cape, a custom-house searcher came on board our ship at Gravesend, and tried to awe us with the dangers that he there met during a strong easterly wind. " Ah !" said he, "when it blows hard, the sea gets rather lumpy here, I can tell you!" He was a cockney, and this had been the limit of his travels.

I had, however, wonderful things to tell, and was obliged to be cautious how I related them, lest my veracity should be called in question : all my precautions were, however, useless. A young Boer, totally illiterate, and more ignorant than the generality of these people, was, in his own opinion, a very clever, sharp sort of fellow, who could not easily be imposed upon.

My story was not about herds of antelopes consisting of thousands, of attacks made on troops of elephants or buffaloes, or of lions carrying off horses from under the very eyes of their owners. I simply wished to tell the Boers what sort of a place London was, which I mentioned as about half its real size, that I might not astonish too much. I gave them a description of the large shops, and at last tried to describe St. Paul's Cathedral. I told them that it was so large that at least four thousand people could stand at the same time inside the building; and that it was so high that if your own brother happened to be at the top, and you at the bottom, you would not be able to recognize him. I was at once told by the young Dutchman that this could not be true; my host, however, came to the rescue, and said that he himself had seen the building, and it was, in reality, even larger than I had stated. The Dutchman would not have it so, at any price, but asked, with a knowing look, " if the wind ever blew in my country," or " if it ever rained." I told him it did both, the latter pretty often. "Then," said he, " that big place that you have spoken to me about cannot exist; it could not be built so strong as to stand more than a week; it would be blown down or washed away. You see that the Deutch mensch (Dutchmen) cannot be humbugged so easily as you thought." Perfectly satisfied at his flattering discovery, he walked out of the room and took his place for the night in his waggon, and I have no doubt communicated to his admiring Hottentot driver how he had shown the Englishman that he was a clever fellow.

I have generally found that the most reasonable men are the purely uncultivated and the most highly educated; the intermediate states appear to carry out the saying, that " a little knowledge is a dangerous thing." A very short time ago I met a gentleman who erred much in the same manner as the Boer. I happened to mention the daring and perseverance of a celebrated African hunter, and that his sporting accounts were very interesting, when the gentleman to whom I refer told me that he had no patience with this hunter. His words were to the following effect: " I am no sportsman, as I never fired off a gun in my life, and therefore I cannot judge of his shooting. But I have read his book, and that story about pulling out the rock snake carried such an air of untruth about the whole thing that I never wish to hear more about him." I asked why a man should not catch hold of a rock-snake if he liked, and in what was the air of untruth. " Why," he sapiently remarked, " it would have stung him to death at once." I immediately withdrew from the argument, but could not help thinking that this gentleman ought never again to be able to look a rock-snake, or any other of the boa species, in the face. The boa has many faults, but to accuse him of possessing poison, which I presume the gentleman meant when he said "sting," is really too bad. Had this snake's ghost known of the accusation that was brought against his whole species, and possessed one-half the wisdom that is attributed to the serpent, he would have risen, and hissed an angry hiss against so barefaced a libel. A man who enacts the part of a critic ought at least to know something of the subject on which he was speaking, and in this case should certainly have been aware that snakes are not rigged with a sting in their tails, like wasps, that none of the rock-snakes or boa-constrictors are poisonous, and that, as a rule, few snakes over eight or ten feet in length have the venom fangs. The want of knowledge neither prevented the Dutchman in Africa from disbelieving the existence of a building like St. Paul's, nor the Englishman in England from casting disbelief on the mode of killing a snake in Africa.

One evening I had strolled to a kloof about three miles from my friend's house, to make a sketch and shoot a guinea-fowl. I walked quietly up the kloof, and sat down amongst some thick underwood, where I could just get a peep at the mountains which I wanted to draw. I selected a good concealed situation, as my bush habits had become so much like nature that I should have considered it throwing away a chance of a shot at something if I had sat out in the open. I had succeeded in putting down the view on paper, and was finishing its details, when I heard a little tap on a tree near me; I looked up, and on the stem, some fifteen feet high, I saw the arrow of a Bushman, still quivering in the bark. I drew back quietly, and cocked my gun by the "artful dodge;" not doubting that these rascals had seen me enter the ravine, and were now trying to pink me with their arrows. I waited anxiously for some minutes, and then saw a Bushman come over the rise, and look about. I knew at once that he must be unconscious of my presence or he would never have thus shown in the open; he turned round, and seemed to be taking the line which his arrow had travelled. As he did so, I saw a rock rabbit (the *hyrax*) hanging behind him, and then knew that he was after these animals, and probably in shooting at one had sent his arrow into the tree near me.

I did not move, as my shelter was so good that even a Bushman's eye would with difficulty see me. He looked about him, and seeing his arrow in the tree, he picked up some stones, threw two or three at it and brought it down; he then walked quietly away over the ridge.

I slipped down the kloof and made the best of my way home, to give my host a caution about his cattle and my horses; as these determined robbers were most dangerous neighbours.

We were not however disturbed. At about nine o'clock in the evening we could see a fire shining from a neighbouring mountain, and we supposed that the Bushmen were having a feast of grilled hyrax for their supper. It was proposed that we should go out and attack the party, but there being no seconder to the proposition, it fell to the ground. My horses after four or five days began to look rather low in flesh; so I bid my host farewell and returned to Pietermaritzburg. On nearing the Umganie drift, I found the river swollen into a complete torrent, occasioned by some heavy showers and storms that had fallen up the country. The rivers of Africa are never to be trusted, for a traveller may pass with dry feet over the bed of a river in the morning, and on returning in the evening find a roaring torrent across his path.

Feeling indisposed for a swim, I accepted the offer of a

shake-down at the house of a Dutchman, a mile or so from the river. He was a very good sort of fellow, but given to grumble. He was in low spirits when I first saw him, as all his cattle had disappeared and he was fearful the Bushmen had carried them off. Upon discovering his loss he at once sent in to the magistrate of the Kaffirs at Pietermaritzburg, who sent a party out in search of the lost herds. The cattle were soon found, as they had only strayed some few miles, attracted by sweet grass. We were sitting at dinner, zee-koe pork (hippopotamus flesh) and tough pudding being the bill of fare; when the Dutchman suddenly jumped up, and exclaimed, "Now I will say the government is good." I looked round and saw that this remark was brought forth by his seeing all his cattle returning under the escort of the police, every head being safe and sound. The man who ought to have watched the cattle while they were grazing had fallen asleep; they walked away, the man awoke, and not seeing them, at once reported to his master that the Bushmen had carried them all off.

The river decreasing during the night, I returned to Pietermaritzburg on the next day.

CHAPTER XVII.

African moonlight—Poor Charley—Want of patience—Blue light in the Bush—Buck killed by a leopard—Strange followers—Porcupine hunt—Practical joke—Foolhardy conduct—A mistake—Kaffir prophet—A dark patriarch—Conjugal authority—Strong-headed individual—Harbour sharks—Fish spearing—Intoxicating root—A suggested experiment—Variety of fish.

THE moonlight nights in South Africa are particularly fine and brilliant; I have frequently read manuscript writing without difficulty, even when the moon has not been quite at the full. Things viewed by its light seem always to be more peaceable and mysterious than by the sunlight. Few, for example, fully appreciate the beauties of the Madeleine in Paris, who have not quietly watched its changing effect during the passage of the lesser light in her bo-peep proceedings with the clouds.

In the bush and plains the animals choose the cool night for feeding, travelling, and drinking. Many an uncouth-looking creature, whose ungainly form is rarely shown to the sun, boldly walks the night without the slightest compunctions for the feelings of the modest moon. Holes, ravines, and hollow trees then give up their inhabitants; and many an animal, who during the day dares not even breathe the atmosphere that man has passed through, gains courage and boldness in the moon's light, and cunningly plots and ably executes an attack on cattle, dogs, or fowls, under the very roof of its day-dreaded adversary. A house situated about four miles from the the Natal flat, and nearly surrounded with wood, was frequently visited by wild beasts; and on one occasion the young ladies, while "doing their back hair" and arranging their nightcaps, happened to cast their eyes above the looking-glass, and there met the impertinent gaze of a large bull-elephant, who was quietly rubbing himself against an orange-tree on the lawn, and pitching the fruit down his capacious throat as boys swallow cherries. My old dog once nearly had his days, or rather nights, terminated by the bold attack of a leopard. My dog for a change, and I also suspect from the irresistible attractions of a fascinating little spaniel named Charley, frequently staid two or three days at a time on a visit at this house; and while taking his repose, about nine o'clock one night, in a back room with his inamorata close beside him, a large leopard came with a spring into the centre of the apartment. A faint shriek from the little dog caused two of the young ladies to enter this room, the whole family being at the time in the front drawing-room. On their approach, the leopard with one bound cleared the window, carrying the dog Charley in his mouth. All entreaties and tears from the young ladies failed in producing the least effect on the feelings of this monster, who never came back; and Charley's tail, and a bit of a foot were all that ever came to light as to the fate of this ill-starred dog.

The elephants, who buried themselves in the most gloomy places during the heat of the sun, stalked about boldly, and took their pleasure during the moonlight. Night after night I rode round the skirts of the bush, moving from one of their fashionable watering places to another, and hanging about the well-worn walks with a praiseworthy perseverance. They were always too cunning for me, and either smelt my approach and dashed away before I could get a shot, or remained inside the cover and grumbled their displeasure, or trumpeted forth a challenge from a stronghold situated a couple of hundred yards within the forest. Finding that they were too wide awake to give a chance by this plan of pursuit, I selected a fine large tree, and taking my desponding friend as a volunteer, we perched ourselves amongst its branches, at about ten o'clock at night. Scarcely had half an hour of silence passed, than my partner voted it a nuisance not being able to smoke; shortly after he complained a little of cramp; and in about an hour voted the whole thing a wild-goose sort of chase, and came to the conclusion that we might as well go home. Seeing great difficulty in maintaining the perfect silence that was so necessary to success, I agreed with him, and we descended the tree.

The walk through the strip of bush, that was dark as Erebus, was anything but pleasant, from the briars and branches scratching face and hands, to say nothing of the chance of finding oneself suddenly lifted up by the trunk of some artful elephant, who might playfully put his foot upon the small of your back by way of caution. We reached our respective homes without an adventure, and on the following day I was pleased to find that the elephants had not been near our tree during the whole night, although the spoor showed that they came in great numbers exactly under it on the morning.

I always found that a Kaffir was the most patient and easily satisfied of my hunting companions. A few evenings, therefore, after my failure with my restless friend, I took Inyovu, and supplying him with a whole box full of the strongest snuff and a thick blanket, took my position once more in the spreading branches of the old tree. I made every preparation for standing a siege, in case the elephants attacked the tree, as was told me would most probably occur, but which I did not for one moment believe. To be well prepared in case of such a contingency, I had filled a small tin saucepan with blue light composition, and having sprinkled over it the tops of a box of lucifer matches to obtain quick ignition, I fixed it firmly in the branches close and handy. I purposed pouring some of this when lighted on the back of any weak-minded elephant who might presume to attempt to haul me down. Unfortunately, all the illumination was wasted on the desert air, for no elephants came to me, although I kept awake and watchful all night. My Kaffir thought me mad, a very common conclusion if one does not do every thing in the old way. Still, although my night was elephantless, I did not consider it as wasted, as the quietness around, only broken by the whispering of the leaves as they affectionately felt each other, and the occasional tiny cries of the ichneumons and other vermin, or the blowing of a buck and rustle of a herd of wild swine, were all music to an ear more easily pleased with the wild side of nature than the crash of omnibus wheels, or the murmur of crowded rooms.

BUCK KILLED BY A LEOPARD.

The monotony of this night was broken by one of those events that must, and do, frequently take place everywhere, and in many cases without the natural excuse that could be pleaded here, "it was the weak oppressed and crushed by the strong."

A red bush-buck had gone out into an open glade, and was quietly taking its dew-refreshed grass supper. I had noticed for some time the innocent way in which it had continued grazing, quite unconscious that a deadly enemy was near, who only refrained from slaying it in the hope that larger game would, by patience, be soon substituted. Suddenly a black looking sort of shadow with a bound was upon it—a shriek, an instant struggle, and all was quiet. My Kaffir whispered to me that he thought we should fire, as leopards' skins were valuable for making tails (the Kaffirs' waist-dress is thus called by the colonists). This whisper was not sufficient to cause alarm, but while moving a little to cock his gun, the Kaffir shook a branch, and the representative of the feline race, taking up his capture, bounded away. We inspected the ground on the following morning and found that there had scarcely been a struggle.

One is frequently curiously attended in Africa by strange followers, and I found myself one night with a footman behind me that might have struck terror into a lady's heart were John Thomas to be thus suddenly transformed. Happening to be at the house famous for the leopard's visit, and going out at about ten o'clock to saddle my horse that I had tied to a tree in the garden, I found him absent; and upon inquiring at the Kaffirs' kraal near, they told me that he had broken his halter and levanted for some time. This was the second trick of the kind that he had played me; on the former occasion, a friend, whose horse had behaved better, accompanied me, and we shared the saddle, turn and turn about, for the four miles that constituted the journey home. On this evening I had to trudge it alone, and what was worse, without my gun; for, having merely gone out to take tea, I had left my usual gun at home. I borrowed an assagy from the Kaffirs and trotted off. The road for great part of the way was lined with bush. A river about three feet deep had to be crossed, and then the flat sands of the Congella, famous for the battle between the Boers and the English troops.

I went on with caution, listening occasionally, as the elephants were near the edge of the bush I had passed in the afternoon, their feeding being clearly heard from the smashing of the large branches. It was not advisable to rub shoulders with these gentlemen unarmed, and in the night, if it could be avoided.

I had passed the little river Umbilo about two hundred yards, when, upon suddenly stopping to listen, I heard something behind me; so dropping to the ground, I placed my head low, and made out the shambling figure of a cowardly hyæna in relief against the sky. I flung a stone at him and he shuffled away. Soon after I heard him behind me again, and he followed at a respectable distance until I reached the village of D'Urban. These brutes, although possessing a strength of jaw capable of grinding an ox's leg-bone to powder, are still such curs as to fly before a dog; and on one occasion, near Pietermaritzburg, four of them were chased for a couple of miles by my old dog, and made such good use of their legs that I could not get near enough for a shot.

During two or three evenings we had great fun near the town of Pietermaritzburg in blocking out porcupines. I nearly ran over one on horseback one day, and narrowly escaped getting his quills in my horse's legs. They spread their quills wide, and run backwards very fast, thus presenting a *chevaux-de-frize* anything but agreeable. This one dodged about round me, now running through the grass quite fast, then stopping and backing, so that I could with difficulty keep my usually well-behaved shooting pony from actually turning tail, and in consequence fired both bullets without any satisfactory result. In a few minutes he came to his hole, a place big enough for a man to live in near the entrance, that had evidently formerly been occupied by some able excavator, probably an ant-bear. I could not get at the "fretful" in this retreat, but on arriving at home consulted with my Kaffirs, who agreed that we would get some dogs, and go out soon after the moon rose. We did so, armed with knob-kerries and assagies; and placing two sentries over the hole, we sent the dogs on the traces, having discovered that he was out for the night. We soon heard the yelping of the curs, and ran to the spot. The porcupine was coming along in a great fuss with the dogs all round him; assagies and sticks were hurled at him, while he dodged amongst the Kaffirs' naked legs, who jumped about with wonderful activity. A blow on the nose at last finished him.

At this place two gentleman attempted to play on me a very silly trick, that might have led to very serious consequences, had it not been for the greatest caution on the part of myself and another individual.

A party of five had been dining together, when, at about 10 P.M., a commissariat officer and I, who were two of the five, left the others, and mounted our horses for the purpose of riding round the edge of the Berea, on the chance of finding an elephant outside it, as I had heard several feeding in the bush as I returned from shooting in the afternoon of this day.

We were much ridiculed by two gentlemen of the party on announcing our intended proceedings, for they seemed to think no elephants were near, and that we were a couple of blockheads for troubling ourselves to go out. Not regarding these remarks, we started, and having been careful to select saddles that did not creak and curb-chains that did not jingle, we advanced with tolerable silence to the part of the forest from whence emanated the sounds that had shown me in the afternoon the presence of a troop of elephants. We halted at about two hundred yards from the tall trees that fringed this part, and listened for any indications. Our patience was not severely tried, as we heard one or two branches smashed as none but an elephant could have smashed them. We immediately took up our position a little nearer, and behind some bushes, so that we might not be seen by any elephants when they came to drink at the pools of water near. We waited for nearly half an hour, plainly hearing the troop feeding at about one hundred yards inside the bush, and apparently coming towards us. Our horses stood like rocks, merely pricking up their ears a little when a louder smash of a branch than usual was heard. It was getting rather exciting, as the elephants were blowing and grumbling very distinctly; and by their moving about a good deal they seemed meditating a march on to the open flat to drink. Suddenly they all became silent, and the finest ear could not discover a sound indicative of a large animal being near. I whispered to my companion, and asked what he thought was the cause. We were not long uncertain, for close under the bush we saw in the gloom two tall objects moving, so there was no doubt that the elephants had come out of the bush, and therefore could now walk silently. We whispered that we would fire together, and both barrels as quickly as possible one after the other. The two objects were little more than eighty yards from us, when we quietly cocked our guns, and were going to deliver our fire.

As I was straining my eyes to catch a glimpse of the glittering ivories, and thereby to judge the position of the elephant's shoulder, I fancied that the step did not appear like an elephant's. The moon was not yet up, consequently we could see but indistinctly. Somehow the thought came across me that perhaps other sportsmen had also come out to try for a shot, and I called immediately to F. "For God's sake don't fire—it is a man on horseback." He said something about "nonsense, it can't be." I called again, rather louder, for him not to fire; and as I did so a roar of laughter came from one of the supposed elephants, and " Sold, old fellow," was facetiously remarked by the other. I was very angry at being thus disturbed, and still more so when I found out the real state of the case. It seemed that, after we left the dinner-table, the first glass of brandy and water (which generally supplies the place of claret or port in Africa) had caused these two gentlemen to decide that our night-ride was ridiculous; the second had proved us two absolute donkeys; the third that we *ought* to be sold. I don't know how many, more or less, it had taken to decide the plan, which was, that they would mount their horses and ride out to where we were waiting, and discover our hiding-place *without our knowing of their approach,* and then commence imitating noises that were to make us think they were elephants! Upon my assuring these gentlemen that a large troop of elephants was really in the bush close by, they either could not or would not believe it, and easily satisfied themselves that their opinion was right; as, after listening a minute or so, and riding round a little way, they declared they only heard a crack of some sort in the bush, and had not seen a single elephant, and that the noises we said we had heard must have been caused by our imagination.

Our opinion had been formed from half an hour's careful listening, *theirs* from two minutes noisy looking round. Is there any self-sufficiency in this sort of conclusions I wonder? I may here relate a ridiculous mistake that I made, and a narrow escape of Kaffir slaughter, both caused by my eagerness for a fine specimen of the black bush-buck.

I have before mentioned one or two little open patches on the top of the Berea. I was riding over these one afternoon, looking for fresh elephant spoor, when I saw, about two hundred yards distant, a black object just visible in the long grass, and there was no doubt in my mind that it was a black bush-buck. I dropped off my horse, and stalked with the greatest care to within about eighty yards of it; I suddenly raised my head to get a peep, and saw only a black back, and recognised a little movement in the tail, which was very buck-like. The object was partly hidden by bushes and grass; the spot was most retired.

I guessed where the shoulders would be, and sent my bullet at them into the long grass; the animal fell over backwards, and I rushed to the spot to discover an old goat, shot directly through the heart. At the same time a little Kaffir sprang up close to the corpse, in a great fright. He informed me that this was the pet ram of an old Kaffir who lived nearly two miles distant; that the grass having been burnt near his kraal, he had sent his boy with the pet to graze on this spot, where the grass was very good. It cost me three shillings to pacify the old fellow, and an extra fee to secure his silence, as the story would not have told well for me. This accident I believe saved a Kaffir's life from being sacrificed to a similar mistake; for I again took for a buck a black object in a most retired part of the forest. I was about firing when I remembered the goat mistake, and approached a little closer to have a better look. I was prepared in case of the buck bounding off, when I gave a little whistle to alarm it, and enable me to have a full view. The object moved when I whistled, and rising to nearly six feet in height, showed itself to me as an old Kaffir man. I was truly thankful that I had not put a bullet into his head. Upon chatting with him, he told me that he was residing two or three days in the bush, previous to his giving a prophecy on some important affair in his kraal. He certainly was no true Kaffir, if he could not tell a thumping lie, after three days getting it up, in the solitude of the bush.

Returning one afternoon from shooting, I saw a party of Kaffirs sitting round my tent, and upon riding up I was informed by one of my dark servants that a chief had come in from the Umzriububu district, to transact some business, and being his particular chief he had asked him to stay and have a talk with me. I was much flattered by this mark of approbation, and at once asked M'untu Umculu into my tent, where we squatted down and took pinch after pinch of strong snuff, until my guest's shining hide became indistinct and shadowy through the tears that forced themselves from the inmost recesses of my eyes.

We said not a word, but the long-drawn sighs that now and then with bellows-like expression emanated from M'untu, gave earnest of his unqualified delight and pure uninterrupted enjoyment.

After half an hour of unsneezing silence, I managed to stutter out, *Chela pela's indaba incosi* (tell me the news, chief), to which M'untu politely replied that "the news should come from me." We had some pleasant and instructive conversation, during which I discovered that the six ladies who were sitting round outside were M'untu's wives, the three men were his servants, and one old fellow, with a very high ring on his head, was his familiar councillor. I ordered an ox's head for their lunch, and expressed a wish that I should see my worthy visitor during the course of the evening. About eight o'clock he came to me in the mud hovel that served as mess-room, and accepted my offer of a seat. He appeared with his retinue of wives, &c. It is strange what different customs exist in different lands. While the princesses of Oude allow not even their beautiful eyes to be seen, the princesses of Kaffirland consider statuesque absence of drapery fashionable. Civilisation prefers the half-way-between-the-two style which many of our ball-room belles now practise. M'untu Umculu appeared wonderfully at his ease, and offered me his snuff-box with the solemnity of a judge. He was decidedly an oracle in his own circle, and although apparently not more than twenty, seemed to have inspired each and every one of his six wives with an awe and a reverence for his word and look, that might give an excellent example to many a man who has only one sixth of his difficulties.

Having on the table a stone bottle of gin, containing about two gallons, I poured out a tumbler-full and offered it to my visitor; he took a little sip, another, then a big draught, and then with one gulp, down it all went. I watched him attentively, but he never even winked his eye. I waited for a short time to watch progress, but M'untu's thirsty nature impelled him to push his tumbler over to me again. I cautioned the Kaffir chief that the spirit which he wished to drink was very powerful, and if he repeated his potation it would probably make him drunk. He, however, still begged for a fresh tumbler full, and finding that he would take no denial, I complied with his request, as I considered that a bad headache in the morning would be a good excuse for me to give a lecture to my tippling guest. I therefore refilled his glass,—in one minute it was bottom upwards, the contents having gone down his throat with a plaintive gurgle—no wink this time either. For quantity and time I could have laid odds on M'untu against any sot of St. Giles's.

I now saw my solemn friend's countenance begin to light up, his tongue's dignity relaxed, and he commenced talking. His wealth and his performances were the theme. The third tumbler brought out the warmth of the savage's heart. Calling each of his wives by name, he made them drop on all fours and crawl up to him; retaining the tumbler in his own hands for security, he placed it to their lips, jerked a little up their noses, and sent them away still crawling and facing him. Oh! what a refreshing exhibition of domestic obedience! Suddenly, with the tone of an emperor, he ordered one of his servants to bring some sugar-cane and honey, both of which he by a wave of his arm indicated were for me and my heirs for ever. A fourth tumbler caused a continuous and indistinct utterance of unconnected sentences in a loud voice, whilst a graceful and unceasing rolling motion pervaded his body. His councillor had tried to stop this jovial proceeding at the third tumbler, but had received a backhander from M'untu that had certainly checked any further interference; the rolling of his body had increased rapidly during the fourth tumbler, and it had scarcely been emptied before M'untu Umculu, chair and tumbler, came with a crash to the ground.

The councillor, who had wisely ordered the wives away as soon as he saw what was going on, now came in, and with the aid of three Kaffirs lifted M'untu up and bore him away, not without considerable opposition, however, as he still held out his broken glass; and its splintered remains were the last thing that disappeared from the door, entreatingly held towards me at arm's length. I soon after sent for the councillor and requested him to remind M'untu Umculu in the morning of the ridiculous exhibition he had made, and to state, that, although my hospitality obliged me to give him what he had requested, I still did not think so highly of him as I had done previously, and warned him against all strong drinks as his greatest enemies. On the following morning, just as the sun was rising, I heard some talking outside my tent, and upon opening the canvass door, saw my drunken guest of last night, sitting down coolly outside. Immediately he saw me he held out his hand and thanked me in a most gentlemanly manner for my kind entertainment of the night before. I asked him if his head ached, but he complained of nothing, and certainly appeared quite right, with the exception of a slight redness about the eyes. What would some of my readers give for a cranium of this strength? Perhaps this child of nature's head did not yet know how to ache. I accepted an invitation to go and hunt in the district that acknowledged M'untu's rule, and with the "united kind regards" of the suite they trudged off; M'untu in the most delicate way having left a gourd snuff-box with my Kaffir, to be presented to me when he was out of sight. I heard that game was plentiful near the kraal of this Kaffir, and shortly after, while the friendship was warm, went down the coast to see him. We had very fair sport with buck and buffalo.

The shooting amusement at Natal could be changed sometimes, as the fishing in the bay was excellent. With a boat anchored in the channel a large number of fish of different kinds were often caught—rock-cod in great numbers especially, and a fish there called a kiel-back, very like a cod in appearance, and weighing generally twenty-five or thirty pounds. Sharks are frequently seen in the bay, and on the bar at the entrance they swarm, presenting anything but an agreeable prospect, in case of an upset in the surf-boat. I have heard that on the outside of the harbour they have frequently taken men down, while inside they are considered harmless. Why they should thus change their dispositions in so short a distance it is difficult to say, but that they do not make a habit of attacking bathers in the bay I am certain, as I was in the water morning and evening, and frequently swam out a considerable distance from the shore—thus offering a good bite to a shark. I believe the reason to be, that inside the bay there are enormous shoals of small fish, so that a shark could feast for months on them and scarcely show that he had diminished their numbers. He does not, therefore, suffer from an unsatisfied appetite so much as his unfortunate brethren, who may not have such comfortable snug quarters, or be able to find their way to them when pressed by hunger.

I never tried a fly in the bay, but am convinced it would be taken very well. There is a fish called a "springer" that makes tremendous leaps out of the water after insects, and would give capital sport. These fish are very cunning and not to be caught like common fish with a simple hook and line; they will come up and look at the bait, swim round it in all directions, but will not even nibble. If you throw a piece of the same substance as your bait overboard, twenty of them make a rush at once to seize it, then have a sniff at your hooked bit, give a kind of chaffing whisk of their tails, and then sail away. These fellows made me very angry; I tried the thinnest lines, but it was no go, the water being so clear; but at last I devised a plan for circumventing them. Having by great practice acquired the art of throwing the assagy, I procured one that had a small barbed end, that the Kaffirs used for fish. I put a piece of lead round the part where the iron joined the wood, and made a piece of string fast to the spear, harpoon fashion. Getting the boat into that part of the bay frequented by these artful fish, I made all ready for a lunge, and told the Kaffir to throw out some little chopped pieces of meat. A dozen springers rose after them at once, close to the boat, and not more than a few feet under water. Allowing for the refraction of the water, the spear was thrown down with great force; it disappeared, but soon came up again near the top of the water, the end violently agitated. A gentle, but steady haul on the line, brought a struggling springer to the boatside, where my Kaffir, slipping his hand in his gills, landed him.

I rarely succeeded in getting more than one at a time by this plan, for the alarm soon spread, and I had then to wait for a day or two for them to forget what had happened, or go to some other part of the bay where they were not up to the dodge.

A root grew on the Natal flat with which I frequently captured fish; it had the effect of fuddling them, and made them jump out of the water, if used in a confined space. It was something like ground-ivy in growth, the long fibres stretching for several feet round; the leaves were small and shaped like clover. The root was discovered by taking hold of one of these creepers and pulling it up until it led to the root, which was then dug up. The root was about a foot long, and half an inch in diameter. When a dozen or so had been collected, they were bruised and fastened on to a long bamboo. The large pools of water left by the high tides on the bluff amongst the rocks, were the scenes of operations, into these the root was inserted, and then stirred round for some time. In less than a minute small and large fish would dart out from the holes in the rocks, and swim about the pool as though greatly perplexed, and would very soon after turn on their backs and float, when they could be taken with the hand. Sometimes with a duck and drake sort of progression they skipped along over the top of the pool and sought the dry land. If they were placed in water that was uncontaminated by this root, they would recover in a few minutes, and might be eaten without the slightest danger. This root was called by the Kaffirs "*Il, o zarni.*" I do not know if botanists are acquainted with it in any way.

The Kaffirs here made large enclosures of bamboo or stakes, driven so close together that no fish could escape, but the water could make its way through. The tops of these dams were covered about two feet deep at high water; and as the rise and fall of the tide were here about four feet, the stakes here were above the water when it went down. Mullet, and many other fish that kept near the surface, amused themselves in these enclosures until too late to escape, when they fell easy victims to the assagies of the Kaffir, who paid his traps daily visits at low water. I think a man might make a capital living by starting at Natal as a fisherman on a large scale, and sending his fish during the cool nights by pack-horses to Pietermaritzburg, where it is almost an unknown luxury. The Kaffirs take some fine fish by spearing. When the tide is half out, there is a long level sand on the left of the bay, with about three feet of water on it. The Kaffirs form themselves into a half-moon shaped line, each with two or three barbed assagies; they keep about ten yards apart and walk slowly along. Should a fish of any size be seen a signal is given, and the outsiders rush round so as to enclose the victim, the others showering their spears at him. He seldom escapes them, as these fellows make capital shots at forty yards. I often bought a heavy cargo of fish from these fishermen, as much as I could carry, for sixpence, or, what they much prefer, a couple of sticks of tobacco.

x

There is a great excitement in the sea-fishing, a title that may be given to the sport in this bay, for one never knows what is coming up when there is a bite—fish of the most ridiculous shapes, and beautiful colours, and all sizes,—now a small rock-cod, then a large parrot-fish; again a tremendous tug at your thick line, and away it flies, with no chance of holding or staying it—some monster has carried off everything. A gallant friend of mine, who was not very careful in the arrangement of his tackle, was near meeting with an accident here. A bite and tug, such as I have mentioned, pulled the line out of his hand, and it flew over the side at the rate of twenty miles an hour. I saw that he had a coil of the line round his body, and had just time, by snatching up a knife, to cut the line, when the whole piece was carried overboard. It must have been a ground-shark or some such monster. My friend would in another instant have been dragged overboard or cut in two, as the line was nearly as thick as my finger, therefore too strong to break before it would have seriously damaged him.

Shoals of porpoises frequently played about in the surf, close to the shore, and good bullet practice might be had at them.

CHAPTER XVIII.

Steeple-chase at D'Urban—The last day's sport—The bar at Natal—Reach Table Bay—Impertinent "pike"-keeper—Chased by a policeman—Dishonest auctioneer—St. Helena—Turtle-catching—Waterspouts—Cintra—Lisbon—Best weapons for the bush—Extra gun-stocks necessary—Recommendation to "used-up" individuals.

A SHORT time before I left D'Urban we had some races on the flat. The horses were not quite equal to those seen at Newmarket; but still, where time is not much noted by the watch, a good race is a good race, although the mile may take more than two minutes in running.

The first race of the day was a mile, over four flights of hurdles, catch weight, any riders. Any riders they were too—as, at the first hurdle, only two out of six got over safely; two jockeys were sent clean out of their saddles, one horse came down on his head, and another refused. Before coming to the second flight, one of the two fortunate horses swerved and missed his fence, but his jock, still keeping on, took the remaining two, and won easily; the race was, however, given against him on account of the slip. All other horses being distanced, the one horse that had fairly gone the course, should, after a walk over, have taken the stakes; but a very powerful-looking jock on a distanced horse, insinuating that he would break any one's head who said he was distanced, seemed to have some influence on the judge, who decided that this man's horse was to be allowed to start in the second heat.

The second heat was therefore merely a match, and the strong-armed man won; he shied his hat in the air and sent his horse home without walking over for the third heat. The owner of the other horse then claimed the stakes, and a regular row seemed the most likely result. I left the course before matters were decided, so do not know what decision this jockey club came to on the knotty question. I should here mention that all the disputing parties, as well as the riders, were English.

I must say that I left the district of Natal with regret, or rather I should say, its sports, climate, and free life. My last day's sport was good, for three bucks were shot, two of them being of the little blue buck species that I have before mentioned. I rode round my old haunts to bid them farewell, and also to look the last on several of my black sporting companions. The Kaffirs were all sorry to hear of my purposed departure, and wished to know where I was going and when I would return. Many of them were much puzzled when they tried to think how people found the road on the sea. They would say, "there were no trails or trees to mark the journey, and the waves were alway saltering their shapes." It was difficult to explain to these unmathematical minds the mysteries of "sights," latitude and longitude, or the use of logarithms. I managed to make them comprehend that by the stars and sun we understood our position; they could not quite make out the system, and seemed to think that there must be *Takata* (witchcraft) about it.

I wondered, as I left these poor black heathens, whether

I should ever again meet in civilized hands as much honesty, truth, and disinterested friendship amongst the uncultivated and ignorant; or whether I should again live for two years amongst a nation, who, although nearly ignorant of Christianity, and the direction towards the right that is given by a knowledge of its simple beauties, still possessed many of those good qualities that are rarely met in the most vaunted Christian countries. I embarked at Natal Bay in a little brigantine; an esteemed brother sportsman being also a passenger. A sulky impudent Dutchman, with his wife and a child, were also sharers of the tiny cabin.

The bar at Natal is not disposed to be always favourable for ingress and egress. Sometimes nine and ten feet of water were found on it, and the next day but seven. So it happened when we were leaving; for on the day before our attempted departure, we were told there were quite nine feet, but on our getting near it we struck. Fortunately there was but a little swell on, but still the ship bumped very heavily, and seemed to bend under us like a wickerwork basket. The Dutchman, who was on deck, looked very white; he dived down below, and soon returned buttoning up his pockets. He looked at us and the skipper, then at the shore, distant about 200 yards, with an intermediate glance of horror at two or three large dorsal fins that were sticking up out of the water, indicative of ten feet long sharks which would not have objected to our attempting a swim. By the aid of the port-boat sent out a-head we managed to get pulled off the bar, and got through another passage, only just then known or practised, which ran for some distance along the coast, and turned out into the ocean beyond.

We soon had a S.E. breeze, set our studding sails, and in seven days dropped our anchor in Table Bay; having completed the voyage in less than one-third of the time that it had taken me to do half the distance on the occasion of my upward journey.

My first experiences of what is called civilization were anything but agreeable. During my stay at Cape Town, while waiting the arrival of a ship to convey me to England, I frequently rode out in the country about Winberg and Rondebosh, and had to pass a turnpike on the road, kept by a goodnatured old man who responded to the name of Peter. We used to give this old fellow a shilling or two, and let him keep the account of the number of times we rode through. He never lost by this arrangement, as I frequently gave him half-a-crown, which would have allowed me to pass nearly twenty times. It so happened, either from thoughtlessness or from having been spoilt by the wilds of Natal, where a stick of tobacco is wealth enough for a long journey, that I rode out one day without any money in my pocket. I discovered its absence when about a couple of miles from home; but knowing that I had a good balance to my credit at the turnpike, I did not trouble myself to return. Cantering on, I passed the gate without a thought, calling out as I went through, "All right, Peter!" and stooping down to show him who I was. I did not see Peter inside, but observed a stranger man come out as I was passing. I paid several *p. p. c.* visits in the country, and returned towards Cape Town. Upon approaching the pike, I saw two men, as though watching me, standing each side of the gate. I, however, rode on, quite unconscious of the storm hanging over my head. Since my last ride through this pike, Peter had been turned out of his place, and a bankrupt butcher installed in office; of this change, however, I was ignorant at the time. As I was passing through the gate, one of the men rushed at me, caught the bridle of my horse, and said, " Come, pay the fare; you ain't going to bilk me a second time!" I asked what he meant, telling him that the pikeman owed me at least a shilling. To this he responded, "You're a blackguard cheat, and I'll pull you off your horse." Suiting the action to the word, he caught hold of my leg and tried to unseat me. I have ever given myself great credit for not having dropped my heavy handled whip on this rascal's head at the time. The man who was standing by said, "No don't strike the gentleman." During the scene, a person, whom I had met but a day or two before at a private house, and who happened to be a man in authority over the police, came out from a building at the back of the turnpike. I told him the case, and that unfortunately I had no money to pay the penny, or twopence, turnpike. With the pomposity of office he pretended not to recognize me, but merely asserted as an axiom, that no one was allowed to ride through turnpikes without paying the fare. The man who had hold of my bridle seemed to consider the sentence as a verdict in his favour, and told me to "pay up without any more humbug." The horse that I was riding happened to be a thoroughbred three year old, lent me by a friend, who had requested me to ride him on the snaffle as he possessed a very tender mouth—a great rarity in Cape horses. I was trying to explain that I would leave my name or my whip, or anything as a pledge for the penny, when the man loudly and angrily repeated his demand for the money, at the same time chucking the horse's mouth with the sharp curb. To this the noble animal strongly objected, and turning round reared straight up. Now had this been my own horse I doubt if I could have borne it quietly, but as it was the property of a friend, such a proceeding was unbearable. The ex-butcher was about repeating his jerk, in the hopes, I have no doubt, of unseating me, when I struck him a blow on the wrist with the loaded end of my whip, that caused him at once to let go of the bridle. I gave the young one a squeeze, who, finding his head free, bounded clear of the attempt to stop him made by the second party. I was so enraged at the whole proceeding, and at having been placed in a false position by the absence of my purse, that I went on for a couple of hundred yards before I recovered my equanimity. I then found that I was riding away from home, and the only other road, which was a long way round, had also a turnpike at which I was not known. Turning my horse into the open furze ground at the side of the road, I made a sweep round across country, and was quietly making my way home, when I saw a policeman on a horse coming after me. Knowing that any attempt to argue the merits of the case would have been useless, I was even obliged to fly. I gave a shake of the reins, and the thoroughbred soon strode away from the blue-coated gentleman, and landed me safe in the castle at Cape Town. The oracular official, however, knew me perfectly well, and had it not happened that the good ship came on the very next day, and carried me out of Table Bay, I have no doubt that I should have seen my name figuring in the Cape Town paper under the head of "Police," and that the crime would have been designated as, "Brutal Assault on a Turnpike-keeper, and disgraceful Attempt at Swindling, by a British Officer."

My other experience was a loss of money only; but still, when one is leaving a colony, and laying in a stock of provisions for a voyage, that commodity becomes singularly useful. I had two guns that, although in good order, I thought would be a drug in England, and therefore asked an auctioneer, to whom I had been introduced, how to turn them into cash. He said they would fetch a good price on the parade at auction, and he would sell them for me, recommending that they should go without reserve. I was hurried in packing up, &c., before leaving, so gave directions to my servant to take the two guns to the auctioneer, and wait for the money. He asked what price I would take, but, relying upon the auctioneer's statement, I named no sum as a reserve. I thought that if I obtained anything like £15 or £20, it would do—one gun originally costing thirty-five guineas, and the other I had bought from a Dutchman, giving a horse and a five pound note in exchange. Upon my servant coming back, I saw that he looked rather queer, and was soon made acquainted with the cause. My two guns, after paying the fees, *realized thirty-six rix dollars, or about two pounds fifteen shillings of English money.* There was no help for it now; but what added to my annoyance was seeing a man carrying my worst gun some hours afterwards, and upon asking him how he liked it, &c., found that he had given ten pounds for it to the very auctioneer who had sold (*alias* bought) it.

There are many men to be found in England who may pride themselves on knowing a thing or two. Let them go to South Africa, and they will find they are perfect babes. I mean not thus to vilify the whole body of the worthy Capeites, but merely their *mauvais sujets*. It is my belief that a thorough Cape "schelm" would give at least two points in the rubber of roguery and beat the best English swindler living. The performances of many individuals in England during the last two years have reduced the odds greatly; and, if we progress as satisfactorily, we may expect shortly to have a very close and interesting match for excellence in this particular.

On leaving Table Bay we had very fine sailing weather, and bowled down to St. Helena in capital style. We stopped two days at this emperor's prison, and had an opportunity of seeing Longwood and the country round. In the island some very pretty green valleys were to be seen, although the coast near the town of St. James was high and rocky. We saw several sharks in the transparent water near, and shoals of small mackerel. It did not give me the idea of a very delightful residence, at least for any lengthened period, unless one happened to have a vast amount of resources within oneself. I thought it was about the last place I would choose in which to settle; but soon had occasion to change my mind, as a view and slight inspection of the island of Ascension made me regard St. Helena as a perfect paradise in comparison.

Ascension might well be compared to a Brobdignag coal-fire suddenly put out. All is black, or reddish brown; only one spot of green is seen on the island, and this is distinguished as the Green Mountain. On walking inland, large bits of rock, that apparently weigh 100 lbs., may be kicked along like footballs; they are really but like cinders. The curiosities of the island are gannet and wide-awake fairs, so called from the enormous swarms of these two birds—a species of gull that there build and reside. The whole ground is covered with the eggs and guano of these birds, while they themselves fly around the heads of the visitor in thousands, uttering threatening cries. I found the wide-awakes anything but correctly named, as I knocked over two or three with my stick, and could have done so to many more had I wished. The great thing at Ascension is turtle; swarms are there found, and the commonest sailor has more than he can eat. Two large ponds, of about 100 feet square, are crammed with the fish, lying two and three deep; the turtle are regularly fed and looked after, ships being supplied with them when required. There are two or three look-out stations in the island, where men watch for the turtle to crawl on shore. Immediately that one is seen, a party is sent out who turn the unwieldy gentleman on his back, where he reposes, flapping his finny legs about until a cart takes him to the prison pond. We had about a dozen sent on board, and in a week were surfeited with turtle-soup, turtle-steaks, turtle-curry, and turtles' eggs; a plain bit of salt junk was for a change quite a treat. As we passed the line, I witnessed a strange collection of water-spouts that were gathered on the horizon near sunset; there were about seven of them nearly close together and moving with different velocities; they had the appearance of columns supporting the dark clouds of heaven. Sometimes they would seem to disperse, and then again, gathering solidity, stalk about like ocean genii.

Our voyage was unmarked by sport. We had a strange death occur on board from chloroform—a man who had a disease of the lungs wishing to have his damaged finger taken off during the influence of chloroform. His wish was complied with, and death resulted. We were expecting to run into the channel and make a very rapid voyage, but were unfortunately met by a strong easterly wind that kept us beating about for a fortnight. Having 500 people on board and but a small supply of water, our position became rather critical; for we were reduced from a quart to a pint of water per man, and having no wine or beer to drink, were in doubt what would come next. Several of the women and children suffered severely from thirst, whilst the able-bodied men had to look at the salt provisions with a hungry forbearance, salt beef, tongues, &c., not being very thirst-quenching articles. I used to sit for a long time with my feet in a tub of sea-water, and fancied that I was not so thirsty in consequence. We tried to run for any port for succour, but upon attempting Vigo, were checked by a two days' calm. A light breeze at length wafted us into the Tagus, and two hours afterwards we dropped anchor opposite Lisbon. I was very shortly up to my neck in a delicious cold bath of the purest fresh water, in one of the most comfortable rooms of the Braganza Hotel, when the buxom Mrs. Dyson sent to know whether I would like the champagne iced for dinner. This was rolling in riches of luxury, after nearly starving of privation, and dying from thirst.

We stayed several days at Lisbon, to enable the ship to be set to rights, and us to get fresh provisions; during the delay I visited Cintra, but I was not as much impressed with its glories and grandeur as Byron seems to have been. This I have no doubt arose from having just left Africa, where parts of the scenery are very similar (with the exception that monasteries are there unknown), only on a much larger scale. Cintra, therefore, looked to my eyes like a pocket edition or model of what I had been accustomed to for nearly three years. I was much struck with the beauty of many of the churches in Lisbon, and also interested with the schools at Belem. It struck me however as cruel, that in one large room, filled with boys, a window looked out into an orange-grove where the ripe fruit hung in clusters within six feet of the glass, against which the boys might flatten their noses in hungry imagination but could not approach nearer to the tempting mouthful; the same style of thing may however be frequently seen near a pastrycook's shop in London.

The opera was amusing—it was "Macbeth," and the Portuguese were not quite "up" in Highland costume.

I was shown over the arsenal by an officer who spoke English; it had very little in it. Feeling, however, that I ought to offer some compliment on its appearance, I remarked "that it was very clean." He said, "Yes; clean of every thing!"

The experimental squadron came into the Tagus while we were there, and caused great consternation in Lisbon by anchoring opposite Black Horse-square instead of lower down the river, thus committing some breach of etiquette or breaking a rule. I was sorry to leave Lisbon, for it was a nice place with a very fine climate, which after all is more than half the battle in this life. One is obliged to seek artificial amusements when every other day is wet, where a few hours of daylight are not regularly supplied, but frequently become mere black, foggy sort of things that are neither days nor nights. If we do get a little fine weather in England we are miserable from knowing that it will not last long, and any change must be for the worse. I am no grumbler, but I do like to see the sun at least 300 days out of the 365. I am fond of green trees, green fields, and even green men. I like to have room to move my elbows without digging them into somebody else's ribs, and I like to be able to open my mouth and shout and have no hearers, instead of having an army jump down one's throat if one merely opens his lips. It is a great comfort to be in a barbarous land where you shake hands with every man you meet (not often troubled by the bye), and can ask this man, black or white, to do you a favour, and meet kindness from him, and probably receive an invitation to shoot or dine with him. It is better than residing in civilized countries, where your most intimate friend will only sometimes know you, near corners, because, perhaps, you don't wear peg-top breeches or Noah's ark coats. I know I am wrong in thinking so; but it all results from having lived with savages.

In the sketches I have written, and the different sporting events that I have recorded, I have endeavoured to give to a novice some information that may be useful to him when he commences his career of sport in South Africa. It has always appeared to me that there was more detail required by people generally than is found in many of the high sporting works already written on South Africa. To fill in this detail has been my endeavour.

I must impress upon all those who purpose a campaign against the *feræ* of Africa the necessity there is for using weapons of a large calibre; a gun with the common sixteen or fourteen bore is a disheartening weapon when used against large game.

It is difficult to say what causes instantaneous death— whether the hole that the bullet makes and the vessels it cuts in its course, or the shock that is given to the stricken animal by its momentum. I am disposed to think it is as much the latter cause as the former, having so frequently witnessed cases in which an ounce-ball striking an animal has merely served to increase its pace, while a two-ounce bullet striking in the same part a similar animal would drop it dead. With elephants the size of the bullet is even more essential—the small ones as Gordon Cumming describes it, "merely telling on their constitutions." It is almost useless to recommend a particular sort of gun, as people generally choose for themselves after all. Were I again to visit Africa, I would take a double-barrelled smooth bore of ten or eight to the pound, having strength and plain good workmanship as its only recommendations. A double-barrelled rifle of about the same calibre would be useful, taking care to have two stocks for each gun, and that the barrels could fit into either stock. I have more than once suffered from smashed stocks, and they are not easily replaced in Africa. A Colt's revolver would also be a very useful weapon, especially when used in the saddle against elands. It might be fired when going at speed, and with greater accuracy than could be attained, under similar conditions, by an ordinary gun.

When I speak of the game in the immediate vicinity of the two towns of D'Urban and Pietermaritzburg, I refer to 1849 and '50, but I am given to understand that there has not been very much decrease since that time. The emigrant has other work to accomplish, and cannot be always shooting. A great deal of hard work must also be gone through before success in sport is certain, and sportsmen therefore are more scarce than would be at first considered probable. During the first three months that I tried my hand at buck shooting, I shot only five. After twelve months' experience, my bag, during ten weeks, was forty-seven; and I had refused several certain shots at antelopes during that time, as I was on the fresh spoor of buffaloes and elephants, and did not wish to disturb the bush.

Far in the interior the game is unlimited in quantity, and the numbers are quite correctly spoken of by Harris, Cumming, and other sportsmen. Any one anxious for pure slaughter may there indulge his fancy to any extent; but I think that the amount of slain is no criterion of the amount of sport.

The sports of Africa are excellent as remedies against attacks of ennui. Should any gentleman feel that he has finished everything in Europe, and is disposed for sport and excitement, let him at once give up white kids and patents, and take to skin shoes and leather breeches; lay out a couple of hundreds in rifles, saddles, and powder, and start for the wilds of South Africa. Thirty days to Australia is now talked about, therefore twenty to the Cape ought to be work easy enough. That man must be composed of strange stuff who does not find a new pleasure in stalking through tropical forests, well stocked with elephants and other large game; or in riding over plains sprinkled with thousands of magnificent antelopes; in dodging the charge of an angry rhinoceros; or escaping the rush of a troop of elephants.

There will be the excitement of midnight hazard, for ivory is plentiful in Africa, although only in the rough at present, while lions' teeth may be looked upon as the "bones," and are nearly as fatal. And if the traveller is not wide awake, the lion will carry off the stakes to a certainty.

A man who has passed through an African shooting campaign, will find that his health is improved; that he is better able to help himself, has a greater trust in his natural gifts, and that trifles cease to annoy him. He will return to England without having lost much of his taste for his native sports. He will enter fully into a five-and-thirty minutes' run across a country at a pace that weeds the mob, or will take his quiet station near the rippling trout-stream, with just the same gusto as before his South-African tour.

My parting advice to all sportsmen is—" Try a shooting trip for a year in the bush, and on the plains of South Africa, the true fairy-land of sport."

ADDENDA.

The Kaffir words given below may be useful to enable some visitor to South Africa to make known to the Kaffirs a few of his wants.

I will not vouch for the correctness of the grammar of which I have made use, but the Kaffirs will understand what may be required from even these sentences.

Each word ought to be pronounced as it is written, the last syllable but one being always rested on longer than the others. The *a, e,* and *i,* are pronounced as in French. The plural is in general formed by prefixing *ama,* and dropping in some cases the first syllable; as, *indoda,* a man; *amadoda,* men; *ihashi,* a horse; *amahashi,* horses. The numerals are more easily explained by holding up the fingers,—*shumi* being ten; *amashumi,* tens. Thirty would be explained as tens, three, *amashumi m'tatu,* or by opening and shutting the hands three times.

The click which is used by the Kaffirs need not be attempted by the beginner in the language,—there are so very few words which require the click, and these few are quite easily understood without it. The ambitious linguist frequently renders himself quite unintelligible to a Kaffir, in consequence of clicking with every word, whether this click is required or not. It is far better to pronounce distinctly the simple word, than to attempt to adorn it by a performance which, as I have before remarked, cannot be perfectly accomplished until the individual has lost nearly all his teeth.

To any person who may wish to advance in the Kaffir language I submit a conjugated verb as a model; but I generally found that *ile*, placed at the end of the infinitive mood, was quite understood by the Kaffirs for the past tense: as, *uku hamba*, to go; *hambile*, gone; *tanda*, to love; *tandile*, have loved, &c.

UKUPOZA, TO DRINK.

PRESENT.

Singular.
1. Diapoza, I drink.
2. Uapoza, thou drinkest.
3. Eapoza, he drinks.

Plural.
1. Siapoza, we drink.
2. Neapoza, ye drink.
3. Paiapoza, they drink.

IMPERFECT.

Singular.
1. Dibendipoza, I drank.
2. Ubenupoza, thou drankest.
3. Ebenepoza, he drank.

Plural.
1. Sibesipoza, we drank.
2. Nebenepoza, ye drank.
3. Pebepepoza, they drank.

PERFECT.

Singular.
1. Dabandapoza, I have drunk.
2. Uabauapoza, thou hast drunk.
3. Eabaeapoza, he has drunk.

Plural.
1. Sabesapoza, we have drunk.
2. Nabenapoza, ye have drunk.
3. Pabepapoza, they have drunk.

PLUPERFECT.

Singular.
1. Dikandapoza, I had drunk.
2. Ukauapoza, thou hadst drunk.
3. Ekeapoza, he had drunk.

Plural.
1. Sikasapoza, we had drunk.
2. Nekanapoza, ye had drunk.
3. Pakapapoza, they had drunk.

ADDENDA.

FUTURE.

Singular.
1. Dopoza, I shall drink.
2. Uopoza, thou shalt drink.
3. Eopoza, he shall drink.

Plural.
1. Sopoza, we shall drink.
2. Nopoza, ye shall drink.
3. Popoza, they shall drink.

POTENTIAL.

Singular.
1. Dingapoza, I may, can, or might drink.
2. Ungapoza, thou, &c.
3. Engapoza, he, &c.

Plural.
1. Singapoza, we may, can, or might drink.
2. Nangapoza, ye may, &c.
3. Pangapoza, they may, &c.

IMPERATIVE.

Singular.
1. Mandipoza, let me drink.
2. Mäupoza, do thou drink.
3. Mäepoza, let him drink.

Plural.
1. Masipoza, let us drink.
2. Manipoza, do ye drink.
3. Mabipoza, let them drink.

Dipozana, do I drink?
Eapozana, does he drink?
&c. &c.
Andipoza, I drink not.

Akupoza, thou drinkest not.
Asipoza, we drink not.
Nosipoza, ye drink not.
Pakapoza, they drink not.

PERFECT NEGATIVE.

Andipozanga, I have not drunk.

A verb receives a prefix corresponding with the first letter or syllable of its nominative; as, *Poza*, to drink; *Inja ipoza*, the dog drinks.

The adjectives and adverbs undergo the same variations, partaking of the prefixes of the substantives with which they may be conjoined; the nouns form diminutives, thus:—

Indoda, a man.
Indodana, a little man.

Intombi, a maid.
Intombazana, a little girl.

Inkosi, a chief.
Inkosana, a young chief, or a little chief.
Di, I.
Wena, you.
Yena, he.
Tina, we.
Zona, they.
Carbo or Hi, no.
Er wer or Yar bo, yes.
Saca bona, a salutation (Good morning).
Hambani gathly or Solaguthly, Good bye.
Uya pina? Where are you going?
Ou vel àpi? Where have you come from?
Uku nika, to give.
Uku hamba, to go.
Uku yenza, to do.
Uku zapa, to come.
Uku biza, to call.
Uku pòza, to drink.
Uku ziza, to bring.
Uku ejla, to eat.
Uku funa, to want.
Uku bona, to see.
Uku èswa, to hear.
Uku tànda, to like.
Uku sika, to cut.
Uku hlànza, to clean.
Uku landèla, to follow.
Uku tènga, to buy.
Uku zingèla, to hunt.
Uku sebènza, to work.
Uku kulùma, to talk.
Uku quela, to ride.
Indòda, a man.
Umfazi, a woman.
Injlu, a house.

Amànzi, water.
Umlilo, fire.
Mùti, a tree, or medicine.
Injlòvu, an elephant.
Imvùbu, a hippopotamus.
Inyàti or Inthùmba, a buffalo.
Impòphu, an eland.
Umsiki, a reitbok.
Impenzi, a duiker.
Ihàshi, a horse.
Inja, a dog.
Imfena, a bahoon.
Inkau, a monkey.
Ingwenie, an alligator.
Inklànzi, a fish.
Inyoni, a bird.
Inyamazàn, small game or bucks.
Lenjlela, a road or path.
Namhla, to-day.
Izòlo, yesterday.
Goomso, to-morrow.
Goomso futi, to-morrow again, the day after to-morrow.
Futi, again.
Izolo futi, the day before yesterday.
Umlungo, a white man.
Isibum, a gun.
Umcizi, powder.
Inyozi, honey.
N'wela, a waggon.
Umculu, great.
N'càni, little.
Cachema, fast.
Gathly, slow.
Ublsi, sweet milk.
Amàsi, sour milk.
Bulala, to wound or shoot.
Ipe, where.
Kona, there.

ADDENDA.

Pezulu, up or above.
Pantsi, below or down.
E'àm, mine.
E'arko, yours.
M'nyama, black.
M'lope, white.
Ebomvu, red.
Inkomo, cattle.

Imazi, a cow.
Inyoka, a snake.
Incwade, a written letter or note.
Egwi, snuff.
Ilanga, the sun.
Inyanga, the moon, a month.
Immali, money.

. By joining some of these words together may be formed many useful sentences; thus:—

Yenza umlilo, Make a fire.
Ziza amanzi nàmi, Bring water to me.
Dia funa ihashi am, I want my horse.
Dia funa uku zingela ama injlovu, I want to hunt elephants.
Mäuzapa nami goomso uku sebenza, Come to me to-morrow to work.

Dia funa uku tenga zinkomo, I want to buy cattle.
Mongàpi? How many?
Ishumi, Ten.
Ubanina? What is the name of?
Ubanina amasondo lè? What is the name of these footmarks?
Engàzi, I don't know.
Chela menà, Tell me.
E-zàpa wena, Come here you.
Hamba kona, Go there.